VOLUME 575

MAY 2001

THE ANNALS

of The American Academy *of* Political
and Social Science

ALAN W. HESTON, *Editor*
NEIL A. WEINER, *Assistant Editor*

CHILDREN'S RIGHTS

Special Editor of this Volume

JUDE L. FERNANDO
University of Arizona, Tucson

 Sage Publications, Inc. *THOUSAND OAKS LONDON NEW DELHI*

Origin and Purpose. The Academy was organized December 14, 1889, to promote the progress of political and social science, especially through publications and meetings. The Academy does not take sides in controverted questions, but seeks to gather and present reliable information to assist the public in forming an intelligent and accurate judgment.

Meetings. The Academy occasionally holds a meeting in the spring extending over two days.

Publications. THE ANNALS of the American Academy of Political and Social Science is the bimonthly publication of The Academy. Each issue contains articles on some prominent social or political problem, written at the invitation of the editors. Also, monographs are published from time to time, numbers of which are distributed to pertinent professional organizations. These volumes constitute important reference works on the topics with which they deal, and they are extensively cited by authorities throughout the United States and abroad. The papers presented at the meetings of The Academy are included in THE ANNALS.

Membership. Each member of The Academy receives THE ANNALS and may attend the meetings of The Academy. Membership is open only to individuals. Annual dues: $65.00 for the regular paperbound edition (clothbound, $100.00). For members outside the U.S.A., add $12.00 (surface mail) or $24.00 (air mail) for shipping of your subscription. Members may also purchase single issues of THE ANNALS for $20.00 each (clothbound, $30.00).

Subscriptions. THE ANNALS of the American Academy of Political and Social Science (ISSN 0002-7162) is published six times annually—in January, March, May, July, September, and November. Institutions may subscribe to THE ANNALS at the annual rate: $375.00 (clothbound, $425.00). Add $12.00 per year for subscriptions outside the U.S.A. Institutional rates for single issues: $70.00 each (clothbound, $75.00).

Periodicals postage paid at Thousand Oaks, California, and at additional mailing offices.

Single issues of THE ANNALS may be obtained by individuals who are not members of The Academy for $30.00 each (clothbound, $40.00). Single issues of THE ANNALS have proven to be excellent supplementary texts for classroom use. Direct inquiries regarding adoptions to THE ANNALS c/o Sage Publications (address below).

All correspondence concerning membership in The Academy, dues renewals, inquiries about membership status, and/or purchase of single issues of THE ANNALS should be sent to THE ANNALS c/o Sage Publications, Inc., 2455 Teller Road, Thousand Oaks, CA 91320. Telephone: (805) 499-9774; FAX/Order line: (805) 375-1700. *Please note that orders under $30 must be prepaid.* Sage affiliates in London and India will assist institutional subscribers abroad with regard to orders, claims, and inquiries for both subscriptions and single issues.

Printed on recycled, acid-free paper

THE ANNALS

Editorial Office: Fels Center of Government, University of Pennsylvania, 3814 Walnut Street, Philadelphia, PA 19104-6197.

For information about membership* (individuals only) and subscriptions (institutions), address:

SAGE PUBLICATIONS, INC.
2455 Teller Road
Thousand Oaks, CA 91320

Sage Production Staff: MARIA NOTARANGELO, KATE PETERSON, and ROSE TYLAK

From India and South Asia,
write to:
SAGE PUBLICATIONS INDIA Pvt. Ltd
P.O. Box 4215
New Delhi 110 048
INDIA

From Europe, the Middle East,
and Africa, write to:
SAGE PUBLICATIONS LTD
6 Bonhill Street
London EC2A 4PU
UNITED KINGDOM

*Please note that members of The Academy receive THE ANNALS with their membership.
International Standard Serial Number ISSN 0002-7162
International Standard Book Number ISBN 0-7619-2467-1 (Vol. 575, 2001 paper)
International Standard Book Number ISBN 0-7619-2466-3 (Vol. 575, 2001 cloth)
Manufactured in the United States of America. First printing, May 2001.

The articles appearing in THE ANNALS are abstracted or indexed in *Academic Abstracts, Academic Search, America: History and Life, Asia Pacific Database, Book Review Index, CAB Abstracts Database, Central Asia: Abstracts & Index, Communication Abstracts, Corporate ResourceNET, Criminal Justice Abstracts, Current Citations Express, Current Contents: Social & Behavioral Sciences, e-JEL, EconLit, Expanded Academic Index, Guide to Social Science & Religion in Periodical Literature, Health Business FullTEXT, HealthSTAR FullTEXT, Historical Abstracts, International Bibliography of the Social Sciences, International Political Science Abstracts, ISI Basic Social Sciences Index, Journal of Economic Literature on CD, LEXIS-NEXIS, MasterFILE FullTEXT, Middle East: Abstracts & Index, North Africa: Abstracts & Index, PAIS International, Periodical Abstracts, Political Science Abstracts, Sage Public Administration Abstracts, Social Science Source, Social Sciences Citation Index, Social Sciences Index Full Text, Social Services Abstracts, Social Work Abstracts, Sociological Abstracts, Southeast Asia: Abstracts & Index, Standard Periodical Directory (SPD), TOPICsearch, Wilson OmniFile V,* and *Wilson Social Sciences Index/Abstracts,* and are available on microfilm from University Microfilms, Ann Arbor, Michigan.

Information about membership rates, institutional subscriptions, and back issue prices may be found on the facing page.

Advertising. Current rates and specifications may be obtained by writing to THE ANNALS Advertising and Promotion Manager at the Thousand Oaks office (address above).

Claims. Claims for undelivered copies must be made no later than six months following month of publication. The publisher will supply missing copies when losses have been sustained in transit and when the reserve stock will permit.

Change of Address. Six weeks advance notice must be given when notifying of change of address to ensure proper identification. Please specify name of journal. **POSTMASTER:** Send address changes to: THE ANNALS of the American Academy of Political and Social Science, c/o Sage Publications, Inc., 2455 Teller Road, Thousand Oaks, CA 91320.

THE ANNALS

of The American Academy of Political
and Social Science

ALAN W. HESTON, *Editor*
NEIL A. WEINER, *Assistant Editor*

——————— FORTHCOMING ———————

COURTHOUSE VIOLENCE:
PROTECTING THE JUDICIAL WORKPLACE
Special Editors: Victor Flango
and Don Hardenbergh

Volume 576   July 2001

REFORMING WELFARE, REDEFINING POVERTY
Special Editors: Randy Albelda
and Ann Withorn

Volume 577   September 2001

DRUG POLICY
Special Editors: Peter Reuter
and Robert J. MacCoun

Volume 578   November 2001

See page 2 for information on Academy membership and
purchase of single volumes of **The Annals.**

CONTENTS

BOOK DEPARTMENT CONTENTS

INTERNATIONAL RELATIONS AND POLITICS

SOCIOLOGY

Children's Rights:
Beyond the Impasse

Nonetheless, if the fundamental rights behind our cause are not sufficient to move people to act, then let it be the economic and social rationale behind it. Either way, we are going to challenge people to act.

—Nelson Mandela and Graça Machel[1]

The ratification of the U.N. Convention on the Rights of the Child (CRC) by a majority of the International Labor Organization's member states technically affirms that "children are born with fundamental freedoms and the inherent rights of all human beings" (UNICEF 2000a, 2) and so should have marked the twentieth century as a century of hope for those children whose fundamental rights are violated across the world. There is, however, widespread concern that, notwithstanding manifold successes in enlisting broad-based societal commitments to safeguard children's rights, there exists neither a universal consensus on the meaning and content of the very concept of children's rights nor sufficient reasons for us to be content with the current status of children's rights worldwide. For instance, the *Report on the State of the World's Children* notes that "for all the gains made, the story of the 20th century is also about failed leadership—a lack of vision, an absence of courage, a passive neglect of their rights, as set forth in the Convention on the Rights of the Child" (UNICEF 2000b, 3).

The widening of the gap between expectations and achievements in the area of human rights raises a fundamental issue: how comfortably does our commitment to children's rights fit with our convictions about social justice? It appears that the current demands for safeguarding various rights have little to do with any comprehensive plan for a new and more just economic and political order, despite the fact that ideals of freedom inevitably entail notions of distributive justice. Although no signatories to the CRC, international donor agencies, or child rights advocates would deny that the present system of distributive justice is mainly responsible for the vulnerability of children, they ultimately shy away from a serious dialogue about alternatives to it.

Even as evidence of the violation of children's rights multiplies at an alarming rate—pointing to the wholesale failure of policies, programs, interventions, and conventions designed to curb these violations—the world remains divided over the fundamental question of what constitutes basic human rights (Ray 1998). We do not even have the language that might grant meaningful agency to children. There seems to be an impasse in the praxis of the discourse of children's rights, where praxis is, in the words of Paulo Freire (1986), "the precise symbiosis between reflective action and critical theorizing" where "critical consciousness" functions as "the motor of cultural emancipation" (6). The reason for such an impasse, according to Fedric Jameson—echoing Francis Fukuyama's notion of the "end of history"—is that in the current context there appears to be a "blockage of the historical imagination" that prevents us from thinking about alternatives to the emergent political economy within which a child-friendly system of distributive justice can be structured (Jameson 1999, 36).

On the positive side, however, the present trends in the debate and advocacy around children's rights have great potential for improving not only the status of children but also the status of other marginalized and exploited social groups because a sound children's rights perspective needs, by definition, to be grounded in a wider understanding of the social, political, and economic order. In the present political context, I think that child-centered demands for distributive justice have a much greater potential in terms of the possibility of building an intercultural consensus as compared with similar demands by other social groups, for example, the working classes and women (although a sound children's rights perspective would make explicit the fact that the situation of children across the world is heavily structured by both class and gender).

The articles in this volume seek to address some of the dominant themes in the current debate over children's rights in order to facilitate new paradigms and directions that could be effective in responding to this most important of issues.

APPALLING FACTS AND A GRIM FUTURE

The sheer frequency and kinds of ways in which children's rights are violated across the globe every day is staggering. Each day, 30,500 children under age 5 die of mainly preventable diseases, and even more children and young people succumb to illness, neglect, accidents, and assaults (UNICEF 2000b). According to estimates by the Joint United Nations Program on HIV/AIDS (1999), more than 3 million children and young people worldwide became infected with HIV in 1998. This included almost 590,000 children under age 15 and more than 2.5 million 15- to 24-year-olds. During 1998, more than 8500 children and young people became infected with HIV each day—six every minute.

In 1999 alone, approximately 31 million refugees and displaced persons were caught in conflicts; their victims are mainly women and children. In the decade since the adoption of the CRC, more than 2 million children have been killed, and more than 6 million have been injured or disabled in armed conflicts. More than 300,000 children are directly or indirectly involved in armed conflicts. These children participate in all aspects of warfare; an increasing number of them serve as suicide attackers and frontline combatants. Millions of others have been forced to witness or even take part in horrifying acts of violence. Children are also likely to be the main victims of the more than 110,000 landmines lying in wait. Children are also the main victims of the economic embargoes that result from interstate conflicts.

The world has more children living in poverty now than it did 10 years ago. Over the last 20 years, as the wealth of the world economy increased exponentially, the number of people living in poverty grew to more than 1.2 billion, or one in every five persons, including more than 600 million children. According to estimates by the International Labor Organization, some 250 million children between the ages of 5 and 14 work in developing countries, with some 50-60 million between the ages of 5 and 11 working in hazardous circumstances (Boyden 1997). As Jo Boyden (1997) notes, in this grim scenario, "childhood is for many a very unhappy time" (191).

Parallel to the exponential increase in poverty rates, the number of street children throughout the world has also grown over the past few decades. Police regularly subject street children to physical abuse and torture. They may be coerced into sexual acts, raped, or even murdered. Often governments treat these children as problems to be eradicated rather than as children to be nurtured and protected. Street children also suffer from chronic poverty, lack of education, and AIDS, and they are often drawn into prostitution and substance abuse. They also make up a large proportion of the children who are at the mercy of the criminal justice system; they are committed to correctional institutions (read "prisons") that are euphemistically called schools (UNICEF 2000a, 2).

The violation of the fundamental rights of children in developed countries such as the United States, despite its unparalleled wealth and advantages, has become more complex. The Blue-Ribbon Commission of the State Board of American Education and the American Medical Association reported that "never before has one generation of Children been less healthy, less cared for and less prepared for life than their parents were at the same age" (quoted in Chomsky 2000, 50). During the past five years, the number of children in need of foster care has increased from a quarter million to nearly 6 million. Widespread incidents of sexual abuse, torture, and neglect in foster care facilities are reported in a number of states. More than 7,500 children are tortured in what are technically government-controlled programs. In New York City, the poor state of social policies has "driven about 40 percent of children below the poverty level, so that they are suffering from malnutrition, disease and so on" (Chomsky 2000, 49). Legal and bureaucratic barriers, profit motives, and a lack of resources in private foster care facilities have left children with limited opportunities for effective care. A recent *Time* magazine report noted that "it is sad legacy of foster care that more children continue to be terribly, terribly scared" (Roche 2000, 82). "None of these things is law of nature. These are consciously selected social policies designed for particular goals, namely enrich the Fortune 500 but impoverish others" (Chomsky 2000, 50).

The international concern over the plight of children made children's rights advocacy one of the most powerful social movements of the twentieth century. Indeed, the efforts of children's rights advocates can be said to have contributed to the near-universal ratification of the CRC. Governments have taken numerous measures to enact legislation and create mechanisms to ensure the protection and realization of the rights of children. Yet these successes are far from being sufficient. The refusal of the United States and Somalia to sign the CRC is still a matter of serious concern because of the former's increasing command over the emerging global political economy and the high incidence of children engaged in armed conflict in the latter. It must also be noted that none of the 191 nations that ratified the CRC have developed an integrated strategy for its implementation.

Governmental bureaucracy and lack of coordination between the international community, the private sector, international organizations, nongovernmental organizations (NGOs), and civil society at large have combined to retard the progress of the CRC (*Children's Rights* 2000, 6). The priorities of the international community in safeguarding the rights of children are well illustrated in UNICEF's *Report on the State of the World's Children 2000*: "In 1996 and 1997, donor nations gave an estimated $350 million each year to combat HIV/AIDS, in meager comparison to the $60 billion that was given by the international community to the Republic of Korea during the Asian financial crisis of the late 1990s" (UNICEF 2000b, 2). To overcome the tragic situation of the world's children, the world "would require a quarter of annual military expenditures of the 'developing countries,' about 10 percent of US military spending" (Chomsky 2000, 135). The international community's formal commitment—to enforce laws and regulations—is undermined by its lack of substantive commitment—to create the economic and social conditions necessary for a better living environment for the majority of the world's children.

The global campaigns and local reforms in search of remedies have resulted in a growing tension between the increasing demands (made particularly by Western countries and addressed to developing countries) to safeguard the rights of children and, on the other hand, the claims of those states accused of violating international standards of children's rights that the CRC's universal standards are ethnocentric or Eurocentric and hence not applicable to societies with different cultural, religious, and social systems. In this view, the CRC's demands for the imposition of a minimum age for employment is an imperialist conspiracy by the West against non-Western states to be understood as a form of protectionism. These tensions have polarized the debate about children's rights between developed countries and developing countries, between the liberal North and the conservative South, between imperialism and fundamentalism, between modernists and postmodernists, and so on. During the course of these debates, the immediate needs of the children have been effectively sidestepped, so much so that these debates appear to include everything but children.

CHILDREN IN DEVELOPMENT
THEORY AND PRACTICE

Rights cannot be safeguarded without meeting the material needs of people and, when talking specifically about children's rights, without dealing with the structural causes of children's vulnerability. Among them, an unsafe environment and chronic poverty are root causes of the tragic situation of the world's children. The insensitivity of conventional development policies to the specific needs of children is now widely recognized as a fundamental reason behind the specific problems that children face. As a result, material poverty among children is becoming a specialized area of development theory and policy intervention, similar to the way in which women, and later, "gender," were mainstreamed in development discourse. I would like to term such a mainstreaming of children as the infantalization of poverty. This means institutionalizing children's poverty as a distinct domain of development policy interventions by isolating it from the poverty of society at large.

This has a number of implications. The discourse on children's rights is fast becoming a technocratic discourse that no longer addresses the issue of power relations that is central to understanding and effectively responding to the needs of children. The danger is that just as the mainstreaming of gender actually peripheralized the needs of women, so the mainstreaming of children's rights may further marginalize the real needs of children. The particularization of children's rights issues—isolating children's rights issues from issues of class, race, and gender—has become a convenient means of avoiding direct engagement with the political and economic realities of the emerging global economy.

Concomitantly, the study of power relations in the current children's rights discourse is structured in binary terms: the powerful versus the powerless. This binary opposition provides ideological legitimacy to oppositional relations between developed countries and developing countries and promotes a paternalistic attitude exercised by the former toward the latter. The very category of powerlessness is defined in terms of Eurocentric/universalist assumptions, where notions of childhood are constructed by combining the biological differences between children with what Chandra Mohanty (1998) has called "Third World difference." This way of homogenizing and systemizing the experiences of children in different contexts, in turn, leads to legitimization of Eurocentric/universalistic policy interventions.

A fruitful analysis of power relations within the context of children's rights is impossible if one isolates children's rights from the demands for rights that are emerging from other groups within society, particularly those defined by class and gender. Put differently, how far can we get if we isolate children from their embeddedness in the class and gender relations that they experience through their relationship with adults? We also need to be cautious about the fact that the excessive emphasis on relativism can encourage various religious, cultural, and political ideologies and practices that are detrimental to the rights of children. A greater emphasis should be given to how the interplay between social and cultural diversity within nations and the homogenizing and centralizing trends of global capitalism impinge upon the production and legitimization of those institutions that are detrimental to the welfare of children. The failure to effectively address these concerns would transform even the most progressive interventions to improve the rights of children into another form of Orientalism. Orientalism, according to Edward Said (1979), is a "systematic discipline by which the European culture was able to manage—and even produce—the Orient politically, sociologically, militarily, ideologically, scientifically, and imaginatively during the post-Enlightenment period" (3).

NGOs AND CHILDREN

The recent successes of NGOs in bringing about an increased awareness of children's issues and in pressuring states to ratify and comply with the CRC have created further space for NGO intervention in the area of children's rights by giving NGOs added legitimacy. The future successes of NGOs, however, are subject to a number of limitations. The continuity of NGOs' efforts is contingent on their ability to raise funds from international donors in developed countries. The overall aid allocations by developed countries to developing countries have been dwindling, and aid flows to NGOs are being increasingly privatized and channeled into those areas that promise quick commercial returns. The trend is well demonstrated by the current shift of NGO programs from education, health care, and advocacy to microcredit. The implicit argument in the NGOs' turn to microcredit is that the economic empowerment of the poor and oppressed is an essential prerequisite for their social and political empowerment; violations of children's rights in the process of economic development are overlooked until the poor and oppressed and their communities become economically self-sufficient.

Ironically, the efficacy of NGO advocacy depends on the ability of the NGOs to enlist the support of the state. Here NGOs are faced with a dilemma: on the one hand, NGOs are registered as legal entities within the institutional parameters of the state. That is, in the final analysis, the autonomy of NGOs is constrained by the political, economic, and cultural ideology of the state. On the other hand, NGOs are widely touted as the most effective institutions through which demands on the state can be channeled (hence their valorization as civil society organizations). The extent to which the state can effectively respond to the demands for distributive justice articulated by an NGO within its jurisdiction is determined by two factors.

First is how the state reconciles such demands with the imperative of remaining competitive on the world market. This imperative—as well as the provisions of structural adjustment policies in most developing countries— has forced the state to reduce resources to areas of social development where there are limited or no direct commercial returns. In the present international political economic order, the priorities of the state have shifted toward disciplining society so as to allow the economy to function according to the logic of the market. The rationale for such a shift in state's priorities is the argument that economic growth is considered an essential prerequisite for the safeguarding of human rights.

The second limiting factor is the extent to which the NGOs' demands and programs for distributive justice challenge state power. Here one finds that the current advocacy efforts by NGOs do not propose a political and economic system that is fundamentally different from that of the state. Instead, NGO claims about state failures in social development partly provided ideological legitimacy for the state to reduce subsidies on welfare and social services such as health and education. NGO activities by no means compensate for the loss of provisions for children due to the dismantling of the welfare state.

Moreover, NGO interventions remain scattered and lack continuity. The private sector does not offer much, if any, hope for the improvement in the status of most of the world's children. Consequently, these children are pushed into an uncertain future in which they are expected to look after their own welfare and, quite often, to support their families as well. This raises the issue as to whether the "NGOization" of children's rights is in fact providing legitimacy for the neoliberal ideology of the state that underpins the reduction of state welfare provisions for children, thereby leaving children in a worse situation than before.

CIVIC HUMANISM VS.
COMMERCIAL HUMANISM

The advocacy efforts of Western consumer groups played an important role in the widespread compliance by states, multinational corporations, and international aid agencies with the CRC. However, due to a number of factors, the fruits of their efforts are limited. First, they have been less sensitive to the realities of children's lives in developing countries. For example, those children who lose their jobs due to closure of sweatshops simply end up worse off. As Jean-Claude Khoury (1998) has put it, the "choice for many families in the developing countries is not between sending a child to a factory and sending a child to a school, but rather between a factory that sells goods for export and a factory that serves only the internal markets" (26). Banning the use of child labor in the formal economy has encouraged the "informalization" of child labor, making the enforcement of child labor laws even more difficult. Informalization has also increased due to the subcontracting of production by multinational firms, which helps the multinational firms escape those responsibilities toward their workers that labor laws used to guarantee.

Second is a widely ignored contradiction in the altruistic concerns of the enlightened consumer. On the one hand, the ideology of consumerism is central to higher economic standards and is linked to the increasing political power enjoyed by consumer rights advocates in industrialized countries. Indeed, on many occasions, consumer advocates have used this power to bring about positive changes in the practices of multinational corporations. On the other hand, since consumerism is at the same time the motor that drives the expansion of capitalist development, it is also central to the economic disparities between developed and developing countries and the resulting human rights violations in the latter. Bluntly put, the poverty of Third World children cannot be understood in isolation from the economic prosperity of those enlightened consumers in the West.

J.G.A. Pocock describes such a dilemma faced by the enlightened consumer as the conflict between "commercial humanism" and "civic humanism," where the former "having abandoned the hard road of republican virtue [now] must seek another root for moral good" (quoted in Eagleton 1992, 131). Now, highly differentiated individuals protest against the violation of human rights that are a direct result of the very processes that have led to their individuation. If one is to think about human rights as virtues, then, according to Eagleton (1992), "virtue and commerce [conducted in a capitalist economy] are thus irreconcilable. . . . virtue in an increasingly commercialized social order cannot be truly exercised in the social, only the political, sphere and so is at risk of appearing restricted and archaic" (133). This is because "it is just that Marxism notes, as commercial humanism does not, that this exhilarated unfolding of human wealth, in both moral and material senses, is also the narrative of an unspeakable tragedy, occurring as it does under the sign of scarcity, violence and exploitation" (137).

Advocacy, even in its most radical forms, does not, per se, undermine the material and power relations against which the human rights advocates are struggling, because there is a clear difference between advocating for an awareness and improvement of the rights of children and striving to create an alternative social and economic order where such violations would not exist. In this context, I would like to suggest two ideas for rethinking the present controversy over rights. One is to view rights as virtues. In the tradition of civic humanism, as Pocock noted, "virtue as devotion to the public good approached identification with a concept of justice; if the citizens were to practice a common good, they must distribute its components among themselves" (quoted in Eagleton 1992, 137).

Second, redistribution of wealth alone is insufficient to address the poverty-related human rights abuses among children. It is far more imperative to engage the process or processes through which wealth is produced, because it is unlikely that the negative impact of the existing modes of production on children's rights can be simply compensated for by (re)distribution. Do the children's rights activists want children in non-Western countries to undergo the same suffering that the children in Western countries experienced during the early stages of the industrial revolution? The bottom line is, Do the majority of Third World countries have the remotest possibility of achieving living standards comparable to those of the developed world? Is it possible for Third World countries to simultaneously maintain a high standard of human rights and achieve economic growth in this era of the dog-eat-dog world market?

What is the probability that current economic policies will even marginally improve the conditions of the majority of the people of the Third World? Has the distribution of wealth between developed and developing countries increased in relation to the global integration of modes of production? If we are to find meaningful answers to these issues, it is important to critically engage with the emerging trends in the global political economy without simply blaming the state, tradition, and multinational corporations for violation of children's rights. More than ever, answers to these issues require a global perspective.

GLOBALLY CONNECTED BUT LONELY

Safeguarding children's rights in particular and human rights in general is predicated upon the informed society, which requires a vibrant information system. Indeed, ongoing improvements in cybernetic and information systems have contributed to the increased global awareness of the state of the world's children and progress in creating a better environment for them.

At the same time, the liberating hope that the communication revolution offers for children is undermined by its underlying economic logic. Children are one of the main targets of the highly commodified cybernetic and information industry that contributes to the widening of the disparity between rich children and poor children and forces the latter into the labor market, delinquency, prostitution, and violence. Some have argued that such forms of violence among children not only are due to structural poverty but also are a result of the consumption of commodities such as video games and toy guns and the negative influences of the cyberworld. Ironically, encouraging children to participate in cyberspace has become a way for parents to shield children from dangerous neighborhoods and streets.

By participating in cyberspace, children can be a part of the global community yet isolated from physical interaction with other children and with the world at large. The increasing celebrations of notions of private property and privacy and of highly personalized toys and entertainment systems and the disintegration of family, kinship, and traditional social ties further contribute to this process of the individualization of children's lives. Such privatization of children's lives has certain costs. As Boyden (1997) notes, "It means that they must become accustomed to a world without movement. They may never play again on the streets" (195). In this highly privatized world of communication, violations of children's rights have become even more complex and uncontrollable.

Commodified communication technologies conceive culture as something that can be modeled according to personal choice. Such homogenization of culture through consumerism not only undermines cultural diversity but also shapes the culture according to the logic of profit. Social groups that are marginalized in this process construe consumerism as a purely Western phenomenon, and the antidote for it is the preservation of traditional cultures.

What might transpire from such demands for the preservation of traditional culture is the reproduction and legitimization of those cultural forms and values that are detrimental to children's rights.

COMMUNITY, STATE, AND THE CHILD

The direct involvement of children in armed conflicts around the world has increased during the past decade. Although the use of children in armed conflicts is common mainly among insurgent groups, in recent years younger and younger children have started to be recruited in government forces (UNICEF 2000a, 26). Both state and separatist groups have reconfigured the identity of these children, projecting them as embodiments and guardians of the nation. While in training, these children (and their parents) are told that they will become the martyrs of their community. When the issue of fundamental rights is raised, they respond that liberation of the community from the "other" is a crucial precondition for the safeguarding of the rights of the individuals and groups of the larger community. Similar processes occurred during the colonial period, when women were told that the liberation of the nation from the colonial state was a prerequisite for the liberation of women. A decade after independence, the failure of the state to improve the status of women was one of the important reasons for the emergence of the second wave of the feminist movement, which sought to independently struggle for women's rights.

Children are placed in a worse situation particularly in countries where there are civil conflicts. Coupled with rapid social change, which often precedes or accompanies war, conflicts lead to a breakdown in the family support networks so essential to a child's survival and socialization, so these children are pushed into vagrancy and prostitution. As Machel notes,

More and more of the world is being sucked into a desolate moral vacuum. This is a space devoid of the most basic human values; a space in which children are slaughtered, raped, and maimed; a space in which children are exploited as soldiers; a space in which children are starved and exposed to extreme brutality. (UNICEF 2000a, 26)

In regions engulfed by conflict, state actors have demonstrated much success in exploiting the notion of sovereignty to prevent international mediation in domestic conflicts. In the aftermath of the Cold War, the international community has become more reluctant to interfere in matters that are essentially within the jurisdiction of sovereign states. The conflicts around the world demonstrate that, as the nations get more integrated, the opportunities for and effectiveness of global institutions to intervene in situations that require global solutions is in fact declining.

The priorities of international intervention in conflict zones continue to be determined by domestic and foreign policy concerns rather than by the concern for anything else, least of all the rights of Third World children. Even

NGOs have demonstrated much reluctance in acting contrary to the foreign policies of their countries, even in situations where thousands of children continue to die due to malnutrition and starvation caused by interstate economic embargoes. In the meantime, separatist militant groups are able to function freely due to the commercialization of the weapons industry, the loosening of state controls over the cross-border movement of arms, and the availability of financial assistance from diasporic communities, showing that globalization is a highly selective—and contradictory—process.

In recent years, state actors in countries where children are involved in armed conflicts have taken active measures to mobilize international condemnation against the recruitment of children for combat by groups that challenge the territorial integrity of the state. Despite their ostensibly good motives, one finds that these state actors are actually exploiting the prevailing international protests against the use of children in combat in order to legitimize military campaigns against those separatist groups that threaten state power. Often, the humanitarian concerns of these states are not corroborated by their sincere commitment to pursue political solutions to the conflicts in question. In such situations, children are exploited as instruments to legitimize the hegemonic projects of the state that are often underpinned by ethno-religious nationalism.

THE POLITICS OF UNIVERSALISM AND RELATIVISM

In recent times, questions have emerged about the analytical potential and political effect of the categories employed by current scholarship to examine the issues relating to children's rights. It is becoming increasingly clear that there is no real consensus on what the term "children's rights" actually means because the very concept, as it exists, is embedded in the Western tradition of political philosophy upon which the U.N. Charter on Human Rights is based and, as such, is far from being an abstract, universal given. The assumption that childhood constitutes a coherent group or a state defined by identical needs and desires, regardless of class, ethnic, or racial differences, lies behind a universalist notion of children's rights. The conventional definition of children's rights, based on an assumed identity of the biological and physiological attributes of children across the world, is challenged by social constructionists who argue that such universalism does not take into account the social, cultural, and political diversity of the meaning of childhood and hence of children's rights in different cultures. The biological determinism of the former does not take into account the fact that the physical characteristics and social competencies of children of the same age vary according to their contextual differences (James and Prout 1997). This view does not, however, completely disregard the fact that childhood has biological aspects; rather, it poses the question as to how this biological immaturity is understood and made meaningful in different cultures (James and Prout 1997, 26). Consequently, childhood is viewed as a social construction; its meaning is negotiated between

different individuals and groups, often with conflicting interests. Thus, childhood is relative (Solberg 1997, 126).

The increasingly contested nature of the very meaning of the term "childhood" raises the issue of whether children can or should be studied as a distinct category of social actors and the possibility of a theoretical space to discuss their issues—a space that lies outside the context of their relationship
with adults. Moreover, how can we do so if it is claimed that the ethnocentric
essentialist and universalistic scholarship on children's rights originating in
the West is colonizing the material, social, and historical heterogeneity of the
lives of children in the non-Western world, thereby producing and representing a singular image of the child—an image that appears to be objective but
nevertheless carries with it the authorizing signature of Western scholarship
and policy interventions?[2]

The claims of the social constructionists and cultural relativists have been
challenged on several grounds. First, could not such relativist arguments in
fact be detrimental to the welfare of children, particularly within the present
global context in which the fundamental determinants of the experience of
childhood are rooted in the transnational political economy? Can cultural relativism actually be helping to absolve the forces of neoliberal globalization of
the responsibility for the negative impact it has on children's lives? Could it
thus be regarded as an ideological counterweight to the challenges posed by
transnational advocates for children's rights? What solutions does such cultural relativism offer in terms of shielding children from the negative impacts
of the emerging global economy?

Relativist notions about childhood—particularly when underpinned by
poststructuralist and deconstructionist ideologies—effectively result in complicity with the status quo and, moreover, make it difficult to effectively deal
with the forces that are working to undermine the quality of children's lives in
the South, forces that are themselves transcultural and transnational in
nature and effect. Terry Eagleton (1992) made the following statement as a
parody of Jacques Derrida, the doyen of deconstructionism: "I am not for
socialism; but I am not against it either. Neither am I neither for nor against
it, nor simply for or against the whole oppression of 'for' and 'against' " (123).
Such equivocation and ambiguity are not always moral virtues, especially
when it comes down to talking about real lives and political choices. Eagleton
reminds us that the truth that "neither liberal nor post-structuralist seems
able to countenance is that there are certain key political struggles that
someone is going to have to win and someone will have to lose" (124).

Relativism's celebration of micro-narratives of childhood as opposed to
macro-narratives—revolving around, for instance, exploitation and violence—
makes it impossible for it to grasp the political, economic, and cultural processes "that are becoming ever more universalizing in their depth, intensity,
reach and power" over the "life worlds" of children. Politically, relativism can
be counterproductive to the welfare of children because under the pretext of
providing the "authenticity to other voices," it "shuts off those other voices

from access to more universal sources of power by ghettoizing them within an opaque otherness, the specificity of this or that language game. It thereby disempowers those voices of [the oppressed] in a world of lopsided power relations" (Harvey 1992, 135).

The main limitation of the current analytical strategies on childhood stems from the fact that children are constituted as a subject in analysis prior to their entry into the orbit of social relations. The fact is neglected that the meaning, or meanings, of childhood is produced through and implicated in these very relations. This is not to deny the importance of the physiological and biological aspects of childhood but to underscore the fact that, if childhood is to be a useful concept in our efforts toward safeguarding the rights of children, it ought to be viewed as a relational category. We should not lose sight of the political usefulness of some forms of determinism and universalism embedded within current notions of children's rights, especially when it comes to constructing and supporting transnational social movements involved in safeguarding children from the negative impact of the forces of neoliberal globalization. What is required today is a constructive dialogue on the issue of childhood and children's rights that does not fall into the twin traps of relativism and universalism, that does not ignore the heterogeneity of children's lives or obscure the commonality of ways in which economic and political forces in an increasingly unstable and polarized world have affected the lives and experiences of these children.

AUTHORS' CONTRIBUTIONS

The articles in this volume are written by an interdisciplinary group of scholars. They explore a wide range of issues regarding child labor within the context of globalization. Two important themes underlying their contributions are, first, the relationship between poverty and the welfare of children and, second, the problematic relationship between universalism and relativism in current debates and policies concerning children's rights.

Allison James and Adrian James's article, "Childhood: Toward a Theory of Continuity and Change," examines the role of law and social policy over time, from an interdisciplinary perspective, and demonstrates that it is no longer possible to see childhood simply as a common and universal biological phase of the life course. However, at the same time, it is being increasingly recognized that although acknowledgment of the social and cultural diversity of children's lives is important, there remain many commonalties that children do share as occupants of the conceptual space of childhood. Although contemporary sociological theorizing about childhood has highlighted this tension, it has offered few solutions as yet.

The international conventions on children's rights play a central role in theoretical and policy debates on children's rights. In ratifying these issues, the United Nations play a key role. Jo de Berry's article, "Child Soldiers and the Convention on the Rights of the Child," provides a critical evaluation of

Article 38 of the CRC, which concerns the prevention of children's active participation in armed hostilities as soldiers. De Berry argues that if the article is to move from ratification to practical implementation there should be consideration of the contexts that influence the phenomenon of child soldiers. De Berry's analysis is based on two contexts: the first is state crisis; the second is the local influences on children's participation in armed conflict in the case of young fighters in the Teso region of Uganda. At both levels, there are global processes that undermine application of the CRC.

Worldwide, untold numbers of children are being systematically deprived of their human rights, dignity, and childhood through child prostitution, child pornography, and other sexploitation. Many of these children are routinely subjected to rape, beatings, displacement, drug addiction, psychological abuse, and other trauma, including exposure to the AIDS virus and a life with no future. Barri Flowers's article, "The Sex Trade Industry's Worldwide Exploitation of Children," examines the current state of international trafficking of children and other child sexual exploitation. Child sex tourism plays a major role in the child sex trade as prostituted youths are routinely lured or abducted into sexual slavery and sex-for-profit by those exploiting them commercially.

Rachel Baker and Rachel Hinton's article, "Approaches to Children's Work and Rights in Nepal," which is based on ethnographic studies, explores the discourse and practice surrounding child labor in Nepal within the context of globalization. The authors point out that current economic and political trends present particular challenges for countries dealing with the development of industry without the social infrastructure needed to uphold citizens' rights. As free trade demands developing countries to compete in global markets, the demand for cheap labor rises. This has specific implications for children, as countries attempt to uphold existing national legislation to provide for children and develop new laws to fulfil the requirements of international mandates.

William Myers's article, "The Right Rights? Child Labor in a Globalizing World," examines some important aspects of the current international debate regarding how to apply children's rights concepts to child labor. He raises a crucial question of what, and whose, ideas about children and childhood provide the foundation for globalized children's rights norms, looking into concerns that international child labor policies may be unjustly dominated by European and North American values and ideas at the expense of more representative worldviews. From this perspective, he reviews the three main international conventions dealing with child labor, discussing certain ideological and strategic differences between them and tracing in their history a gradual movement away from the dominance of North ethnocentrism and toward more culturally inclusive and flexible formulations of children's rights standards. In his conclusion, Myers points out that "the case of child labor suggests that globally representative children's rights just might indeed be possible, even if it takes a few tries to get them right."

The article by Sudharshan Canagarajah and Helena Skyt Nielsen, "Child Labor in Africa: A Comparative Study," provides a detailed and systematic analysis of the determinants of child labor in Africa as inferred from recent empirical studies conducted in three different African countries, namely, Côte d'Ivoire, Ghana, and Zambia. The authors find some support for the popular belief of poverty as a determinant of child labor. However, they emphasize the importance of other determinants. Operating within the realm of neoclassical economics, the authors point out that school costs and transportation costs have the greatest effect on child labor and school attendance, whereas the hypothesis of imperfect capital markets and that of household composition generally find some support.

Children have lived on and worked in city streets since time immemorial. But in recent years, free-market policies have led to a growing gap between rich and poor, unprecedented urbanization, and the fracturing of traditional social structures. One result has been the development of entire subcultures made up of children, including many whose family ties have been cruelly cut. Childhood is supposed to be a time of safety, of laughter, and of learning. But these children lead stunted lives characterized by fear, shame, and discrimination. Based on fieldwork conducted in Ghana and Brazil, Kathleen McCreery's article, "From Street to Stage with Children in Brazil and Ghana," provides an insightful story of street children in Ghana. In that article, McCreery's play *When I Meet My Mother* offers a glimpse into the lives of a gang of Brazilian street children in one 24-hour period. McCreery makes a strong case for using drama as a means of helping these children develop their potential and tell their own stories.

Steven Hick's article, "The Political Economy of War-Affected Children," examines the effects of armed conflict on children in relation to the rapidly changing nature of armed conflicts since the rise of globalization and the end of the Cold War. The article discusses the impact of war in relation to refugee and internally displaced children and child soldiers, the sexual assault and exploitation of girls, and children traumatized by war. How the international community should respond to protect children and prevent war is explored in relation to the political and economic context within which wars occur. This article demonstrates that the exploitation of people and natural resources by transnational corporations is increasing poverty and other social problems and that the need for equitable and sustainable development, at an international level, is a prerequisite for reducing global conflict.

Transnational movements and NGOs have become an important component of an emerging and relatively recently theorized transnational civil society in the field of international relations. Geeta Chowdhry and Mark Beeman's article, "Challenging Child Labor: Transnational Activism and India's Carpet Industry," examines the role of the transnational human rights movement in relation to child labor in the carpet industry in India. Although the intersection of child labor with the carpet trade from India was utilized effectively by Indian and German activists to bring about changes in child labor use, the more foundational impact has been the creation of Rugmark, a label that certifies child-labor-free carpets and provides services for rehabilitative and educational responses to child labor in the carpet industry. It is also important to remember that the flow of human rights norms related to children, in the Rugmark case, was not from the liberal states to India; rather, it was the effort of social activists from India that initially guided German activists.

Steven Hick and Edward Halpin's article, "Children's Rights and the Internet," explores the impact of the Internet on the discourse of children's rights. The authors argue that the Internet is no substitute for strong and vibrant communities and societies but that it does provide a new and effective means for different people of the world to connect with one another. If the Internet is to become a force of development, democracy, and justice then it must be accessible to all people of the world. Primarily, people and organizations in richer industrialized countries promote the rights of children and connect others with their struggles through use of the Internet. The Internet will never be an instrument of justice if it remains out of the hands of the poor and oppressed.

Saadia Toor's article, "Child Labor in Pakistan: Coming of Age in the New World Order," is a critical evaluation of how consumer protests and boycotts in the North led to initiatives being taken by various national and international organizations. By posing the issue of child labor as a function of poverty and lack of education (of children) and awareness (of families), Toor argues that it is impossible to understand, let alone address, the child labor problem without placing it against the backdrop of the dynamics of the current neoliberal international political economic system. She concludes by arguing that the only way in which the issue of social and labor rights can be once more given precedence in an increasingly socially disembodied world economy is through political engagement with the forces of globalization—the World Bank, the International Monetary Fund, and the World Trade Organization.

If we seriously mean to improve life conditions for children what is urgently needed today is to bring children back to the center of society's efforts to create a better world for them. This requires at least three conditions. The first condition is to avoid excesses of both universalism and relativism in the current theoretical debates and policy practices concerned with the rights of children. Second, theoretical and policy approaches regarding children's rights should not be particularized so that they are treated in isolation from issues concerning class, race, and gender. The third condition is to work toward a comprehensive system of distributive justice that would guarantee the basic economic needs of children so that the formal equalities granted for them in the political domain will not be undermined by the inequalities of the economic domain. In such a system of distributive justice, the dominant economy ought to become a "field for the flourishing of public virtue" where "virtue and commerce thus ceases to be antithetical" (Eagleton 1992, 27).

JUDE L. FERNANDO

Notes

1. UNICEF 2000c.
2. A similar observation was made about Western feminist scholarship by Chandra Mohanty (1998).

References

Boyden, Jo. 1997. Childhood and the Policy Makers: A Comparative Perspective on the Globalization of Childhood. In *Constructing and Reconstructing Childhood*, ed. Allison James and Alan Prout. London: Falmer Press.
Children's Rights: Time for Governments to Fulfil Promises Made Ten Years Ago. 2000. Available at http://www.savethechildren.org/press/pr99_childrenrights.html.
Chomsky, Noam. 2000. *Chomsky on Miss-Education.* Ed. Donaldo Macedo. Boston: Rowman and Littlefield.
Eagleton, Terry. 1992. Deconstruction and Human Rights. In *Freedom and Interpretation: Oxford Amnesty Lectures.* New York: Basic Books.
Freire, Paulo. 1986. *Education for Critical Consciousness.* New York: Continuum.
Harvey, David. 1992. *The Conditions of Post Modernity.* London: Blackwell
James, Allison and Alan Prout. 1997. A New Paradigm for Sociology of Childhood? Provenance, Promise and Problems. In *Constructing and Reconstructing Childhood*, ed. Allison James and Alan Prout. London: Falmer Press.
Jameson, Fedric. 1999. *The Cultural Turn: Selected Writings on the Postmodern, 1983-1998.* London: Verso.
Joint United Nations Program on HIV/AIDS (UNAIDS). 1999. Report, Feb., p. 12. Available at http://www.unaids.org/wac/1999/eng/facts-e.htm.
Khoury, Jean-Claude. 1998. The Reemergence of Sweatshops. *Business Ethics: A European Review* 7(1):26-27.
Mohanty, Chandra. 1998. Under the Western Eyes: Feminist Scholarship and Colonial Discourse. *Feminist Review* 36(Autumn):61-89.
Ray, M. 1998. *The Human Rights Reader: Major Political Writings, Essays, Speeches, and Documents from Bible to the Present.* New York: Routledge.
Roche, Timothy. 2000. The Crisis of Foster Care. *Time*, 13 Nov.
Said, Edward. 1979. *Orientalism.* New York: Vintage Books.
Solberg, Ann. 1997. Negotiating Childhood: Changing Constructions of Age for Norwegian Children. In *Constructing and Reconstructing Childhood*, ed. Allison James and Alan Prout. London: Falmer Press.
UNICEF. 2000a. *Impact of Armed Conflict on Children.* Available at http://www.unicef.org/graca.
UNICEF. 2000b. *The State of the World's Children 2000.* Available at http://www.unicef.org/sowc00.
UNICEF. 2000c. *Why Global Partnership?* Available at http://www.unicef.org/initiative.

ANNALS, *AAPSS*, **575**, May 2001

Childhood: Toward a Theory of Continuity and Change

By ALLISON JAMES and ADRIAN L. JAMES

ABSTRACT: The socially constructed character of childhood is, by now, recognized as an important factor in shaping children's everyday experiences. It is no longer possible to see childhood simply as a common and universal biological phase in the life course. However, at the same time, it is being increasingly recognized that although acknowledgment of the social and cultural diversity of children's lives is important, there remain many things that children do share as occupants of the conceptual space of childhood. Although contemporary sociological theorizing about childhood has highlighted this tension, it has, as yet, offered few solutions. In this article, it is proposed that by examining the role of law and social policy over time from an interdisciplinary perspective, it is possible to account for both change and continuity in childhood as a structural space and, in turn, to see this as being the source of the diversities and commonalties that pattern children's everyday lives.

Allison James is a reader in applied anthropology at the University of Hull. Her research interests are in the anthropology and sociology of childhood, and she has published widely in this field.

Adrian L. James is a professor of applied social sciences at the University of Bradford. His research background is in the evaluation and analysis of social policy and sociolegal studies.

NOTE: An earlier version of this article was given at the Third International Congress on Childhood, at the University of Ankara, October 2000.

THREE basic premises lie at the heart of contemporary childhood studies. Derived originally from theoretical and empirical research in the social sciences (see Prout and James 1990), these constitute its basic building blocks. The first premise is that childhood is socially constructed, the second is that children are worthy of study in their own right, and the third is that children are competent social actors who may have a particular perspective on the social world that we, as adults, might find worth listening to. But the different ways in which these ideas have been taken up have helped shape an increasingly varied profile for this interdisciplinary arena, one that now encompasses sociology, anthropology, psychology, geography, history, philosophy, theology, education, sociolegal studies, and literature.

In this respect, the history of childhood studies mirrors the pattern of growth of cultural studies or women's studies (Alanen 1988). Nonetheless, it is fair to say that the study of childhood still draws heavily on the pioneering work carried out within the sociology and anthropology of childhood, and it is from this perspective that we address a key issue of contemporary childhood studies: the problem of how to reconcile, at one and the same time, the commonalities and the diversities of childhood. This is a problem not only of theory but also very much of practice, as those working in developing situations in the context of the U.N. Convention on the Rights of the Child know all too well (Boyden 1997; Woodhead 1996). However, though

this question can be quite simply stated, providing an answer to it that is both theoretically sound and practically useful is a little more problematic. Here we begin to explore how we might begin to address this by developing a theoretical perspective on childhood and change.

WHAT IS CHILDHOOD?

The foundational work of the new childhood studies is traditionally located in the work of Phillipe Aries (1962), whose historical research first underlined the socially constructed character of childhood. Through his assertion that "in mediaeval society childhood did not exist" he argued that while younger members of the species clearly existed, in mediaeval society they were not granted a special or distinctive social status (125). Once weaned, they participated in society according to their abilities, just as adults did. Aries argued that what was lacking at this time was an awareness that children might require a different and specific kind of social experience and that this awareness only gradually emerged from the fifteenth century onward. In his view, the dawning consciousness of children being different and particular can be seen marked out over time in the gradual social, political, and economic institutionalization of the idea of children's needs. This can be illustrated, for example, in the rise of schooling (Hendrick 1997) and the development of pediatrics and specialized children's clinics (Armstrong 1983).

Though the precise details of Aries's claim have been, and still are, subject to critique (see, for example, Pollock 1983), the broad framework of his argument remains foundational. First, "childhood" cannot be regarded as an unproblematic descriptor of a natural biological phase. Rather, the idea of childhood must be seen as a particular cultural phrasing of the early part of the life course, historically and politically contingent and subject to change. Second, Aries's thesis underlined the point that how we see children and the ways in which we behave toward them necessarily shape children's experiences of being a child and also their responses to and engagement with the adult world.

In sum, what has been central to the development of childhood studies is the twin recognition that childhood is, at one and the same time, common to all children but also fragmented by the diversity of children's everyday lives. That is to say, childhood is a developmental stage of the life course, common to all children and characterized by basic physical and developmental patterns. However, the ways in which childhood is interpreted, understood, and socially institutionalized by adults through their engagement with children and childhood varies considerably across and between cultures and generations. And, importantly, it varies with regard to the concepts of child-specific needs and competencies that are made evident in law and social policy as well as in the more mundane and everyday social interactions that take place between adults and children.

Given this variation between concepts of childhood and, thus, the variation in children's social experiences, it might be argued that childhood is always best understood in terms of its local,[1] diverse context; that it is no longer practical or even possible to speak, as has often been the case in the past, of the child as a universalized and apolitical subject of the modern world; and that, instead, it is best to concentrate on exploring the local diversities and cultural variables that fracture the coherent sensibilities of the notion of the child as a common and shared category status.

However, there is an inherent danger in overemphasizing cultural differences and local diversity. In doing so, we risk losing sight of the commonalities that *do* unite children. And to lose sight of these commonalities would mean dispensing with the political and policy agendas that might be brought into play to serve all children's interests, both globally and within the context of a single society. There is, then, some ambivalence, both in the academy and in the real world of practitioners and policymakers, with regard to how we might manage and perhaps even begin to work toward some resolution of these twin aspects. In this sense, childhood studies may be at a crossroads in terms of the direction in which it is heading.

What this draws attention to is, therefore, that the theorizing that has taken place to date has failed to specify adequately the mechanisms and processes through which childhood or, as we would wish to argue, culturally and politically diverse "childhoods" have emerged historically. Thus, a number of key questions arise: while we have much empirical evidence of the growth in or the emergence of the concept of childhood, how, exactly, did that take place? What were the key social and political processes that led to the gradual social, political, and economic institutionalization of the idea of children's needs? Why is it that these needs were differently and differentially institutionalized in different cultural contexts and historical eras? What role do children themselves play in shaping how childhood is understood, and what is the impetus for continued change and development in conceptions of childhood? Are we simply dealing here with the messy and chaotic path of history and random chance, or can we, instead, identify some key process that might allow us to offer a more general theory of childhood change that extends beyond the specificity of particular localities? By adopting a more dynamic interdisciplinary approach, we suggest that this might indeed be possible, and, in this article, we offer a theoretical approach to childhood change that builds on the creative tension that exists between the commonalities and diversities of childhood.

In what follows, we first set out the ways in which the study of children and childhood is being approached by contemporary researchers and then go on to develop some of the insights that arise from these perspectives with respect to understanding processes of change—and, indeed, those of continuity—in children's experiences of childhood.

KEY THEMES AND DEBATES IN CHILDHOOD STUDIES

James, Jenks, and Prout (1998) have outlined four models of childhood that, they argue, inform contemporary sociological research. These models emerge out of two particular research perspectives that engage in rather different ways with the conundrum of how to manage the apparent gulf between the commonality and diversity of childhood to which we have previously referred. The first perspective strongly asserts children's competence and stresses the importance of seeing children as social actors; the second addresses, equally strongly, a rather broader set of questions about how childhood is structured as a social space for children. It could be said, therefore, that the first perspective pays more attention to diversity in childhood research through its emphasis on children's individual and social action, while the second, by emphasizing structural issues, works toward explanations of what is common for all children. However, despite their apparent diametric opposition to one another, each approach does recognize, implicitly, the necessity of acknowledging both the commonalities and diversities of childhood.

Turning first to the perspective of the child as social actor, as James, Jenks, and Prout (1998) note, those working from this perspective have adopted two rather different models of childhood, what they term tribal and minority group. In both models of childhood, it is taken for granted that children are competent social actors and people with informed and informing views of the social world. But for those working with a tribal model, most attention is paid to the ways in which that competence is acknowledged and expressed or how is it disguised and controlled in and through children's everyday relationships—with each other, with their families, and with adults. In the tribal model, the commonalities of childhood are downplayed, and the diversities wrought by age, gender, class, health, and ethnicity are highlighted (see, for example, Corsaro 1979; Thorne 1993). It is argued that only by looking inside the different social worlds of children can their competence be revealed and explicated. Thus, within this perspective, to be able to see children as competent means exploring the ways in which children themselves, in and through their own social relationships, actively construct a child's world, distinctive and unique in its form and content. Children's own culture, their local play traditions, and language are thus key foci for researchers working with this model of childhood.

This concentrated focus on children as active learners and socializers also marks the second agency-focused perspective—the minority group—but here finds translation through more engagement with what is common to all children. Children's competencies, for example, are regarded as shared human competencies rather than as a child-specific set of abilities that are simply of and about the concerns of children. In this way, children are visualized as taking on the characteristics of a minority group vis-à-vis the adult population, separated and often discriminated against by the very institution of childhood itself (for example, see Mayall 1996; Alderson 1993). Research explores the ways in which children are united as members of the social category "child"—united by factors such as young age, lack of citizenship status, and lack of political, economic, and social rights. Within such a perspective, then, children as social actors are understood against the backdrop of a shared commonality that is envisaged as being akin to that of other minority groups.

Turning to the second perspective on childhood, which examines how childhood is structured as a social space for children, we find comparable variation. Once more, the differences center on the extent to which the particularity or diversity of children's childhoods, as revealed in children's everyday actions, is acknowledged within the more overarching paradigm that stresses the commonality of childhood as a social space. James, Jenks, and Prout (1998) suggest that, working from this more structural perspective, one strand of research is concerned with exploring the ways in which the social space for childhood is marked out in society, seeing this as a constant and recognizable component of all social structures. Beginning from the assumption that children are common to every social system, such research has as its central focus the commonality of childhood. The status identity of the child is examined in its inter-relationship with other status categories—adolescence and adult-hood, for example—as a structural feature of the life course and, there-fore, as a more general feature of the social system. Such a perspective on childhood permits work to be carried out at a national and a global level through adopting a comparative framework within which the status of the child is taken as is, and is not, in itself, made a matter of dispute (see Qvortrup 1994).

This body of work is comple-mented by the final model of child-hood. Representing childhood as a social construct, this model explores the diverse ways in which childhood comes to be constituted in society for children. Rather than taking the child for granted, this radically rela-tivistic body of work examines the discourses through which the idea of the child and childhood is produced. It asks, What is the child in the local context? How is the status of the child understood locally? What fea-tures of the child are highlighted as important and attributed with sig-nificance? Such work does not assume, therefore, that there is a set of naturalized competencies that allows us to define the child from the outset, and, in this sense, it is diamet-rically opposed to the model of growth and maturation offered from within developmental psychology while nonetheless being focused on the structures through which ideas of childhood are articulated (see, for example, Jenks 1996; Stainton-Rogers and Stainton-Rogers 1992; Gittens 1998).

UNDERSTANDING CHILDHOOD CHANGE

The four models outlined above are but variations on a theme. The differences between them constitute differences of emphasis, rather than of kind, with the major difference being the extent to which the com-monality or diversity of childhood is acknowledged and revealed in the pictures they offer of children's everyday lives and childhoods. Each kind of approach highlights some fac-ets of child life and downplays others. There is, therefore, much common ground.

However, foundational to all of these approaches (whether explicitly acknowledged or not) is, we suggest, one rather more basic axiom: that children are not only shaped by cul-ture but also help shape it. To put it another way, childhood not only shapes children's experiences, but children also help shape the nature of the childhood that they experience. Thus, the challenge, as we see it, is to demonstrate and explain the links between such structure and agency perspectives. And in doing so, as we shall argue, we can also show how commonality and diversity are, simultaneously, at work in all chil-dren's everyday experiences of child-hood. This, however, also requires us to acknowledge and to incorporate into our analysis the fact that child-hoods are also shaped in part by adults.

On the face of it, such a standpoint is hardly new, for what we are argu-ing is that the different approaches to contemporary childhood research are, in essence, engaging with the structure and agency debate that has long bedeviled social science; that neither structure nor agency perspectives are sufficient; and that what in fact we need is to do both—simultaneously. What is needed, in effect, is to find some empirical evidence in children's everyday lives to support Gidden's structuration theory or Bourdieu's theorizing about the "habitus" (see James forthcoming).

There is, however, a twist here: it may be that childhood does indeed represent a unique context for doing this. And here time itself is the key, for the very materiality of the biological base of childhood—its universality and commonality as a temporal phase in the life course of all children—can be said to work as a kind of structural constraint on action-centered perspectives for understanding childhood that stress locality and diversity. Thus, as much as we might wish to see children as authors of their own histories, we do, nonetheless, have to acknowledge two things about children and childhood. First, all children do eventually grow up and change and become adults. That is to say, all children leave childhood. Second, and despite the passage of children in and out of it, childhood, as a social space, remains. However—and this is important—as this temporal space in the life course is itself historically located, the nature of childhood inevitably changes and thus so do children's experiences of that space. Our concern here is to reveal the medium through which such processes of

change take place and to suggest how they can be accounted for theoretically.

In brief, to engage with the dynamic interplay between structure and agency perspectives, it is necessary, we argue, to make the temporality of childhood a central and uniting theoretical strand. This involves first exploring how it is that discourses of childhood and the child—for example, those evident in the law, in social policies about family and parenting, and in educational policy or political rhetoric—are given practical form in children's day-to-day experiences through the shaping and reshaping of the category of the child and the generational space of childhood (James and James 2001). Second, it involves asking how children themselves encounter and respond to these versions of the self-as-child and of childhood that they meet on an everyday basis in their social relationships with adults and, indeed, with their peers. Framed in this way, we can tack between structure and agency perspectives and, in empirical research, engage with the commonalities as well as the diversities of childhood through giving sensible documentation of the institutional and social mechanisms that shape the process of socialization and thus the process by which children grow into and out of childhood (see James forthcoming).

At a theoretical level, therefore, we are suggesting that there is a highly dynamic and symbiotic relationship between the conceptualization of childhood as a particular generational and cultural space and children's actions as the occupants of that space; that children are social members of the category "child" who, through their interactions and engagement with the adult world, help form both the categorical identity of the child with which they are ascribed and the generational space of childhood to which they belong; and that this relationship delineates the "how" of the socialization process. In this sense, discourses of childhood are never simply discourses; they are and indeed have to be enacted, given practical realization and material form through the minutiae of the everyday social practices that take place between adults and children in the home, at school, in the community, or in the doctor's office. Moreover, we argue that such discourses do not stand alone or emerge from nowhere; they represent the culminated history of social policymaking with regard, for example, to the protection and welfare of children, policies both predicated on and helping to promote particular ideas of children's needs as well as ideas of what children are or normally should be (see Hendrick 1997; Stainton-Rogers and Stainton-Rogers 1992).

This, however, raises a key question that, as we suggested earlier, requires us to draw on other disciplines if we are to explain and understand more fully the relationship between children, childhood, and the adult world. If the categorical identity of the child and the social and generational space of childhood to which children belong are created through their interactions and engagement with the adult world, is

it sufficient to see these as simply the product of everyday social practices, or does such a process require the specification of a more powerful institutional mechanism than this that can explain how this takes place over time? Our answer must be that it does and that the clue to understanding this mechanism lies in both the threats and potentialities that the commonalities and diversities of childhood bring to and for children, and adults' responses to these, since it is through the combined effect of these that both the changes and continuities of childhood arise.

CHILDREN, CHILDHOOD, AND SOCIAL ORDER

As we have argued, recent research has made it clear that children are not simply passive objects and the product of universal biological and social processes but are active participants in their own social worlds and in those of adults. The very fact that this is so is evidenced by the changing historical (both short- and long-term) emphasis on the regulation and control of children and childhood, in concerns about children's impact on social order, and in the ways in which these ebb and flow over time. For example, as James, Jenks, and Prout (1998) note, changes in conceptions of children and childhood pattern history with images of the child as evil or innocent, the child as immanent, or alternatively, the child as developing naturally, images that become concretized and made "fact" through the different ways in which children's lives are ordered and controlled.

Thus seventeenth-century Puritanical regimes that controlled and ordered the evil child were gradually replaced by less strict regimes designed to foster the child's natural innocence (see also Hendrick 1997). And now in the United Kingdom, at the turn of the century, the natural, spontaneous innocence of children is becoming, once more, subject to regimes of surveillance and new forms of ordering (James and James 2001). The net of social control threatens increasingly to restrict children's everyday lives and activities. But the question is, Why and how does this change occur?

Turning to our models of childhood, we might begin to tease out an explanation. For example, by focusing on the child as social actor within the tribal model of childhood, we can see children exercising their agency within local contexts and in response to local particularities. And in doing so, we might see how it is that this exercise of agency creates some of the diversities that, as noted, are just as much a part of childhood as are its commonalities. As Bluebond-Langner (1978) so graphically described, the prospect of imminent death serves to give children a self-confidence and competence in dealing with the adult world that would in other circumstances not be theirs. The dying or chronically sick child's childhood represents one kind of diversity. Alternatively, we might explore how the common social space of childhood positions children as members of a minority group, united as actors in a shared and particular position within the social structure, and how, as a consequence of such

perceptions of commonality, exceptions emerge—for example, the child who exceeds expectations of an age-based competency, the child carer, the child worker, and the child soldier. But—and this is significant—the emergence of such exceptions has, potentially, two rather different consequences: it can reinforce existing models of the child, but it can also lead to the reconsideration of these models. Change and continuity in thinking are thus both possible: the question of which will occur is determined by prevailing social, political, and cultural conditions.

It might be postulated, therefore, that, over time, in such instances the pressure for greater regulation and control of children's actions and agency will vary, along with adult perceptions of the priority to be given to reinforcing the social order and/or to producing new, uniform but culturally specific social constructions of childhood. An example from the United Kingdom would be the demand made for new forms of control over childhood and, indeed, the emergence of new constructions of children's nature and competencies that followed in the wake of the James Bulger case in 1993, when two 10-year-old boys murdered a younger child after abducting him from a shopping precinct in Bootle (see James and Jenks 1996).[2]

At a theoretical level, then, what we have here is an explanation of childhood change, envisaged as a reflexive and evolutionary process, that is driven forward by an interaction between adults' perceptions of different models of childhood and of children's agency. Childhood is imaged as a social space that is continuously located within and shaped by the social structure of a given society but that is also shaped by the actions of successive generations of children who succeed in creating and re-creating diversity within this common socially constructed category.

What we wish to add to this analysis is an explanation of why and how this happens. Central to this process is, we suggest, the regulatory mechanism of law since it is law that defines the rights and responsibilities of, and therefore the relationships between, citizens in any given cultural and political context. It is law that creates and sustains the regulatory frameworks that define childhood and therefore also the social practices that encapsulate and systematize everyday interactions between adults and children. Law is therefore an integrative mechanism: it formalizes and mitigates conflicts and facilitates social interaction by regulating the relationships between the differentiated parts of social systems (Roach Anleu 2000, 41), a perspective developed in somewhat different contexts by social theorists such as Parsons (1962, 1978) and Habermas (1996). Since law also comprises and reflects cultural knowledge, however, it is quintessentially normative and therefore also provides an important means of communication between citizens by defining their legal rights, freedoms, and responsibilities, both to the state and to other citizens, be they adults or children, as well as seeking to regulate these.

Thus, we are suggesting that law, be it religious or secular, emerges as

the key mechanism that mediates between, but also preserves, the boundaries between adulthood and childhood. Further, if we think of law in a generic sense, it is one of the primary mechanisms for social ordering, comprising a system of principles that reflect the social construction of a wide range of phenomena, behaviors, and relationships. It is through law that children's everyday lives as children are constructed and regulated (James and James 1999). Therefore, we would argue that what the concept of childhood represents is, in effect, the cumulative history of the formulation of social policies expressed as law in response to the activities of children in their engagement with the adult world. It is through the operation of law that social order is produced and reproduced and through which diverse realities are mediated by reference to common principles. Law thereby accommodates both diversity and commonality in allowing change but also ensuring continuity.

CHANGING CHILDHOOD
AND CHILDHOOD CHANGE

Viewed from within the theoretical framework outlined above, the significance of law in relation to childhood change can be exemplified by the U.N. Convention on the Rights of the Child, since this seeks to define those very commonalities that constitute the social space of childhood and to specify criteria by which the child might be protected. At the same time, however, the convention seeks to allow sufficient space for the existence of culturally and politically specific constructions of childhood.

It is also important to acknowledge, however, that in recognizing the existence of culturally and politically specific constructions of childhood, and by seeking to encourage nation-state signatories to locate the principles of the U.N. convention within their own jurisdictional frameworks, law works to accommodate diversity. It does this not only at the macro level of cultural and political specificity but also by acknowledging law as a mechanism that is uniquely equipped to adjudicate on individual and local issues in the context of generally held principles. Thus, if we take any area of law that contributes to the definition of "childhood" and "the child," whether this be family law, employment law, education law, or whatever, each nation-state's judicatory system has the function of testing the facts of individual cases, involving individual children in their relationship with the adult world, against the general principles by which childhood is defined in relation to adulthood in that particular cultural or political context.

Law does not, however, exist in a vacuum, and it is not, as some theorists would argue (for example, Teubner 1989; King 1990), an entirely closed and self-referential system (James 1992). It, too, is a social and cultural construct that mediates between the state and the individual and, therefore, between the state's desire for the achievement of conformity and commonality through regulation, on the one hand, and the individual's desire for

diversity and the freedom to explore and express agency, on the other. This tension is held in the sphere of social policy, be this in terms of the promulgation of policies defining the rights and responsibilities of citizens in a secular society or the promulgation of doctrines that define the rights and responsibilities of believers in a religious-based society, since such policies, whether defined by the secular or the religious state, are the ultimate source of law. Importantly, of course, such polices change over time, in response both to internal and external pressures, and thus law also changes, along with the childhoods it serves to regulate. We would contend, therefore, that law is a dynamic mechanism that articulates and mediates the relationship between the individual and the state, between adults and children, between adulthood and childhood, between the common and the diverse, and between social policies and social practices, while also providing the continuities between pasts, presents, and futures.

CONCLUSION

The strides made in the development of childhood studies in recent years have been immense. There is now widespread if not universal acceptance of the premise that childhood is indeed socially constructed; that children are worthy of study in their own right; and that children are competent social actors who may have a particular perspective on the social world that we, as adults, might find worth listening to. These strides have been made possible by the reflexive relationship between theory and research. What has eluded us so far, however, has been the identification and articulation of a mechanism that mediates between the diverse and apparently contradictory perspectives that the study of childhood have revealed and that allows us to reconcile the commonalities and diversities of childhood. What has also been problematic to explain is the fact that if we are fully to understand childhood, we must consider both structure and agency, as well as account for and explain the process that enables childhood to change while also ensuring that certain aspects continue.

What we have outlined in this article is a theoretical proposition that, we believe, reconciles these tensions and mediates different perspectives that characterize the field of childhood studies. The challenge now is to demonstrate this empirically.

Notes

1. In this context, we are using "local" to mean both local in the global context as well as local in the national and regional context.

2. The difference here between the Bulger case and the case of child-to-child murder in Trondheim, Norway, is interesting. The Norwegian case led to no reconceptualization of childhood and no changes in regulation or calls for increased control. The Norwegian child killers were regarded as victims rather than perpetrators of violence, and there was no public debate about the nature of childhood as there was in the U.K. case. The exercise of agency can thus give rise to both continuity and change.

References

Alanen, L. 1988. Rethinking Childhood. *Acta Sociologica* 31(1):53-67.

Alderson, P. 1993. *Children's Consent to Surgery*. Buckingham: Open University.

Aries, P. 1962. *Centuries of Childhood*. London: Jonathan Cape.

Armstrong, D. 1983. *The Political Anatomy of the Body: Medical Knowledge in Britain in the Twentieth Century*. Cambridge: Cambridge University Press.

Bluebond-Langner, M. 1978. *The Private Worlds of Dying Children*. Princeton, NJ: Princeton University Press.

Boyden, J. 1997. Childhood and the Policy Makers: A Comparative Perspective on the Globalization of Childhood. In *Constructing and Reconstructing Childhood*, 2d ed., ed. A. James and A. Prout. London: Falmer Press.

Corsaro, W. A. 1979. We're Friends Right? Children's Use of Access Rituals in a Nursery School. *Language in Society* 8:315-36.

Gittins, D. 1998. *The Child in Question*. London: Macmillan.

Habermas, J. 1996. *Between Facts and Norms: Contributions to a Discourse Theory of Law and Democracy*. Cambridge: Polity Press.

Hendrick, H. 1997. Constructions and Reconstructions of British Childhood: An Interpretive Survey, 1800 to the Present. In *Constructing and Reconstructing Childhood*, 2d ed., ed. A. James and A. Prout. London: Falmer Press.

James, A. Forthcoming. The English Child: Towards a Cultural Politics of Childhood Identities. In *The Best of British*, ed. N. J. Rapport. Oxford: Berg.

James, A. and C. Jenks. 1996. Public Perceptions of Childhood Criminality. *British Journal of Sociology* 47(2):315-31.

James, A., C. Jenks, and A. Prout. 1998. *Theorising Childhood*. Cambridge: Polity Press.

James, A. L. 1992. An Open or Shut Case? Law as an Autopoietic System. *Journal of Law and Society* 19(2):271-83.

James, A. L. and A. James. 1999. Pump Up the Volume: Listening to Children in Separation and Divorce. *Childhood* 6(2):189-206.

———. 2001. Tightening the Net: Children, Community and Control. *British Journal of Sociology* 52(2): 211-28.

Jenks, C. 1996. The Postmodern Child. In *Children and Families: Research and Policy,* ed. J. Brannen and M. O'Brien. London: Falmer Press.

King, M. 1990. Child Welfare Within Law: The Emergence of a Hybrid Discourse. *Journal of Law and Society* 18:303-22.

Mayall, B. 1996. *Children, Health and the Social Order.* Buckingham: Open University Press.

Parsons, T. 1962. The Law and Social Control. In *The Law and Sociology: Exploratory Essays,* ed. William M. Evan. New York: Free Press.

———. 1978. Law as an Intellectual Stepchild. In *Social Systems and Legal Process,* ed. Harry M Johnson. San Francisco: Jossey-Bass.

Pollock, L. A. 1983. *Forgotten Children: Parent-Child Relations from 1500 to 1900.* Cambridge: Cambridge University Press.

Prout, A. and A. James. 1990. A New Paradigm for the Sociology of Childhood? Provenance, Promise and Problems. In *Constructing and Reconstructing Childhood,* ed. A. James and A. Prout. London: Falmer Press.

Qvortrup, J. 1994. Childhood Matters: An Introduction. In *Childhood Matters,* ed. J. Qvortrup. Aldershot: Avebury.

Roach Anleu, S. 2000. *Law and Social Change.* London: Sage.

Stainton-Rogers, R. and W. Stainton-Rogers. 1992. *Stories of Childhood: Shifting Agendas of Child Concern.* London: Harvester Wheatsheaf.

Teubner, G. 1989. How the Law Thinks: Towards a Constructivist Epistemology of Law. *Law and Society Review* 23:727-57.

Thorne, B. 1993. *Gender Play: Girls and Boys in School.* New Brunswick, NJ: Rutgers University Press.

Woodhead, M. 1996. In Search of the Rainbow: Pathways to Quality in Large-Scale Programmes for Young Disadvantaged Children. In *Early Childhood Development: Practice and Reflections,* vol. 10. The Hague: Bernard van Leer Foundation.

ANNALS, *AAPSS*, **575**, May 2001

The Right Rights?
Child Labor in a Globalizing World

By WILLIAM E. MYERS

ABSTRACT: This article examines some important aspects of the current international debate regarding how to apply concepts of children's rights to child labor. It begins with the question of what, and whose, ideas about children and childhood provide the foundation for globalized children's rights norms, looking into concerns that international child labor policies may be unjustly dominated by European and North American values and ideas at the expense of more representative worldviews. From this perspective, it then reviews the three main international conventions dealing with child labor, discussing certain ideological and strategic differences between them and tracing in their history a gradual movement away from the dominance of Northern ethnocentrism and toward more culturally inclusive and flexible formulations of children's rights standards.

William E. Myers is a visiting scholar in the Department of Human and Community Development at the University of California, Davis, and a former official of the ILO and UNICEF.

G LOBALIZATION is cultural and political, as well as economic, and in recent years primarily European and North American concepts of global human rights have been promoted throughout the world as political and cultural products that should be adopted by rich and poor countries alike. As part of this movement, the rights of children have become an increasingly important subject of international concern and action, and the U.N. Convention on the Rights of the Child (CRC), adopted in 1989 and now ratified by all countries except Somalia and the United States, has become the most widely subscribed human rights treaty ever. This convention has effectively focused and globalized international discussion of children's rights and established a set of principles and responsibilities to which nearly all countries are now officially committed. UNICEF and various nongovernmental child defense organizations are dedicated to securing the CRC's effective implementation. Because of its unparalleled official reach, the CRC can be seen as a globalized response for protecting children in a world becoming increasingly smaller and more interdependent. Since it is now the prevailing general framework for most international action on children's rights, many have assumed that its legal provisions are supported by equally global concepts of what children's rights are and how to observe them. However, experience with interpreting and implementing the convention in different political, economic, and cultural settings has revealed considerable diversity of thinking about children's rights and how to implement them, even among groups that strongly support the CRC.

Child labor has in recent years been perhaps the most visible single issue generating discussion about how children's rights are to be defined and observed in an era of globalization. It is currently the subject of heated national and international debate, and much of the controversy revolves around the questions of who should decide what is best for children and determine the policies and programs intended to protect them, and according to what criteria. Much of the polemic about child labor is couched in terms of children's rights. In this case, however, the children's rights discourse draws not only on the CRC but also on other rights concepts about children and child work, some of which precede the CRC by more than a century. Even a cursory review of the international discussion of child work reveals marked divergence of opinion regarding what constitutes a right, who gets to claim or impose rights, and which rights should be preferred over others. Moreover, as I will explain in the following sections, not even internationally mandated standards addressing child work are fully compatible with each other; choices are inescapable. Ideological and policy differences sometimes escalate into competition over whose ideas, objectives, and political agenda will win out by being formally or informally accepted as rights or at least as recommended strategies for achieving rights already recognized. Given the competing rights discourses, policymakers interested in applying a children's rights perspective to the solution of child labor problems are immediately faced with the quandary, Which rights are the right rights? This question is now at the very heart of current international debate concerning how to define and deal with child labor.

THE GLOBALIZATION OF IDEAS ABOUT CHILDHOOD

Current debates about the application of children's rights to child labor have their roots in the thorny problem of reconciling uniform global rules with the protection of cultural diversity and international democracy. How should a children's rights approach based on specified international standards of social conduct deal with infinite variation in how societies think about children and childhood in general and about child work in particular? On the one hand, there is today a renewed emphasis on multiculturalism, on the importance of maintaining cultural integrity, and on raising children to appreciate and fit into their own social milieu as well as in an expanding world. On the other hand, however, most thinking on children's rights has for a century been based on a homogenizing concept of childhood as a biologically driven natural phenomenon characterized by physical and mental growth stages that are everywhere roughly the same, even if culturally inflected. Recent experience and scholarship suggest that this homogenizing notion is too simplistic. Practical experience demonstrates the existence of an

international divide between rich and poor societies, according to which the industrialized countries of Europe and North America (and often Western-educated elites in poorer countries) tend to conceive of childhood and raise their children differently than the less economically developed societies of Africa, Asia, and elsewhere. For instance, Northern societies tend to rigorously separate childhood from adulthood by keeping children dependent through adolescence and discouraging their participation in certain adult concerns such as economic maintenance of the family. Many Southern societies, on the other hand, stress family unity and solidarity, equip their children to play mature roles by adolescence, and include children in contributing to the family livelihood. They often reject Northern-influenced international child labor standards because the views of children and childhood implicit in such do not adequately fit with the realities of developing countries (Boyden, Ling, and Myers 1998; White 1994, 1996; Woodhead 1998).

Diversity is also a principal theme in research from the academic disciplines of social science and social history, in which childhood is increasingly understood to be every bit as much a culturally constructed concept as it is a natural phenomenon of biological immaturity (for example, Aries 1965; Burman 1994; Cole 1996; Cunningham 1991, 1995; James and Prout 1997; Rogoff 1990; Valsiner 2000). In fact, many historians and social scientists no longer treat childhood as a universal phenomenon that merely has different cultural expressions. They find it more useful to think instead in terms of many different childhoods linked to particular contexts, "neither timeless nor universal but, instead, rooted in the past and shaped in the present" (James and Prout 1997, 232). If children are raised by different methods to make their way in societies having different values, goals, and challenges, what is the legitimate basis for international children's rights standards such as those articulated in the CRC? A perspective emphasizing the diversity of childhood raises some cogent questions about whose values and what processes should orient globalized children's rights standards, and no children's rights issue has so far raised them more clearly than does that of child labor.

These questions were explored by Oxford anthropologist Jo Boyden in a now classic 1990 critique of the globalization of ideas about children and childhood (Boyden 1997). She noted that European and North American urban, middle-class concepts of children and childhood have been promoted worldwide as a standardized universal model of childhood assumed to apply to all societies. It is presumed that these culture-specific notions represent universal childhood as it is rather than as it is imagined to be from a particular cultural perspective. Despite the lack of evidence that these ideas are necessarily correct or somehow better for children than other people's notions, child-raising practices from these same rich, capitalist, politically democratic, mostly Judeo-Christian societies are being held up as universal norms applicable also to societies of developing countries whose economic conditions, social structures, and cultural and religious traditions are vastly different. European and North American middle-class notions of what constitutes a proper childhood in their own societies are ethnocentrically projected globally as criteria by which to judge how well all the other world's societies tend to their own children.

Boyden (1997) contended that the ethnocentrism of industrialized countries, bolstered by their superior political and economic power, was unjustly dominating the international discourse on children's rights. She pointed out that ideas useful primarily within the cultural and economic context of northern Europe and North America end up being globally institutionalized through international instruments, such as the CRC, which was being readied for adoption at the time she wrote. Concepts and values perhaps more important in the developing world were not equally represented. Boyden intended not to defend relativism or discourage international agreements to defend children's rights but to point out that the institutionalization of a particular Western model of childhood as the basis for global rights disenfranchises poor and working-class children—by far the world's majority—by making their lives seem deviant, inferior, or even pathological just for departing from an inappropriately imposed culture-biased norm. She cited work as a central element of many developing-country childhoods, which tends to be unjustly neglected or condemned by rich-country ethnocentrism.

Seven years after her seminal article first appeared, Boyden took the occasion of a second edition to add a substantial postscript updating her observations in the light of experience with the CRC, which had by then become the primary international framework for discussing children's rights. She again called attention to child labor as an area in which Northern ethnocentrism combined with vested economic interests, imposed on the South in the name of children's rights, can easily injure the very children supposedly being protected. As an example, she cited a well-documented case in which thousands of children working in Bangladesh garment factories were summarily dismissed from their jobs when the U.S. Congress considered legislation prohibiting the importation of products made with the involvement of workers under 15 years of age, citing international child labor standards. Since the United States was by far the largest export market for the industry, which also contributed over half of Bangladesh's foreign exchange, nervous owners unwilling to risk access to their best market quickly dismissed workers thought to be under or even near that minimum age. Nongovernmental organizations concerned with the children's welfare soon reported that fired children were not returning to school as U.S. advocates of the measure had expected they would but were instead moving from comparatively safe, well-paid garment factory employment into forms of work at once less remunerative and

more dangerous for children, a situation confirmed by International Labor Organization (ILO) and UNICEF follow-up studies (Boyden and Myers 1995).

Boyden held up the Bangladesh case of misguided good intentions as a warning about the consequences of simplistically applying rich-country assumptions and remedies to poor-country situations without adequate attention to differences of social and economic context. She worried that the pat formulas of much children's rights discourse would substitute for rigorous attention to the specifics of children's situations and lead to generic, simplistic solutions likely to be ineffectual or counterproductive for the children involved. She pointed out that the ultimate impact of the CRC will depend as much on the style of its implementation as on the content of its text, and she insisted on the need for basing international children's rights standards on more objective and culturally inclusive criteria. She suggested that effective protection of children from workplace abuse often depends less on preventing them from working, per the European and American solution unilaterally imposed on Bangladesh, than on protecting them in their work and creating more alternatives for economic and social advancement. Child work tends in much of the world to be more deeply embedded in family life than is typical in rich countries, and interventions in it may therefore have important consequences for how children are perceived and treated by their parents and other caregivers. Those intervening in children's work need to keep in mind likely consequences beyond the workplace.

Work has been shown by anthropologists, sociologists, and psychologists to relate to children's welfare and development in diverse ways that vary with social, economic, and cultural factors and even with the particular characteristics of children themselves.[1] While there is no evidence that engaging in work is necessarily bad for children—in most societies, it remains an important means of teaching and socializing them—very large numbers of children are involved in kinds of work and working conditions that are clearly detrimental to them. However, often what is damaging about such work is less its intrinsic nature (for example, processes exposing children to toxins or unsafe machinery) than its organization or the social relations surrounding it (for example, working too many hours or in competition with school, harsh and demeaning supervision, or disparagement by adults for working or choice of occupation). The same kinds of work, or protective interventions in work, can and do have very different impacts on children's lives and development depending on how society constructs the meaning and value of the work in question. Even children in stressful kinds of work have been found to thrive surprisingly when they and the work they do are esteemed by family and community, and children in far less stressful work situations may become more vulnerable when they and their work are denigrated by others (Boyden, Ling, and Myers 1998).

Sensitivity to culture and the way it mediates the effects of experience on children by no means invalidate the idea of global child labor standards but do suggest the need to carefully distinguish between values based on a broad representation of human experience and those that are merely Euro-American ethnocentrism projected by economic and political power onto a global arena. Modern social science thinking about children and childhood would suggest that beneficial international standards for dealing with child labor need to be able to accommodate diverse models of childhood and ways of raising children while at the same time establishing widely accepted norms by which societies can be held accountable. Also, practical experience suggests that valid global standards also should reflect widely shared values and avoid ethnocentric impositions by the rich and powerful. Many have recognized these dilemmas as the central problems of establishing meaningful children's rights. Philip Alston (1994), a leading authority on children's rights, has said that it is necessary to point the way toward "approaches which involve neither the embrace of an artificial and sterile universalism nor the acceptance of an ultimately self-defeating cultural relativism" (2).

Is it realistically possible to draft and negotiate international agreements to meet so demanding a criterion? Is it feasible to walk a children's rights tightrope suspended between ethnocentric cultural imperialism at one extreme and unaccountable relativism at the other? In order to find out, let us consider the history of the main international conventions pertaining to child labor.

THE NATURE AND ROLE OF INTERNATIONAL CONVENTIONS

International political action against child labor is closely linked to international conventions, a form of treaty that carries the force of law in signing nations, sponsored through the U.N. system and subscribed to by countries through a formal process of ratification. National governments claim the right to define international norms through the assertion that governments are the legitimate representatives of their citizens (including children) and that the conventions they draft and ratify speak for everyone. However, conventions dealing with social matters usually are negotiated by professional bureaucrats and diplomats instead of experts, and they balance the agendas of the various interested groups and institutions according to their relative power. Accordingly, they tend to be instruments of political rather than technical consensus, informed more by opinion than research, and are more responsive to interests than experience. As such, they signify what countries say they agree to do, not necessarily what they really are willing to do or what qualified experts would think should be done. These conventions establish international guidelines and standards that ratifying countries commit themselves to follow in their own national policies. Social conventions of the type dealing with children's rights and child labor, unlike some security and trade conventions, are purely voluntary and have no enforcement mechanism to make countries behave according to their obligations. Countries can, and frequently do, pay little or no attention to high-minded conventions that they may have ratified for any of a variety of reasons, which may or may not include serious commitment to the objectives and principles involved. Some conventions have reporting processes in which an international panel periodically reviews each member country's performance against its history and commitments, issuing findings that may come to public attention via the media. For example, the CRC is overseen by an international committee that receives and reviews country reports on progress in implementing the convention. Although social conventions such as we will deal with here are often considered to be weak because of their lack of enforcement powers, they can in fact exert a strong influence on policy by shaping and establishing reference points for international debate and action. Therefore, they are important even if they are weak, and for that reason may actually be more influential than they at first appear.

Three international conventions comprise the main global reference points for national and international policy regarding child labor: the ILO Minimum Age Convention (No. 138) of 1973, the already mentioned 1989 U.N. Convention on the Rights of the Child, and the new ILO Worst Forms of Child Labour Convention (No. 182) of 1999.[2] Each of the two ILO conventions is accompanied by a set of recommendations regarding how to implement it. Together, the three conventions reflect competing and progressively changing notions of childhood and the role of work in it, as will be described in the following sections. Let us review these conventions, examining their provisions and the models of childhood and the sources of values they incorporate.

The ILO Minimum
  Age Convention

The earliest of these three conventions is the ILO Minimum Age Convention (No. 138), which in 1973 updated and replaced a series of earlier child labor conventions going back to the founding of the ILO in 1919. This agreement perfectly exemplifies the attempt to globalize Northern ideas and values and the problems this globalization engenders. That characteristic is explainable by its roots in the early days of the ILO. The ILO was at its outset a Europe-centered agency whose original purpose included, among other things, the political objective of halting the spread of radical socialism by providing a democratic alternative based on a tripartite collaboration of government, industry, and labor. The elimination of child labor was considered such an important element of this strategy that the Treaty of Versailles authorizing establishment of the ILO mandated as one of its main tasks "the abolition of child labor and the imposition of such limitations on the labor of young persons as shall permit the continuation of their education and assure their proper physical development" (quoted in Cunningham 1999, 10). During its early years of mostly European focus, the

ILO logically enough drew on accumulated European concepts and experiences to create its international child labor standards and policies. However, when developing countries began somewhat later to enter the organization in greater numbers after decolonization, the ILO merely reinforced and disseminated its existing Europe-derived policies rather than reconceive them to fit new realities. As a result, the various successive ILO conventions regulating the work of children have essentially globalized European (and now also North American) history, conceiving of child labor in primarily urban-industrial terms and looking to the state for the same remedies that had been at the center of child labor reform in the rich countries. These were primarily legal mechanisms requiring a well-developed legislative apparatus credible with the public, an honest and well-organized public sector labor inspectorate for enforcement, and compulsory education in a well-developed public education system able to provide all children with a worthwhile alternative to work. It goes almost without saying that this industrial conception and legalistic approach are anachronistic in most of today's developing countries, where child employment is overwhelmingly agricultural, where social welfare laws have relatively little impact on the everyday life of the poor, where labor inspection services tend to be precarious and corrupt, and where national governments have extreme difficulty extending full primary education coverage to the rural and urban periphery areas where most working children live.

Convention 138 is best understood in this historical light. Although nowhere does it use the term "child labor," it starts from the original Northern idea, first developed in late-eighteenth-century and early-nineteenth-century England, that children have a natural right not to work and that their very presence in the workplace is the crux of the child labor problem (Cunningham 1991, 1995). This position also reflects fears that the economic participation of children undermines adult jobs and income, a proposition still widely believed and asserted, although it receives little support from the available evidence, which is ambiguous. It needs to be remembered that the Minimum Age Convention was not intended to be just about children or to serve only their interests; it is equally about protecting labor markets and adult economic interests. The abolition of child labor has therefore long been understood by the ILO to mean removal of underage children from economic activity, which is felt to be properly the exclusive province of adults. Accordingly, Convention 138 prohibits children from engaging in any economic activity (child care and housekeeping chores are considered noneconomic) below certain specified minimum ages. The only exceptions are for work in educational institutions (as part of training) and on small family farms producing for local consumption. The convention standards apply even to children working for themselves in odd jobs or for their parents in small family-run

businesses. A general minimum age for admission to "employment or work" is set at 15, but in no case is it to be less than the age up to which children are obligated by law to be in school. In the poorest countries, the minimum age may be temporarily set a year younger. Children may do "light work," defined as safe part-time work that does not interfere with schooling, beginning at age 13 or, in the poorest countries, at age 12. Below these ages, economic activity of any type or amount is proscribed. Children below age 18 may not engage in hazardous work, although those at least age 16 may do so if properly protected and instructed. Countries have some discretion in deciding what work activities should be covered by or exempted from minimum age laws, but this discretion is limited since the convention dictates certain kinds of work that must be covered. It should be noted that the convention's style is relatively detailed, going beyond principles and objectives to specify a variety of different universal age standards to the precise year.

Although Convention 138 is strongly influenced by the historical notion that children should have a right not to work, it does not explicitly represent its provisions as rights; indeed, there are those who question whether restricting children's room for choice can be considered a right at all. Nor does the convention condition its provisions by what is in children's best interests, although it is safe to surmise that a majority of the delegates adopting the convention in 1973 thought that at least preadolescent children would benefit by being excluded from work. The convention also implies a very traditional view of children as helpless victims or potential victims needing adults to intervene on their behalf; it makes no pretense about giving children a say in what happens to them.

As might be expected, Convention 138 has met resistance in societies whose child-raising values include introducing children to work at an early age rather than excluding them from it. In many traditional African societies, for example, properly raised children are supposed to be introduced to various work roles and skills at a young age, and idle children are considered to be victims of parental neglect. The precise age standards, which are widely perceived to reflect industrialized-country norms more than developing-country realities, have also caused many problems. In many developing-country rural areas, for instance, children starting school at 6 years of age can finish all the education (typically the primary level) locally available to them by age 10 or 11, well before even the reduced standard would permit them to work. In many places, girls are allowed to marry and assume responsibility for a household at an age younger than this convention would allow them to work.

Given such incompatibilities, it is hardly surprising that, for its first quarter-century, the convention languished with fewer than 50 ratifications, very few of which were from developing countries having noteworthy child labor problems. Although the huge majority of the world's working children are in Asia—half are thought to be in South Asia alone (Bangladesh, India, Pakistan, Nepal, and Sri Lanka)—no Asian country ratified Convention 138 until the Philippines did so in 1998. By September 2000, however, the convention had been ratified by 100 countries, 6 of which are from Asia but still none from the critical region of South Asia. Nor, interestingly enough, has the convention been ratified by any of the three North American countries (Canada, Mexico, and the United States). Why the sudden rush of new ratifications? The only plausible explanation is a campaign of firm political pressure from the ILO, which has recently promoted this convention as one of the core conventions all of its members are expected to ratify in solidarity with basic ILO principles. Also, the ILO's International Programme for the Elimination of Child Labor (IPEC) insists that countries receiving its financial and technical assistance begin the process of ratifying Convention 138 if they have not already done so.[3] For poor countries, this is a cheap price to pay for needed money and technical assistance. One could be forgiven, however, for questioning the practical impact of such pro forma ratifications, especially in light of the expanding ideological influence of the CRC.

The wisdom of a global child labor standard prohibiting all work below a given age has in recent years also been increasingly called into question by expert sources as varied as nongovernmental child defense agencies (for example, Badry Zalami 1998; Johnson, Hill, and Ivan-Smith 1995; Marcus and Harper 1996), the

World Bank (Basu 1999; Fallon and Tzannatos 1998; Grootaert and Patrinos 1999; Miljeteig 2000), and independent researchers (for example, Boyden, Ling, and Myers 1998; White 1994; Woodhead 1998, 1999). In brief, it has been observed that this approach does not work very well for protecting children and may sometimes even be counterproductive, not only in developing countries but even in Britain, where it was originally invented (Hobbs and McKechnie 1997; Lavalette 1999). The case generally is argued that economic incentives, improved education, public information about work hazards, targeted income generation projects, local monitoring of child work, the organization of working children, and other interventions are likely to be more effective in protecting the majority of working children (for example, Anker and Melkas 1996; Boyden and Myers 1995; Grootaert and Kanbur 1995; Grooteart and Patrinos 1999; International Working Group on Child Labour 1998; Myers and Boyden 1998; Schiefelbein 1997). While this line of thinking is clearly on the rise, the Convention 138 goal of excluding children from economic participation still is fiercely defended by, most notably, the trade union movement, with support also from the ILO and some government and nongovernmental organizations in both industrialized and developing countries.

*The U.N. Convention on
the Rights of the Child*

The CRC was adopted in 1989, 16 years after the ILO Minimum Age Convention, and one can see in it both similarities and profound differences. Like the 1973 ILO convention, it is clearly conceived along the lines of Euro-American notions of childhood and how to protect it. Even the very idea that there should be a single, formalized children's rights convention consolidating existing rights and creating new ones is entirely a product of the North; no such demand would be likely to surface from the South. Its creation was in fact largely a northern European initiative, especially from Poland and Sweden. Although it still retains the strong Northern influences that worried Boyden, it is nevertheless more accommodating of diversity than is Convention 138. Part of the reason lies in its different style; rather than prescribing details, it articulates objectives and principles, leaving more room than does the Minimum Age Convention for members to implement it in ways appropriate to their situation. Also, the opening paragraph of its main provision on child work (Article 32) proposes not to exclude children from economic participation altogether but to protect them "from economic exploitation and from performing any work that is likely to be hazardous or to interfere with the child's education, or to be harmful to the child's health or physical, mental, spiritual, moral or social development." By targeting only work that is detrimental to children, this approach fits poorer societies that are mostly agricultural (virtually all farm children have to help out with chores), and in which children often must help secure the family's survival, much better than does the ILO blanket prohibition on children working. At the same time, it prohibits children from engaging in work that is harmful to them, an objective that can be reached even in the context of poverty. Even if children must work, their safety and education can be secured. Other clauses in this article call for regulating the hours and conditions of child employment, as well as the legal penalties needed to make enforcement effective. However, one provision retreats a bit from this concept by calling for establishment of a minimum age, or minimum ages, for admission to employment, though no particular age is suggested.

Other CRC articles are also directly relevant to child labor, such as those guaranteeing rights to education (Articles 28 and 29), to rest and leisure (Article 31), to protection from all forms of maltreatment and exploitation by caregivers (Article 19), and to freedom of association and assembly (Article 15), to mention but a few. There are also several overarching provisions that cut across all sectors of concern, two of which have been very much at issue in addressing child labor. The first is Article 3, which provides that "in all actions concerning children, whether undertaken by public or private social welfare institutions, courts of law, administrative authorities or legislative bodies, the best interests of the child shall be a primary consideration." The second is Article 12, which in part assures "to the child who is capable of forming his or her own views the right to express those views freely in all matters affecting the child, the views of the child being given due weight in accordance with

the age and maturity of the child." It also grants children the right to be heard in administrative and judicial proceedings affecting them. CRC advocates, including UNICEF, insist that the convention should be treated as a whole and that all the rights bearing on a particular problem need to be given equal weight. In the case of child work, for instance, this means that all the articles mentioned in this paragraph—plus, perhaps, others—should be considered as of equal importance to Article 32. Such an approach makes the convention extremely difficult to implement, and many have remarked that, by trying to do too much, it may end up accomplishing very little.

The effect of both the specific and overarching provisions is to make the CRC application to child labor more child centered than is ILO Convention 138, partly by specifying children's rights as such, partly by granting those rights priority over adult interests, and partly by opening opportunity for working children to participate in and have effect on decisions affecting them and their work. The growing influence and extensive ratification of the CRC, in conjunction with its more contemporary and widely adaptable concepts of child labor, now seems well on the way to displacing Convention 138, which looks increasingly anachronistic, as an intellectual force. Attempts by UNICEF, the ILO, and others to semantically reconcile, or at least bridge, important differences between the CRC and Convention 138 have not been very credible. Despite some overlap, the two are widely and sensibly perceived to be in tension (Hanson and Vandaele 2000).

One can argue that the CRC is gradually expanding beyond its original status as primarily an international legal instrument for reorienting national child welfare and protection codes to become a cultural force rooted perhaps more solidly in civil society than in government. If one consults the thick and widely disseminated UNICEF handbook for implementing the CRC, one will note that it deals almost exclusively with legal issues of the sort that would be of interest to government lawyers writing or interpreting national legislation to bring it in line with CRC guidelines (UNICEF 1998). In the case of child labor, however, it is increasingly accepted by virtually all parties everywhere that the direct impact of government is limited and that providing children with the protection against detrimental work mandated by the CRC must involve families, communities, and civil society as well. As a result, much of the most effective advocacy for the CRC is by nongovernmental organizations and mobilizes civil society. Working children themselves are in many places becoming mobilized to articulate and defend their own rights, sometimes through their own highly effective associations or unions (Miljeteig 2000; Swift 1999; Tolfree 1998). Workshops, media campaigns, and other activities aimed at bringing social behavior in line with rights guaranteed by the CRC are now common, and in some places schoolchildren now receive instruction about their rights under the CRC as part of their regular curriculum. Child work is, in many places, one of the most important topics discussed in the CRC context.

One can perceive in different CRC articles and clauses divergent visions of children and childhood, which sometimes clash with each other. While some provisions imply a traditional Euro-American view of children as primarily passive, helpless, dependent, and in need of close adult direction, others are more in tune with today's emergent social science understanding, still Euro-American, of children as more active, competent, capable of independent initiative, and needing adult partnership more than imposed supervision. Articles providing for enabling rights—the right to be heard, the right to receive information, the right to association, and so forth—open opportunities for children to exert more control over their own lives. These articles have had remarkable resonance with children and grassroots organizations in many developing countries where working children are increasingly undertaking advocacy, mobilization, action projects, and even surprisingly sophisticated research on their own behalf. Organized and expressive, working children are an increasingly influential new element now being felt in international debate and action on child labor (Swift 1999). U.S. readers may find this assertion difficult to credit, which is understandable since America is not sensitive to the CRC (which it has not ratified) and since its organizations interested in child labor are little involved in international research and debate on the subject. However, the influence of working children's "protagonism" (the prevailing term for children's own initiatives) shows every sign of expanding as UNICEF, nongovernmental organizations, educational institutions, and even unlikely outfits such as the World Bank—which has recently published a study of working children's protagonism (Miljeteig 2000)—accept and act upon children's role as essential actors and stakeholders in defending their own rights.

The Worst Forms of Child Labour Convention

By the mid-1990s, the ILO had taken note of the various problems with Convention 138, delicately terming it too "complicated." It also noted that the social and political environment had been changed by the nearly universal ratification of the CRC, which also had a stronger claim as the main international guideline for child protection policy. It was increasingly clear that the ILO, stuck with an uninspiring child labor convention and competing with the more compelling vision and broader authority of the CRC, stood to lose its international leadership on child labor issues. It responded to this challenge in a highly creative and socially constructive manner, proposing an altogether new convention to focus world attention and resources with priority on "the most intolerable forms of child labor" (International Labor Office 1997). Although the ILO may have been prodded by events, this action was not primarily a case of bureaucratic one-upmanship, for a reasonable policy basis for prioritizing the worst

forms of child labor had already been laid through IPEC activities and an ILO publication—jointly produced with UNICEF—calling for such a policy priority (Bequele and Myers 1995). Moreover, the ILO took care, as did CRC advocates, to work with international nongovernmental organizations and others to lay a politically popular groundwork for a new convention. The grassroots activities came to a climax in a "global march," consisting of country-level workshops and demonstrations and a very media-friendly convergence of child delegates on the Geneva ILO headquarters when the new convention came up for adoption.

The resulting Worst Forms of Child Labour Convention (No. 182), with its accompanying Recommendation No. 190, was adopted in 1999 and commits all ratifying members to "take immediate and effective measures to secure the prohibition and elimination of the worst forms of child labor as a matter of urgency." It targets all forms of slavery, child prostitution, and the use of children in other illicit activities such as the drug trade, as well as work that "is likely to harm the health, safety or morals of children." These are forms and conditions of work that no group or country could credibly defend and that virtually all societies are able to condemn from within their own value systems. The new convention commits ratifying countries to prevent or remove children from engagement in the targeted forms of child labor and to provide education, vocational training, or other viable alternatives to inappropriate work. It directs member countries to "identify and reach out to children at special risk" and to "take account of the special situation of girls." It also demands that each member state prepare an action plan, and it calls for international cooperation in support of implementation.

The content and style of ILO Convention 182 suggest the impact of the CRC, which it specifically references as an antecedent, and of lessons learned from experience with the Minimum Age Convention. One could argue that this convention has come closer to expressing a genuinely global consensus on child labor than has either the CRC or Convention 138, and anthropologist Ben White (1999) interestingly notes that it "appears . . . to represent an attempt to incorporate relativist principles in a global standard-setting exercise, and therefore perhaps to have side-stepped the issue of cultural relativism" (141). This achievement is remarkable in several ways. First of all, Convention 182 was so skillfully negotiated to garner support from both industrialized and developing countries that it became the first ILO convention ever adopted by unanimous vote. It got there by rigorously targeting the worst aspects of a major global social problem in a way that all the essential actors can agree to, which is no small achievement. If ratification proceeds as expected—38 countries already had ratified by October 2000, a quick pace compared to the usual time lag—the new convention will rest on unusually solid political ground. Because of its broad support, it already is attracting substantial donor investment toward implementation. Second, the Worst Forms of Child Labour Convention is positioned to become one of the most basic of global human rights agreements and should encounter little trouble in being widely accepted as such. Third, it articulates its objectives and the ratifying states' responsibilities in terms that are general but able to be monitored and that leave ample room for different societies to work toward its implementation within their own concepts of childhood and child raising. Fourth, the accompanying Recommendation 190 provides for "taking into consideration the views of the children directly affected by the worst forms of child labor." Here it buys into the CRC concept that children are competent to act on their own behalf. It responds to the CRC Article 12 provision for children's participation in public decisions affecting them, as well as to pressure exerted on the ILO by international child defense organizations, working children's own associations, and others insisting that the new convention be consistent with at least key provisions of the CRC. While we have yet to see how this new convention will be implemented, it is impressive to note that national and international nongovernmental organizations, governments, and bilateral and multilateral development assistance programs are now in the process of gearing up to focus on the rights of children in the most harmful child labor situations.

CONCLUSION

The story of how three conventions have, in the short space of just 26 years, struggled to bring a workable children's rights perspective into global action on child labor suggests the presence of a learning process. Comparison of these three conventions in their historical sequence indicates a progression of children's rights thinking about child labor, first from globalized Northern ethnocentrism (ILO Convention 138), to a more open and culturally adaptable approach still set within Northern concepts of children's rights (the CRC), and from there to a more democratic model better structured to accommodate diversity while focusing on a realistic social objective against which progress can be monitored (ILO Convention 182). However, the sequence is one of emphasis only, for all three conventions are simultaneously in force.

Perhaps one could sum up the history of the three conventions by saying that, after a false start followed by a solid but relatively unfocused step forward, a workable center of gravity for global action against child labor has finally been found. The "right rights" seem not to be those imposed by the rich and powerful but those that are more broadly defined and more democratically adopted. The case of child labor suggests that globally representative children's rights just might indeed be possible, even if it takes a few tries to get them right.

Notes

1. This fairly large and complex literature is extensively reviewed in Boyden, Ling, and Myers 1998 and thus will not be cited here.

2. These conventions are available on the Internet. Those from the ILO may be downloaded from www.ilo.ch and the CRC from www.unicef.org.

3. Some readers may wonder why the ILO places so much importance on ratification of Convention 138 since its obvious limitations and anachronisms have long been recognized and criticized from both outside and within the ILO. Although official emphasis on the core conventions is real, an alternative explanation that many find equally compelling is that Convention 138, and its objective of removing children from the labor market, is especially dear to the heart of organized labor, a pillar of this tripartite organization. No new policy or convention can be adopted without agreement of all three partners, which is inherent to the corporatist political model on which the ILO is founded—that is, progress and stability are to be achieved through negotiation and agreement between government, capital, and labor. It is widely accepted (but undocumented) that internal politics dictated a deal promoting a push on Convention 138 ratifications in return for organized labor's support for a new convention against the worst forms of child labor. Many in the ILO felt that such a new convention was necessary to revitalize a flagging child labor program and to retain ILO policy leadership in the area, but representatives of labor were initially cool to the idea and worried that prioritizing the worst cases would detract from the ILO's traditional commitment to exclude all underage children from labor markets. They accurately perceived that many ILO colleagues considered Convention 138 to be at least unrealistic and that there was growing demand for a more pragmatic position that could mobilize greater consensus for action. The reported end bargain was to attempt both at once, the cost of which has been to internalize policy inconsistencies and to paper over conflicting views of childhood and child labor.

References

Alston, Philip, ed. 1994. *The Best Interests of the Child: Reconciling Culture and Human Rights*. Oxford: Clarendon.

Anker, Richard and Helina Melkas. 1996. *Economic Incentives for Children and Families to Eliminate or Reduce Child Labour*. Geneva: International Labor Office.

Aries, Philippe. 1965. *Centuries of Childhood*. New York: Random House.

Badry Zalami, Fatima. 1998. *Forgotten on the Pyjama Trail: A Case Study of Young Garment Workers in Meknes Dismissed from Their Jobs Following Foreign Media Attention*. Amsterdam: International Working Group on Child Labour.

Basu, Kaushik. 1999. International Standards and Child Labor. *Challenge* 42(5):80-93.

Bequele, Assefa and William Myers. 1995. *First Things First in Child Labour*. Geneva: International Labour Office.

Boyden, Jo. 1997. Childhood and the Policy Makers: A Comparative Perspective on the Globalization of Childhood. In *Constructing and Reconstructing Childhood: Contemporary Issues in the Sociological Study of Childhood*, 2d ed., ed. Allison James and Alan Prout. London: Falmer Press.

Boyden, Jo, Birgitta Ling, and William Myers. 1998. *What Works for Working Children*. Stockholm: Radda Barnen.

Boyden, Jo and William Myers. 1995. *Exploring Alternative Approaches to Combating Child Labour: Case Studies from Developing Countries*. Innocenti Occasional Papers, CRS 8. Florence: UNICEF International Child Development Centre.

Burman, Erica. 1994. *Deconstructing Developmental Psychology*. London: Routledge.

Cole, Michael. 1996. *Cultural Psychology: A Once and Future Discipline*. Cambridge, MA: Harvard University Press.

Cunningham, Hugh. 1991. *Children of the Poor: Representations of Childhood Since the Seventeenth Century*. Oxford: Blackwell, 1991.

———. 1995. *Children and Childhood in Western Society Since 1500*. London: Longman.

———. 1999. The Rights of the Child and the Wrongs of Child Labour: An Historical Perspective. Paper presented at the IREWOC Workshop on Children, Work and Education, Nov., Amsterdam.

Fallon, Peter and Zafiris Tzannatos, 1998. *Child Labour: Issues and Directions for the World Bank*. Washington, DC: World Bank.

Grootaert, Christiaan and Ravi Kanbur. 1995. Child Labour: An Economic Perspective. *International Labour Review* 134(6):187-203.

Grootaert, Christiaan and Harry Anthony Patrinos. 1999. *The Policy Analysis of Child Labor: A Comparative Study*. New York: St. Martin's Press.

Hanson, Karl and Arne Vandaele. 2000. Working Children and International Labour Law: A Critical Analysis. Paper presented at the International Conference on Rethinking Childhood: Working Children's Challenge to the Social Sciences, Nov., Bondy, France.

Hobbs, Sandy and Jim McKechnie. 1997. *Child Employment in Britain: A Social and Psychological Analysis*. Edinburgh: Stationery Office.

International Labor Office. 1997. *Combating the Most Intolerable Forms of Child Labour: A Global Challenge*. Background document prepared for the Amsterdam Child Labour Conference. Geneva: International Labor Office.

International Working Group on Child Labour. 1998. *Working Children: Reconsidering the Debates*. Amsterdam: Defence for Children International and the International Society of the Prevention of Child Abuse and Neglect.

James, Allison and Alan Prout. 1997. Re-presenting Childhood: Time and Transition in the Study of Childhood. In *Constructing and Reconstructing Childhood: Contemporary Issues in the Sociological Study of Childhood*, 2d ed., ed. Allison James and Alan Prout. London: Falmer Press.

Johnson, Victoria, Joanna Hill, and Edda Ivan-Smith. 1995. *Listening to Smaller Voices: Children in an Environment of Change*. London: Actionaid.

Lavalette, Michael, ed. 1999. *A Thing of the Past? Child Labour in Britain in the Nineteenth and Twentieth Centuries*. Liverpool: Liverpool University Press.

Marcus, Rachel and Caroline Harper. 1996. Small Hands: Children in the Working World. Working Paper No. 16, Save the Children, London.

Miljeteig, Per. 2000. Creating Partnerships with Working Children and Youth. SP Discussion Paper No. 0021, World Bank, Washington, DC, Aug.

Myers, William and Jo Boyden. 1998. *Child Labour: Promoting the Best Interests of Working Children*. London: Save the Children Alliance.

Rogoff, Barbara. 1990. *Apprenticeship in Thinking: Cognitive Development in Social Context*. Oxford: Oxford University Press.

Schiefelbein, Ernesto. 1997. *School-related Economic Incentives in Latin America: Reducing Drop-Out and Repetition and Combating Child Labour*. Innocenti Occasional Papers, CRS 12. Florence: UNICEF International Child Development Centre.

Swift, Anthony. 1999. *Working Children Get Organized: An Introduction to Working Children's Organizations*. London: Save the Children Alliance.

Tolfree, David. 1998. *Old Enough to Work, Old Enough to Have a Say: Different Approaches to Supporting Working Children*. Stockholm: Radda Barnen.

UNICEF. 1998. *Implementation Handbook for the Convention on the Rights of the Child*. New York: UNICEF.

Valsiner, Jaan. 2000. *Culture and Human Development*. Thousand Oaks: Sage.

White, Ben. 1994. Children, Work and Child Labour: Changing Responses to the Employment of Children. *Development and Change* 25(4):849-78.

———. 1996. Globalization and the Child Labour Problem. *Journal of International Development* 8(6):829-39.

———. 1999. Defining the Intolerable: Child Work, Global Standards and Cultural Relativism. *Childhood* 6(1):133-44.

Woodhead, Martin. 1998. *Children's Perspectives on Their Working Lives: A Participatory Study in Bangladesh, Ethiopia, The Philippines, Guatemala, El Salvador and Nicaragua*. Stockholm: Radda Barnen.

———. 1999. *Is There a Place for Work in Child Development? Implications of Child Development Theory and Research for Interpretation of the UN Convention on the Rights of the Child, with Particular Reference to Article 32, on Children, Work and Exploitation*. Stockholm: Radda Barnen.

Children's Rights
and the Internet

By STEVEN HICK and EDWARD HALPIN

ABSTRACT: The Internet is having a profound impact on children's rights around the world. Its impact is both negative, such as with the proliferation of child pornography, and positive, in providing child advocates with new tools to promote and protect the rights of children. This article examines how international collaboration and the linking of legal systems are required to combat abuses of children's rights on the Internet. It also explores how children's rights organizations use the Internet to combat abuses of children on the Internet and to provide information on all children's rights issues, respond quickly to the abuse of children's rights, and connect children and youths in different countries to empower them to advocate for their own rights. The Internet is no substitute for strong and vibrant communities and societies, but it does provide a new and effective means for different peoples of the world to connect with one another.

Steven Hick is associate professor at Carleton University, founder and director of War Child Canada, and director of a diversity studies research center. He is a humanitarian activist with interests in human rights, social work, and the Internet. He has written extensively on educational technologies, online activism, and human rights, including two books.

Edward Halpin is a senior lecturer in the School of Information Management at Leeds Metropolitan University. His research interests are in the areas of human rights, racism and extremism on the Internet, privacy, and social exclusion. His publications include Human Rights and the Internet *(2000) and* The Use of the Internet by the European Parliament for the Promotion and Protection of Human Rights *(1998).*

THE instruments available to protect the rights of children have changed dramatically in recent times. At the beginning of the twentieth century, children virtually had no rights. Children were considered to be merely little adults who could be easily enslaved as factory workers. They had few rights and were afforded no special kindness. Children were not considered to be in a special stage of development that required nurturing and care. However, at the end of the twentieth century, the U.N. Convention on the Rights of the Child (CRC) was created. The convention is the most universally accepted human rights instrument in history: every country in the world except two has ratified it. As the world increasingly connects and interrelates, the need for such universal instruments is paramount.

The world is undergoing rapid economic, technological, and political change. Globalization is increasingly taking hold. In this article, the concept of globalization is seen as the newest development in the expansion of global capitalism. It is a new manifestation of an old system of market liberalism, only this time it is occurring on an international, rather than national, level. The rise of the global economy is often partly explained by the rise of new information and communication technology (ICT),[1] of which the Internet is a major component. The Internet is frequently seen as a key enabling factor for global capitalism. It is, therefore, crucial in any discussion of globalization and children's rights to examine the impact of the Internet.

The Internet has important implications for the rights of children throughout the world. The Internet and all future forms of global electronic information and knowledge dissemination and communication indisputably affect children's rights. Reviews of the impact of the Internet on children often emphasize the negative consequences of online child pornography and pedophilia. These are serious issues, and they should be discussed. The Internet offers new and highly sophisticated opportunities for lawbreaking and creates the potential to commit traditional types of crimes in nontraditional ways. The Internet, however, has also played a key role in connecting people and organizations around the world to promote and protect the rights of children. It offers human rights workers and activists new opportunities to promote children's rights. In this article, we will explore both the positive and negative consequences—or opportunities and hazards—that the Internet holds for children's rights.

What new benefits and threats does the Internet make possible? Is it a force for good, alleviating poverty, creating new opportunities, ensuring that the voices of oppressed and displaced children are heard, or alternatively, will it intensify existing poverty, deny new opportunities, and create a society no better than that which we already have? Perhaps the answer will remain unclear, but the new technologies we consider here are clearly having an influence and must be carefully explored.

This article will provide a brief overview of some of the issues associated with the development and use of the new ICTs and how they relate to children's rights. The major themes to be considered include an examination of the situation of the world's children and the nature of threats to or violations of children's rights online, mechanisms of protection, globalization and ICTs, and finally, the use of ICTs by human rights organizations for the promotion of children's rights. At the outset, it is crucial to emphasize that any evaluation of the impact of the Internet must take into account the fact that as a phenomenon the Internet is in a state of constant and rapid evolution and any analysis of the affects on children's rights will quickly shift.

THE SITUATION OF THE WORLD'S CHILDREN

Conflict, poverty, homelessness, social instability, and preventable diseases such as HIV/AIDS threaten the human rights of children around the world. The following excerpts from the most recent yearly UNICEF report, *The State of the World's Children* (2000), captures the plight of children today.

The number of people living in poverty continues to grow as globalization proceeds along its inherently asymmetrical course: expanding markets across national boundaries and increasing the incomes of a relative few while further strangling the lives of those without the resources to be investors or the capabilities to benefit from the global culture. The majority are women and children, poor before, but even more so now, as the two-tiered world economy widens the gaps between rich and poor countries and between rich and poor people.

Slave-like also describes the lives of millions of other children throughout the world. There is no way to calculate the exact number of young boys and girls whose lives are endangered by their sale and trafficking, by debt bondage, serfdom, forced or compulsory labour, forced or compulsory recruitment into armed conflict, prostitution, pornography or by the production and trafficking of drugs. Efforts to eliminate these gross violations have been ongoing and have been energized by the 1999 Worst Forms of Child Labour Convention. But, according to estimates by the International Labour Organization (ILO), some 250 million children between the ages of 5 and 14 work in developing countries and some 50 million to 60 million children between the ages of 5 and 11 work in hazardous circumstances. The challenges of preventing and eradicating these extreme violations of children's rights illustrate the layers of want, discrimination and exploitation that drive humanity's poorest children into obscure and dangerous worlds.

Some people wrongly assume that the rights of children born in wealthy nations are never violated. It is mistakenly believed that these children have no need for the protection and care called for in the convention. To varying degrees, at least some children in all nations face unemployment, homelessness, violence, poverty, and other issues that dramatically affect their lives.

GLOBALIZATION AND THE INTERNET

The emergence and growth of new technologies for communication over the later decades of the twentieth century is often regarded as having created a new form of society, often referred to as the information society. The process leading to the development of these new and (if we are to believe the hype) revolutionary technologies can often be traced back to research and development within the military establishment. The Internet is a case in point; a very good description of its development is provided in *The Internet and Society* (Slavin 2000, 11). The Internet has rapidly become a key element for communication in this so-called global information society.

International Internet usage is rapidly growing, but the growth is concentrated in North America and Europe and, to a degree, parts of Asia. As recently as 1996, "it was estimated that the Internet had some 60 million users world-wide and that this number was doubling each year, evolving from a government and academic network to a vital element of modern business and commerce, whilst providing new educational and leisure opportunities" (Brophy and Halpin 1999, 352). More recent estimates suggest that the "total number of Internet users worldwide by 1999 was . . . between 150 and 180 million," with estimates that the "expected numbers would rise to one billion by 2005" (Slavin 2000, 40).

This enormous growth in Internet connectivity, in association with the development of other electronic communication technologies, has resulted in changes in many spheres of society, including children's rights. The nature of human rights abuse requires rapid action in response to violations. The Internet—a global interconnected network of computers—and other ICTs provide the tools for rapid, cheap, and accurate information with which to respond. This might well explain why many organizations have quickly adopted this technology as a tool for their work. Increasingly, the Internet has become a tool for the promotion and protection of children's rights, being used to obtain, communicate, and disseminate information. Web pages and e-mail have become fundamental tools for the promotion and protection of human rights.

The Internet has become a key element in what we term the globalization of society, providing technology that recognizes no national boundaries, that has no single owner, and that is not regulated or controlled by any single national or international legal framework. Yet the Internet is found in every nation, providing information and contact instantaneously to anybody at any point of the globe. Connectivity to the Internet, with the advantages it provides for rapid information flow, has ensured that every nation is now connected. All major businesses have adopted it as a means of communication, and nongovernmental organizations (NGOs) have found it to be an invaluable tool. The reality of this globalization might, however, be somewhat less clear. What is the extent of connectivity, and who really has access to the global information society?

The U.N. Development Programme's (UNDP) *Human Development Report 1999*[2] discusses the global distribution and connectivity of new technologies. The report suggests that the current global information society is "elitist," with "income, education, gender and geography as the major fault lines." The report goes on to suggest that there is a "two tier technological society" in which "the first society has access to plentiful information at low cost and high speed. The second society has its quality of access impeded by time, cost, uncertainty of connection and outdated information." This notion of a two-tier technological society fits well with an analysis of connectivity, with North America, Europe, and some parts of Southeast Asia having full access, while areas such as sub-Saharan Africa lack adequate access. The UNDP report concludes that there are "seven goals that must be targeted to achieve an information society. These are connectivity, community, capacity, content, creativity, collaboration and cash." The analysis provided by the UNDP report clearly questions the notion of globalization in the sense that we traditionally think about it. What we see is the stratification of global economies being repeated—the traditional haves and have-nots being replicated. For children's rights work, this is a major concern. Clearly, we are seeing a continuation of the economic and social exclusion that has plagued the world for so long, with additional barriers being created along the way.

ABUSES OF CHILDREN'S
RIGHTS ON THE INTERNET

Child pornography on the Internet is a growing and spreading problem. Those struggling against it are facing particular technical and legal challenges, given the rapid pace of technological change and the ability of images to move across borders. A response requires resolute international cooperation between nations, law enforcement agencies, the Internet industry, complaint hot lines, and NGOs. While it is the responsibility of each nation to ensure the application of existing laws (pertaining to criminal acts, intellectual property, and the protection of minors), the Internet's technical features, worldwide extension, and unlimited accessibility make the application and enforcement of existing rules difficult. In many cases, a concerted international effort is required.

Defining child pornography on the Internet, which traverses many different legal territories, is complicated. A background paper for the 1999 International Conference on Combating Child Pornography on the Internet (1999, 15) defined child pornography as graphic material featuring naked or sexually active children that is used for sexual gratification. It also maintained that, in the online pedophile community, the images have different functions beyond that of sexual gratification. The paper reports that, in the pedophile community, child pornography, and the composition of it, is used to validate and celebrate adult interest in child sexuality as well as to seek commercial profit. The pedophile community has become expert at circumventing attempts at Internet regulation, exploiting any weakness in Internet legislation at the national or international level.

There is a disjunction between the scope of the Internet and the reach of legal systems. The Internet operates internationally, while our laws function on a territorial basis. Material can be accessed locally, yet it can be housed on computer systems outside local jurisdictions. Determining the extent to which national law applies can therefore be complex. Legal liability frequently depends on the extent to which any particular party controls, or is aware of, illegal content. The concept of being aware, or knowing, has its own difficulties, given the nature of the Internet.

To protect children from harmful Internet content, the international community must respond at the legal, industrial, and educational levels and must take into consideration protective measures. Any effective response will need to center on high levels of international cooperation. National responses to child pornography often empathize national (especially criminal) law, without taking into account alternative protective measures. However, even in the legal field, there are considerable problems. In fact, despite the successful efforts of international and supranational organizations, the various national laws have remarkable differences, uncertainties, and loopholes, especially with respect to the criminal law provisions on privacy infringement, hacking, trade secret protection, and illegal content.

UNICEF and UNESCO have held several important meetings on Internet safety. At the International Conference on Combating Child Pornography on the Internet, a declaration and an action plan were created calling for an international task force on child pornography and pedophilia on the Internet. The action plan called for concrete actions such as universal ethics and self-regulation standards to be developed by Internet service providers and the creation of national hot lines and "electronic watchtowers" to report cases of pedophilia and child pornography on the Internet. Also, the United Nations passed a resolution proposed by the special rapporteur on child pornography, Ofelia Calcetas-Santos, calling on member states to criminalize the production of child pornography and to ensure the prosecution of those who profit from it.

The effective investigation and successful prosecution of those who make child pornography available on the Internet require international collaboration. Since the technology used is global, the response must be global. This year, member states started elaborating the U.N. Convention Against Transnational Organized Crime. Many children's rights organizations hope the process will apply to groups engaged in making child pornography available on the Internet, and the full array of international cooperation measures introduced by the convention would therefore apply. Law enforcement agencies, prosecutors, and the judiciary of U.N. member states could then collaborate in collecting evidence, arresting perpetrators, and bringing them to justice (Arlacchi 1999, 3).

In 1998, the United States enacted the Child Online Protection Act, which criminalizes the commercial distribution via the Internet of material considered harmful to minors. The U.S. law calls for warnings and protective screens (such as "Are you under 18? If so, click here") to discourage and warn children before they continue to a harmful Web site. The passage of this act elicited immediate protests from freedom-of-speech groups claiming that the act may be an infringement of the First Amendment, which is a constitutional rule forbidding the enactment of legislation that inhibits freedom of expression. Others claimed that the law does not go far enough, that the protective screens are only minor hurdles for persistent surfers and curious children. Also, the U.S. law primarily protects children from viewing harmful content, but it does not address the problem of child pornography more generally.

The European Union (EU) countries have agreed on the need to make a distinction between illegal content and harmful content. They believe that the different categories of child pornography require different approaches, particularly regarding the use of the law to combat offenders. In the EU, illegal content will be dealt with by existing law enforcement agencies according to existing national law. Industry is also being encouraged to adopt properly functioning systems of self-regulation, such as codes of conduct and establishment of hot lines for complaints. In fact, the EU approach tends to emphasize nonlegal efforts, which enables Internet users to filter out content they themselves deem harmful. The use of content rating systems and filtering technology is encouraged. The 1998 EU action plan for promoting the safe use of the Internet provided funding for complaint hot lines and for the development of filtering systems rating systems (White 1999).

Both the U.S. and EU approaches emphasize the end user and not the persons placing illegal or harmful content on the Internet. In part, this is due to the inherent difficulties of proving who actually controls content on the Internet. It also stems from fears that limits on freedom of expression will either be challenged in the courts or may be used by authoritarian governments to curtail other nonharmful speech and expression. While there are doubts as to how effective these laws can be enforced, there are also apprehensions about laws that limit the freedom of expression.

PROMOTING THE RIGHTS
OF THE WORLD'S CHILDREN

Children's rights abuses necessitate rapid responses from the people in the nation in which the abuse is taking place and from people and nation-states worldwide. Oppressive regimes and totalitarian dictators can be affected when the international community registers a complaint or when children's rights workers launch a campaign. Frequently, the speed of response by organizations deters or stops the abuse of children's rights. The advent of the new ICTs, and in particular the Internet, has enabled both rapid and effective responses to children's rights abuses around the world, supporting the work of those who fight for justice and fairness. As Stephen Hansen (1998) points out, "Human Rights groups are relying on the Internet more and more to speak out, document, and draw the world's attention to human rights violations" (3).

The definition of human rights is perhaps best understood from the codification found within legislative provision rather than by a lengthy examination of the literature available on the subject. Perhaps the best known codification can be found in the 1948 Universal Declaration of Human Rights, which encapsulates the essence of fundamental human rights in the following basic statement of the expectations for freedom and dignity in a free and just society:

Disregard and contempt for human rights have resulted in barbarous acts which have outraged the conscience of mankind, and the advent of a world in which beings shall enjoy freedom of speech and belief and freedom from fear and want has been proclaimed as the highest aspiration of the common people. (United Nations 1948)

The CRC further codifies rights that are particular to children. The CRC incorporates the full range of human rights—civil and political as well as economic, social, and cultural—for all children. The underlying values—or guiding principles—of the CRC guide the way in which each right is fulfilled and respected and serve as a constant reference for the implementation and monitoring of children's rights. The CRC outlines in 41 articles the human rights to be respected and protected for every child under the age of 18. The convention's four guiding principles are as follows:

1. Article 2, on nondiscrimination, states that no child should be injured, privileged, or punished by, or deprived of, any right on the grounds of his or her race, color, or gender; on the basis of his or her language, religion, or national, social, or ethnic origin; on the grounds of any political or other opinion; on the basis of caste, property, or birth status; or on the basis of a disability.

2. Article 3, on the best interests of the child, states that the best interests of the child shall be a primary consideration in all actions concerning children, whether undertaken by public or private social welfare institutions, courts of law, administrative authorities, or legislative bodies. In each and every circumstance, in each and every decision affecting the child, the various possible solutions must be considered and due weight given to the child's best interests. "Best interests of the child" means that legislative bodies must consider whether laws being adopted or amended will benefit children in the best possible way.

3. Article 6, on survival and development, addresses children's right to life, survival, and development. The survival-and-development principle is in no way limited to a physical perspective; rather, it emphasizes the need to ensure the full and harmonious development of the child, including at the spiritual, moral, and social levels where education will play a key role.

4. Article 12, on participation, is the principle affirming that children are full-fledged persons who have the right to express their views in all matters affecting them and requires that those views be heard and given due weight in accordance with the child's age and maturity. This article recognizes the potential of children to enrich decision-making processes, to share perspectives, and to participate as citizens and actors of change.

The exponential growth of the Internet and other new ICTs has changed the work methods of organizations pursuing the guiding principles and goals of the CRC. The growth in technology and its application has also provided us with a tide of new descriptive words—such as "information superhighway," "cyberspace," and even "digital democracy"—that often express hyperbole and create certain expectations (Hague and Loader 1999, 1). These words are commonly used, and the benefits they imply are taken as matters of fact. It can appear that we live in a world in which technology can provide us with almost everything we need, be it shiny new products or the latest news of the suffering of others, through famine or war, around the world. Almost instantly, news is brought to us, with pictures as it happens, informing us of human rights abuses and atrocities, not just as news but also as entertainment or perhaps even infotainment. Is the image of the child of war information, or is it being used for entertainment purposes? Perhaps this question is irrelevant so long as the message is delivered. The Internet, ICTs, and tools of mass communication seem to be ubiquitous in the Western world, with new manifestations of their existence being utilized daily. The utility of the Internet for children's rights organizations is clear in that it aids the communication so vital to the work. However, might the Internet also be the harbinger of new risks and threats, particularly for some of the children of the world?

CHILDREN'S RIGHTS AND
THE USE OF THE INTERNET

The availability of ICTs is a means of achieving some of the aspirations of the CRC and the Universal Declaration of Human Rights. Children affected by war, street children, exploited children, and children of poverty do not have access to the United Nations to put their cases forward. Often they do not have a voice at all but rely on their champions. These champions, or advocates, are those who observe, support, listen, and act as the children's representatives. They are primarily from NGOs or nonprofit organizations. They shine light into the dark corners of our society, and increasingly they use the Internet to ensure that we see the abuses.

However, the reality of children's rights abuses is substantially different from the sentiments expressed in the declarations and pronouncements of governments around the world. Denial of the most fundamental human rights continues to be a problem throughout the world, with abductions, sexual exploitation, recruitment as soldiers, beatings, rape, imprisonment, torture, and summary executions still taking place on a daily basis. For children, the abuses include forced labor, sale as a commodity, sex crimes, involvement in wars as tools of the military, false imprisonment, and the experience of poverty created by powers way beyond them. These abuses are well documented in the reports of well-respected human rights NGOs—such as Amnesty International[3] and, in the case of children's rights, the Child Rights Information Network (CRIN)[4]—that provide evidence of the extent and type of abuses that occur.

The reality is that human rights declarations mean little to a victim; however, the knowledge that one's situation is being communicated across the world may provide hope, and it is against this background that human rights activists work, increasingly using ICTs and the Internet, in the full knowledge that

the nature of human rights abuses necessitates rapid responses: oppressive regimes do not wait for the international community to grant permission or for human rights workers to register a complaint. The quicker that human rights organisations can respond, the more likely that illegal detention and other abuses can be stopped. (Brophy and Halpin 1999, 356)

In the article "Information Technology and Human Rights," Metz (1996) underlines the importance of information to human rights work, commenting that "accurate and timely information is an indispensable tool and an essential precondition for effective responsive action and the pro-

motion of human rights, whether by organisations, individuals, governments or international institutions" (705).

The Internet provides children's rights NGOs and activists with the ability to promote and protect human rights. The Internet aids detection by being an immediate means of information as situations develop, ensuring early warning through rapid flows of information and enabling decision making. Through these mechanisms, preventive action can be initiated using rapid response networks and campaigning and by the provision of reports to governments and the mass media. The tools provided by the Internet—Web pages to promote causes, e-mail to provide rapid communication, discussion groups to allow informed debate, and lists of the world's latest human rights situations—all play a role in the work of human rights activist online.

Children's rights activism is difficult to contain within the borders of individual states; by its very nature, it has involved transborder responses to the abuses that occur. The Internet is therefore a ready ally for children's rights activists because it exists beyond the normal geographical constraints applied to previous modes of communication and provides global coverage.

The world of children's rights is difficult to classify; it contains a diverse range of organizations, from the international to the very local, the large to the very small, with activists often occupying multiple roles within a range of different groups and organizations. The Internet is a mechanism for change in the work of children's rights activists. Hierarchical communication structures are increasingly being replaced with more vertical and democratic structures. Evidence of this exists in organizations such as Amnesty International and is displayed in the work of CRIN. The Internet has also enabled the increase of specialist groups of activists, such as lawyers, journalists, social workers, and doctors, who have formed specific children's rights groups, often transcending the borders of traditional nation-states and responding directly to rights abuses (Brophy and Halpin 1999, 354). Alexander and Pal (1998) suggest that the impact of ICTs is changing the nature of the state. ICTs

— stimulate growth in the number of formal and informal information groupings of people, because they allow them to mobilize more effectively and more cheaply;

— encourage the development of broad coalitions and networks which nonetheless remain quite decentralized;

— permit huge amounts of information to be circulated through networks and encourage co-production of that information; [and]

— constrain the capacities of governmental agencies through the empowerment of NGOs and the reduction of monopolies of knowledge and expertise.

Alexander and Pal's analysis certainly applies to human rights organizations. With new organizations formed and coalitions built, the Internet has created a ready method to support such activities. CRIN's global network of 1100 organizations makes it possible to see how the Internet offers the ability to communicate effectively and efficiently. Since the Internet is being used by children's rights NGOs, it is worth understanding why they have adopted it and how they are using it.

CHILDREN'S RIGHTS
ORGANIZATIONS
ON THE INTERNET

The following brief case studies look at the Web presence of three human rights organizations currently active and working to promote and protect the human rights of children. The analysis has been undertaken by examining the Web sites of the organizations, evaluating how the organizations carry out their work using the Web sites, and, when possible, interviewing staff members. We acknowledge that this is a limited analysis; however, it is appropriate because the Web sites could be said to provide one public image of each of the organizations. The analysis illustrates quite different uses of the Internet.

Children's Rights
Information Network

CRIN emphasizes the use of the Internet to disseminate information useful to children's rights organizations and activists. One of the crucial benefits of the Internet for this function is the ability to inexpensively distribute volumes of information to people no matter where they may be in the world in a timely manner. A key disadvantage to the use of advanced technology is the inequitable access of those in poorer countries.

CRIN has a membership and network of over 1100 child rights organizations around the world. CRIN works to "improve the lives of children through the exchange of information about child rights and the UN Convention on the Rights of the Child. CRIN's network furthers the discussion on critical child rights issues."[5] The organization began its work in 1995, supported by funding from UNICEF and Save the Children in both Sweden and the United Kingdom. The organization originated at a time when the use of the Internet by human rights NGOs was very much in its infancy, the Web providing a tool for campaigning and promoting the rights of children, while e-mail provided a ready tool for communication.

While CRIN uses the benefits of new technology in its work, the organization also acknowledges the importance of more traditional methods of communication, such as paper-based publications and fax communication. At present, CRIN is working on the development of an integrated approach to its communications strategy, with technology being a key aspect. However, with about 55 percent of the user population being from the developing world or the South (22 percent in Africa and 14 percent in Asia), and their feedback indicating that these member organizations may not be as technologically advanced or advantaged as members in the North, CRIN's strategy includes three mediums: e-mail, Web, and paper. An integrated and strategic approach using these three mediums can ensure that the organization functions globally. It recognizes that where electronic communication can provide quick, cheap information flows in the North, there may be slower and more expensive communication flows to the South; therefore, paper remains integral to global coverage and inclusion of all partners.

Amnesty International
  Children's Human
  Rights Network

Amnesty International[6] and Human Rights Watch (HRW) use the Internet in different ways. These organizations tend to emphasize the distribution of urgent action alerts. When a child's basic rights are being violated, Amnesty International and HRW react as quickly as possible, distributing the news and recommended action via the Internet.

The following outlines how Amnesty-USA undertakes its work on children's rights. The Web site states that

AI [Amnesty International] has often highlighted individual cases of children who have been the victims of human rights violations such as torture, ill treatment or extrajudicial execution. But too often, AI's work on children has been incidental to its core research and campaigning. As a result, children have often been invisible in AI's coverage of human rights violations in the adult sphere. In recent years, AI's membership forums have recognized the need for AI to increase its work on children and adapt its research and campaigning strategy so that we can play a wider and more constructive role in promoting and protecting children's rights. In the process, AI is hoping to forge closer links with other institutions and NGOs working in this field.[7]

The Web site provides a very strong focus on campaigning for the rights of children but also clearly indicates how the Web site is combined with e-mail in order to mount activist campaigns. This mirrors the way in which Amnesty International generally uses the Internet, though the organization also tends to use these technologies in conjunction with other means of delivering information about its campaigns and activism. Amnesty International has mounted campaigns where information is delivered into countries with little Internet connectivity via the Internet and is then disseminated by more traditional means. These types of cases can be found in the work of Halpin and Fisher (1998, 13). The site encourages activist participation in "Action Appeals," providing information about specific abuses and then seeking to act upon them by sending letters or e-mail to the relevant authorities.[8]

In an interview, one volunteer said the following about the advent of ICTs:

The ability to exchange information rapidly and to respond immediately to human rights violations is a giant leap forward in this arena, and it is one that I hope will as quickly as possible be available to human rights defenders worldwide. Amnesty International has from its beginnings stated that the best weapon against human rights violations is spreading the news that they are hap-pening and holding the violators responsible in front of the whole world community. The Internet makes it possible to do this virtually instantaneously. For those of us who do that work, it means a morale boost from stepping out of our isolated little rooms. For the victims of those violations, it can mean the difference between life and death.

War Child Canada

War Child Canada[9] uses the Internet to further its work in helping war-affected children in new and innovative ways. Beyond its use of the Internet to disseminate information about the organization, projects, and the issue of war-affected children, War Child Canada uses the Internet to connect youths around the world to advocate for their own rights. The organization is finding innovative methods to engage youths from every corner of the world. War Child Canada has used the Internet to "webcast" concerts and to hold live Web chat sessions with musicians and politicians. For example, the organization recently had live chats on the Internet with Canadian Minister of Foreign Affairs Lloyd Axworthy and with hip-hop musician Rascalz. Another innovative use of the Internet is live webcast reporting of field experiences. The organization has webcasts and chat sessions with youths affected by war, from schools, from camps, and on the streets, and with peacekeepers and politicians. It also webcasts important conferences on the topic of war-affected children.

War Child Canada also recognizes the digital divide as an important barrier to the inclusive use of technology in promoting and protecting the rights of war-affected children. Toward alleviating this, the organization is providing Internet access points in various communities in war-torn countries. War Child Canada recognizes that this is only a small step in bringing down the digital divide, but the organization also sees the real benefits of connecting youths around the world to advocate for their rights.

In all these case studies, there is strong evidence of the importance of technology in the fight for the human rights of children, with a reliance on good-quality, accurate, and timely information being vital to the work. The organizations use technology in three primary ways:

— disseminating timely information on the issues,
— distributing urgent action alerts, and
— connecting children and youths in innovative ways to enable them to advocate for themselves.

These organizations recognized that technology is only one means of delivering their stated aims. They all recognized the difficulties of using the Internet when so many people in the South do not have access. They all believed that traditional communications mediums still play an important role.

CONCLUSION

Mechanisms and efforts to protect and promote children's rights have significantly advanced in the last century. The century began with children being isolated and enslaved, having no rights at all, and ended with children connecting worldwide to advocate for their own rights. The situation of the world's children, however, still has a long way to go. The abundance of rights issues discussed in this volume illustrates this. Progress is being made on a number of different fronts, one of which is the innovative and extensive use of the Internet to connect people and communities, disseminate timely information inexpensively, and alert the world's population to violations of children's rights. The Internet also has its dark side for children's rights, as exemplified by online child pornography. In fact, the very features of the Internet that make it so effective as a human rights tool also enable it to be a destructive and hard-to-control force.

If the Internet is to become a force of development, democracy, and justice, it must be accessible to all people of the world. The Internet is used primarily by people and organizations in richer industrialized countries to promote the rights of children and to connect other people with their struggles. The Internet will never be an instrument of justice if it remains out of the hands of the poor and oppressed.

Notes

1. The wider term "information and communication technologies" (ICTs) is also used here, as the Internet is only one of a number of technologies used by the human rights world. The Internet, however, will be the primary technology considered in this article.

2. Reported in the Nua Internet survey, "UN Examines the Global Internet Society." Available at http://www.nua.ie/surveys/?f=VS&art_id=905355021&rel=true.

3. See http://www.amnesty.org (site visited 10 July 2000).

4. See http://www.CRIN.org (site visited 25 Oct. 2000).

5. From http://www.CRIN.org (site visited 25 Oct. 2000).

6. See http://www.amnesty-usa.org/children/about.htm (site visited 27 Oct. 2000).

7. From http://www.amnesty-usa.org/children/future.html (site visited 27 Oct. 2000).

8. See http://www.amnesty-usa.org/children/about.htm (site visited 27 Oct. 2000).

9. See http://www.warchild.ca (site visited 2 Nov. 2000).

References

Alexander, Cynthia J. and Leslie A. Pal. 1998. *Digital Democracy: Policy and Politics in the Wired World.* Toronto: University of Toronto Press.

Arlacchi, Pino. 1999. Address to the International Conference on Combating Child Pornography on the Internet, Vienna.

Brophy, P. and E. F. Halpin. 1999. Through the Net to Freedom: Information, the Internet and Human Rights. *Journal of Information Science* 25(May):351-64.

Hague, B. and B. Loader. 1999. *Digital Democracy: Discourse and Decision Making in the Information Age.* London: Routledge.

Halpin, E. and S. M. Fisher. 1998. *The Use of the Internet by the European Parliament for the Promotion and Protection of Human Rights.* Luxembourg: European Parliament.

Hansen, S. A. 1998. *Getting Online for Human Rights.* New York: American Association for the Advancement of Science.

International Conference on Combating Child Pornography on the Internet. 1999. Background paper. 29 Sept.–1 Oct., Vienna.

Metz, J. 1996. Information Technology and Human Rights. *Human Rights Quarterly* 18:705-46.

Slavin J. 2000. *The Internet and Society.* Cambridge, MA: Polity Press.

UNICEF. 2000. *The State of the World's Children.* Available at http://www.unicef.org/sowc00.

United Nations. 1948. *Universal Declaration of Human Rights.* Geneva: United Nations.

White, A. 1999. Freedom of Information in the Face of World-Wide Concern About the Sexual Abuse of Children, Paedophilia and Pornography on the Internet. Paper presented at the meeting Sexual Abuse of Children, Child Pornography and Paedophilia on the Internet: An International Challenge, UNESCO, Paris.

ANNALS, *AAPSS*, **575**, May 2001

Child Labor in Africa:
A Comparative Study

By SUDHARSHAN CANAGARAJAH and HELENA SKYT NIELSEN

ABSTRACT: This article analyzes the determinants of child labor in Africa as inferred from recent empirical studies. The empirical analysis is based on five country studies undertaken in three different African countries, namely, Côte d'Ivoire, Ghana, and Zambia. Some support is found for the popular belief of poverty as a determinant of child labor; however, other determinants are of similar importance. Among school costs, transportation costs have the greatest effect on child labor and school attendance, whereas the hypothesis of imperfect capital markets and that of household composition generally find some support.

Sudharshan Canagarajah works as a senior economist at the World Bank. Before joining the World Bank in 1993, he held teaching and research positions in universities in North America and Britain. His publications cover development issues in sub-Saharan Africa and Asia and include topics such as child labor, poverty, public expenditure and social protection.

Helena Skyt Nielsen holds a research position at the Aarhus School of Business in Denmark. She has published research on development and labor issues in the Journal of Population Economics *and* Economics Letters, *among others.*

NOTE: The views expressed in this article are those of the authors and should not be attributed to the World Bank or its affiliated organizations.

71

CHILD labor is widespread in the developing world. The International Labor Organization (ILO) estimates that in developing countries the total number of working children age 5-14 years is 250 million. Of these, 120 million work full-time, and 24 million are below the age of 10. In absolute terms, child labor is most prominent in Asia because approximately 150 million working children live in Asia. However, in relative terms, child labor is more widespread in Africa. Even though Africa accounts for only one-third of the working children in the developing world, labor force participation rates exceed 30 percent in many areas (see ILO 1997; UNICEF 1997).

Formal surveys and anecdotal data indicate that the agricultural sector has the highest concentration of child labor. Although agriculture is a large consumer of child labor all over the developing world, there are distinct differences between the sector composition of child labor in Africa, Asia, and Latin America. In Africa, child labor is considered primarily a rural phenomenon, while in Asia and Latin America, which are more urbanized, child labor is also considered an urban phenomenon. In Africa, child labor is concentrated in subsistence farming and is often associated with large, rural households. Children primarily tend livestock or assist adults during the harvest season. In addition to subsistence farming, African child laborers are also employed in commercial farming, which is concentrated in two geographical regions: the countries of coastal West Africa and the East African plateau.

For several reasons, the large number of child workers in the developing world is troubling. Child workers are equally susceptible to the dangers faced by adult workers under similar conditions, but they are more seriously affected because of their different anatomical, physiological, and psychological characteristics. The working conditions of children are far below those of adults: children work longer hours for lower wages and under more dangerous conditions. Unlike adults, children do not fight against their oppression through unions (see, for example, World Health Organization 1987).

In addition to being hazardous and harmful to children's health—in fact, more children are believed to die from exposure to pesticides than from all the most common childhood diseases combined—child labor interferes with education. Either school attendance is forgone in favor of work, or learning is inefficient because the children are not allowed to spend time doing their homework or because they are unable to pay proper attention in school because of fatigue. When directly asked, child workers find that school attendance is not the greatest problem of child labor; instead, they respond that they need leisure time to be children (see UNICEF 1997).

As mentioned previously, the problem of child labor in Africa is more pronounced than elsewhere in the developing world. While statistics in this field are far from reliable, it is assumed that in some regions of Africa labor force participation rates for children might be as high as 30 percent (for data, see ILO 1997;

UNICEF 1997). Furthermore, cost-benefit analyses show annual gross domestic product (GDP) losses of 1-2 percent because of the loss in human capital stock due to the use of child labor (see Nielsen 1998; Canagarajah and Coulombe 1998). Hence, there is enough motivation to find out what determines whether children work or attend school. To appropriately respond to the problem, it is necessary to explore characteristics of the households, economy, and society that may offer an explanation for the high incidence of child labor in Africa.

This article is an attempt to understand causality, and to influence policy, in order to promote the school enrollment of at-risk African children. It describes African child workers and investigates the socioeconomic characteristics associated with child labor. The conclusion offers policy suggestions to reduce child labor in Africa.

For purposes of this analysis, the concept of child labor is defined as children age 7 to 14 who are involved in economic activities for cash, kind, or nonwage incentives. Economic activities can include working in the household enterprise, farming, street vending, or wage work. Attempts to classify home care rarely succeed in distinguishing between household chores and taking care of siblings from idle time. As noted by UNICEF (1998), this results in a gender bias in the statistics because working female children more often perform full-time housework than working male children do.

Although children are involved in hazardous and harmful tasks, as well as other tasks that are less harmful, this article considers child labor in the broadest sense. This is because of the difficulty of making the distinction between different kinds of child labor, as described in the data, and the perception that even harmless child labor may interfere with a child's education and hence have harmful consequences.[1]

The country studies that form the basis of this article are based on household surveys collected by governments. Although they may not be the best instruments to analyze child labor, these surveys are likely to be unbiased because they are based on representative population samples.

The article is organized as follows: The next section examines the contributions that explain child labor from the standpoint of economics literature and derives five specific hypotheses to be tested in the empirical analysis. The third section presents some empirical evidence of the extent and the determinants of child labor and school attendance in Africa. The five hypotheses are tested based on evidence from the three African countries. The fourth section concludes with a discussion of the policy implications of the analysis and puts the findings in the perspective of policies pursued by international organizations.

CHILD LABOR HYPOTHESES

This section reviews the economics literature on child labor and derives five main hypotheses to explain its use. Both supply-side and demand-side issues are important when confronting the economics of child labor. Because it is based on data from household surveys, the empirical part of this article focuses on supply-side issues. However, some demand-side factors are discussed briefly at the beginning of this section.

Employers argue that children are irreplaceable because of their "nimble fingers." Following this argument, only children with small fingers have the ability to make fine, hand-knotted carpets; only children can pluck the delicate jasmine flowers without breaking branches; and similarly, only physically small individuals are able to climb mine tunnels. Although children, in general, have low productivity and are mostly unable to produce high-quality products, employers still tend to consider them to be cost-effective labor due to their low salary level (see U.S. Department of Labor 1995). On the other hand, Levison et al. (1996) find that children are not necessary for the Indian carpet industry to survive and that only minor changes in the financial arrangements between loom owners, exporters, and importers could reduce the incentive to employ children.

If the children do not have irreplaceable skills and if they are only marginally less costly than adults, the question remains as to why industries continue to hire children, especially in the face of growing global resistance to products made using child labor. Levison et al. (1996) suggest that the answer can be found in children's nonpecuniary characteristics. Children are less aware of their rights, less troublesome, more willing to take orders and

to do monotonous work without complaining, more trustworthy, less likely to steal, and less likely to be absent from work.

If the employer is the household of residence and if the household is poor, child labor may be used as cheap labor that makes it possible to maintain the budget (see Mehra-Kerpelman 1996). This could be in the form of either help in the household enterprise or in the home in order to free adult household members for economic activities elsewhere.

A final note on the demand side is increased school enrollment in years of bad harvest. While increases in harvest-related poverty and school attendance normally correlate negatively, the demand-side reduction in the agrarian sector in poor harvest years may liberate children's time and allow them to attend school.

The supply side of the market for child labor provides a different set of explanations for the prevalence of child labor. In the field of economics, the supply of child labor is explained in the context of the theories of investment in human capital and allocation of time.[2] The two primary contenders for children's nonleisure time are school and work. In a standard human capital model (see, for example, Ben-Porath, 1967; Siebert, 1990), each individual chooses the level of consumption and the allocation of time that maximize the discounted expected future utility. The standard human capital model is not sufficient to describe child labor in developing countries. The decision maker is often not the child but may be the household head, who allocates the time of all the household members.[3] Also, maximization is constrained by the fact that households have no access to borrowing and that consumption should exceed a certain subsistence level. In the developing world, and especially in Africa, a large proportion of households live at a minimum level of expenses. In this extended human capital model, child labor would be present in either of the following situations:

— Household consumption is equal to the subsistence level, and the marginal benefits of child labor may or may not exceed the marginal costs of child labor.
— Household consumption exceeds the subsistence level, and the marginal benefits of child labor (earnings and saved costs of schooling) are higher than the marginal costs of child labor in terms of the forgone return to human capital investments.

The first set of conditions is fulfilled for households living at the subsistence level and sheds light on why child labor may coexist with a good education system and a high demand for skilled labor. This set of conditions explains why poor households make use of child labor and why child labor may be used even in off-seasons in agricultural areas.

The second set of conditions would be fulfilled if school costs were high or if the return to schooling was low. The return to schooling is low if, for instance, the quality of schooling is low (for example, Glewwe 1996) or if the expected future demand for educated labor is low.[4] Also, a situation of high demand for unskilled labor and, consequently, child labor would satisfy this condition. An example is the case of agriculture during peak seasons.

If households are risk averse, poor parents would receive a high marginal benefit (marginal utility) from child labor income, and they would be more likely than risk-neutral agents to supply child labor. The use of child labor is a way of augmenting income such that the risk of suddenly falling below the subsistence level of consumption is reduced. For instance, for subsistence farmers, child labor is a way of reducing the potential impact of a bad harvest, whereas for urban households, child labor might reduce the potential impact of job loss or rising food prices. For households living close to the subsistence level, the impact of income interruptions, such as a bad harvest or job loss, are more severe; thus this risk management argument explains why these households may be more inclined to use child labor.

To simplify, one may say that three main hypotheses emerge from the human capital framework: a poverty hypothesis, a school costs hypothesis, and a school quality hypothesis. In the existing literature on child labor, all three hypotheses find some support. Bonnet (1993) focuses on poverty as an explanation, and this is also found to be important by Cartwright (1998) and Sakellariou and Lall (1998). However, the analysis in the next section of this article moderates that result, and Hiraoka (1997, chap. 2), in her thesis, asks whether poverty really is the main explanation for child labor. Both Lavy (1996) and Jensen and Nielsen (1997) find that transportation costs of schooling are important. Gertler and Glewwe (1990) refine this conclusion by investigating the willingness to pay for reducing the distance to school. They find that both the rich and the poor are willing to pay the price for reducing the distance to schools to less than 1 kilometer. Lavy (1996) finds some evidence of an effect of low school quality on school attendance, although the effects are relatively small in magnitude. Bonnet (1993) argues that failure of the education system is an important explanation for the prevalence of child labor. When parents do not expect children to learn much in school, they decide to give them informal education in terms of work experience.

Another strain of the literature focuses on household issues such as the quantity of children and their level of education and the age-gender division of domestic and other work. These issues, which are described next, are summarized in a hypothesis of household composition.

The household decision to allocate children's time is often seen as a joint decision dependent on the number of children (Becker and Lewis 1973). Both the number of children (quantity) and well-educated children (quality) represent potentially high household income, and when household welfare is maximized, the household decision maker faces a trade-off between the two. Patrinos and Psacharopoulos (1997) find some evidence of a positive effect of the number of siblings on the probability of going to work; however, a

simultaneous equation system is needed before concrete conclusions can be made about this relationship. Rosenzweig and Wolpin (1980) simulate the structural model, which was suggested by Becker and Lewis (1973), and confirm that an exogenous increase in fertility decreases child quality. However, Montgomery, Kouamé, and Oliver (1995) state that the existence of a trade-off between quantity and quality has not yet been established in the case of sub-Saharan Africa. In addition, it is hard to accept that lifelong horizons, family planning, and economic rationality govern fertility and educational decisions in traditional Africa.

As discussed by Rosenzweig (1977), children's role in household production is of great importance in relation to child labor. This is especially true in the substitutability between the work of female children and their mothers: when mothers work, girls stay home to take over their duties. Levy (1985) and Rosenzweig (1981) show that a 10 percent increase in women's wage rates would decrease the female child's labor force participation by as much as 10 percent. Sakellariou and Lall (1998) and Cartwright (1998) reach a similar conclusion. This effect can go far toward explaining the incidence of child labor in subsistence households, although regional and sector differences in the intensity of this effect have also been noted in the literature.

Age and age distribution of siblings are important variables in understanding the incidence and nature of child labor (see, for example, DeGraff, Bilsborrow, and Herriman 1993). One common finding is that the incidence of child labor is higher for the older children than for the younger children. Another common finding is that having older siblings in the labor market decreases the likelihood of younger siblings being involved in child labor.

Another factor affecting the choice of school versus labor is the parents' employment. A central ILO concern has been that the demand for child labor in certain areas is higher than or even reduces the demand for adult labor and thus forces children into the role of family income providers. Ironically, this is a vicious cycle in which children replace adults in the labor force, and the children of the displaced adults are forced to join the labor force to support the family.

If children are regarded as pure investment goods, textbook economics would tell risk-averse parents to diversify the investments in children's education. Therefore, they invest in formal education by allowing some children to get continuing education and invest in informal education (experience) by giving some children a primary education or no education at all. Lloyd (1994) and Patrinos and Psacharopoulos (1997) find some evidence for this sort of diversification.

Continuing to view children as pure investment goods, a capital market hypothesis can be formulated. Human, physical, and financial capital can be regarded as competing investment alternatives. In developing countries, the degree of rationing and borrowing constraints on the financial capital market is high; thus, this market is not perfectly competitive. To a lesser degree, the human capital market may also be characterized by rationing since the supply of schools may be limited. The human capital market differs from the two other markets in that parents do not have absolute control over the outcome of an investment in human capital because the children may leave the household after they have finished their education (Parsons and Goldin 1989; Andvig 1997). Households without access to the financial capital market and without physical assets may be forced to "take loans" on the human capital market if they experience a sudden income drop. Withdrawing children from school and letting them work represents a loan in this market. Hence the capital market hypothesis might contribute to explaining child labor.

The previous discussion gives rise to five different hypotheses explaining child labor: poverty, school costs, school quality, household composition, and capital market. In the following section, evidence for and against the five hypotheses are presented based on case studies in Africa.

EMPIRICAL EVIDENCE

This section presents empirical evidence for the extent and determinants of child labor in Africa. Figure 1 illustrates the amount of child labor in Côte d'Ivoire, Ghana, and Zambia, together with that of other low-income African countries. Both Côte d'Ivoire and Ghana seem to be representative for their income group with regard to the level of child

FIGURE 1
CHILD LABOR IN LOW-INCOME AFRICAN COUNTRIES

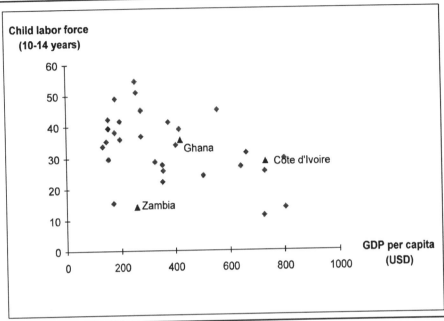

SOURCE: World Bank 1997. Numbers from 1995 or the most recent available figure is used. For Côte d'Ivoire, Ghana, and Zambia, the numbers are calculated from the Ghana Living Standards Survey 1991-92, Côte d'Ivoire Living Standards Survey 1988, and Priority Survey II 1993, respectively.
NOTE: Child labor is defined as the share of the children in the 10-14 age group that is active in the labor force.

labor. However, Zambia has a much lower level of child labor than other countries with a similar GDP per capita. Actually, the extent of child labor in Zambia is at about the same level as in Egypt and Swaziland, where the GDP per capita is much higher.

In the following section, a number of empirical studies of child labor in Côte d'Ivoire, Ghana, and Zambia are surveyed. The choice of countries is constrained by the availability of data and the existence of relevant empirical studies, and these countries may not be representative of Africa as a whole. After a brief description of the studies that are used for the survey, each of the five hypotheses is tested in turn.

The five studies

Table 1 briefly presents the five studies that form the basis for the survey of child labor in Côte d'Ivoire, Ghana, and Zambia. The main difference between the studies emanates from the choice of econometric methods.

Table 2 presents summary statistics describing the reported child activities in the samples that form the basis for the five studies. Some

TABLE 1
OVERVIEW OF THE FIVE STUDIES

		Grootaert (1998)	Coulombe (1998)	Canagarajah and Coulombe (1998)	Bhalotra and Heady (1998)	Nielsen (1998)
Country		Côte d'Ivoire	Côte d'Ivoire	Ghana	Rural Ghana	Zambia
Data		CILSS 1988	CILSS 1988	GLSS 1991-92	GLSS 1991-92	PSII 1993
Age group		7-17 years	7-14 years	7-14 years	7-14 years	7-14 years
Method		Sequential probit and multinomial logit	Bivariate probit	Bivariate probit	Tobit	Bivariate probit

NOTE: CILSS = Côte d'Ivoire Living Standards Survey; GLSS = Ghana Living Standards Survey; PSII = Priority Survey II.

characteristics are similar in all the studies. First, there is more child labor and non–school attendance in rural areas than in urban areas. Second, if children work in urban areas, they are more likely to combine work with school attendance than to only work. Third, the proportion of children that are neither attending school nor working seems to be about 20 percent. Grootaert (1998) argues that these children are doing home care activities, since "in the context of Côte d'Ivoire, it would be most unusual for children in the age group 7-17 to not attend school and to make no contribution at all to the household" (21).

The numbers confirm the statement made previously that child labor in Africa is mainly a rural phenomenon. A lower bound on the estimate of child labor in rural areas is 21 percent, which is the case in Zambia; the other studies report estimates greater than 30 percent.

For Côte d'Ivoire, the figures in the two studies are quite different. This is due to the different age groups and different definitions of child labor. Coulombe (1998) defines child labor as the proportion of children who worked during the last week before the survey, whereas Grootaert (1998) uses the proportion of children who worked during the last year.

Bhalotra and Heady (1998) restrict their sample to children who reside in households that cultivate land, and they analyze the hours of farm work. Therefore, they use only about half of the rural sample, which explains the difference in the numbers in the two Ghanaian studies.

The descriptive statistics in Table 2 represent the dependent variables of the analysis. To explain the variation in the dependent variables, the authors use different sets of explanatory variables, most of which come under the heading of one of the following hypotheses: poverty, school costs, school quality, household composition, or capital market. Starting with the poverty hypothesis, which is traditionally viewed as the most important, each of the five hypotheses is tested in turn.

Poverty hypothesis

In the surveyed papers, it is difficult to find clear evidence for the supposed dominating importance of

TABLE 2
REPORTED ACTIVITIES IN THE FIVE STUDIES (in percentages)

	School Only	School and Work	Work Only	Neither	All
Côte d'Ivoire*					
Grootaert (1998)					
Rural	18.8	25.8	34.4	20.9	100
Urban	34.3	36.4	6.5	22.8	100
All	25.3	30.2	22.8	21.7	100
Coulombe (1998)					
Rural[†]	37.8	0.4	33.9	27.9	100
Urban[†]	69.3	0.4	5.1	25.2	100
All	52.2	0.4	20.8	26.6	100
Ghana					
Canagarajah and					
Coulombe (1998)					
Rural[‡]	42.2	25.4	12.1	20.2	100
Urban[‡]	77.9	4.9	3.4	13.7	100
All	53.9	18.8	9.3	18.1	100
Bhalotra and					
Heady (1998)					
Rural[§]	37.4	31.3	13.1	18.2	100
Zambia					
Nielsen (1998)					
Rural	59.9	7.0	13.6	19.4	100
Urban	85.8	1.1	0.7	12.4	100
All	70.4	4.6	8.4	16.6	100

*Coulombe defines child labor as the proportion of children who worked during the last week before the survey, whereas Grootaert uses proportion of children who worked during the last year.
[†]Calculated from Tables 4 and 8 in Coulombe (1998).
[‡]Calculated from Table 3 and Annex 2 in Canagarajah and Coulombe (1998).
[§]Work is farm work, and the numbers are computed from Table 3 in Bhalotra and Heady (1998).

poverty as an explanation for child labor. To test for the importance of poverty, Canagarajah and Coulombe (1998), Coulombe (1998), and Nielsen (1998) base their income measures on total household expenditure and correct for potential endogeneity. The remaining two studies correct for potential endogeneity in the definition of the income measure rather than in the estimation procedure. Grootaert (1998) uses an indicator variable to determine if household income (excluding income from child labor) is in the lowest quintile, whereas Bhalotra and Heady (1998) use household food expenditure per capita to approximate household income per capita.

When estimating a sequential probit model for rural areas, Grootaert (1998) finds that poverty is not important for the first-stage decision that concerns whether or not the individual attends school only. However, it is important in the second-stage decision, which is between attending school and working at the same time as opposed to working only or taking part in home care activities. Belonging to the lowest income quintile decreases the probability of combining work with school attendance by 27 percentage points for the average person. Estimating the multinomial logit model confirms this finding. The effect seems considerable, although it is difficult to assess because of the broad reference group and the relative definition of poverty. For urban areas, poverty is found to exert a significant effect on both the first-stage decision (attending school only) and the second-stage decision (combining work with school attendance) in the sequential probit model. However, the magnitude of the effect is somewhat smaller (9 and 13 percentage points, respectively).

In their tobit estimation for hours of work for rural Ghana, Bhalotra and Heady (1998) find a bell-shaped effect of income for girls and no effect for boys. This is in conflict with the negative effect of poverty, which is often taken for granted. However, they argue that alternative characterizations must be sought before they are confident of their result.

Studies that estimate a bivariate probit model generally indicate that the effect of the income measure on school attendance is always significantly positive, whereas the effect on child labor is less clear-cut. Canagarajah and Coulombe (1998) and Coulombe (1998) both use a welfare indicator, defined as the logarithm of household expenditure per capita, to account for poverty. In Côte d'Ivoire, the elasticity of the probability of working is about 0.3, although the effect is not always significant.[5] In Ghana, the effect of welfare on child labor follows an inverted U-shape curve with the maximum just below the median expenditure. Therefore, the expected negative effect of income only prevails in the upper end of the income distribution. This characteristic is observed to be very strong in rural areas. In the case of Zambia, the effect of household income on child labor has the expected sign, although it is only significant for rural areas, and the elasticity is less than 1. This means that huge income subsidies or many decades of widespread economic growth are needed to reduce child labor considerably.

Canagarajah and Coulombe (1998), Coulombe (1998), and Nielsen (1998) reject exogeneity of income in most estimations. Hence correcting for endogeneity might be crucial for obtaining reliable results with respect to the effect of poverty. Nielsen mentions that the effect of income on child labor has increased significantly after correcting for endogeneity.

As an explanation for the weak support of the popular belief that the poor use child labor more often than others do, Bhalotra and Heady (1998) and Canagarajah and Coulombe (1998) suggest some conflicting evidence. Poor households may be more likely to be located in regions with a sluggish economy, which results in a generally low demand for labor (including child labor). Furthermore, the poor and their children are more likely to be affected by slack seasonal labor demand patterns and constraints in terms of other inputs and availability of credit. However, some of the reported studies (see, for example, Nielsen 1998; Bhalotra and

Heady 1998) have already controlled for regional effects, landownership, and credit availability.

To recapitulate, the empirical studies cast doubt about the traditional, simplistic view that poverty is the main factor that pushes African children into the labor market. In many cases, a significant effect of poverty on child labor is found, but usually, the magnitude of the effect is moderate. Similar conclusions may be drawn about the effect on school attendance; although the effect is always significant, the order of magnitude is moderate.

Costs hypothesis

All studies but Bhalotra and Heady (1998) use the cluster mean of education expenses, including fees, teaching material, uniforms, and other expenditure, as a measure of school costs. Grootaert (1998) finds a very weak effect when estimating a multinomial logit, but he finds no effect at all when estimating a sequential probit. Coulombe (1998) finds the opposite signs of what would be expected, whereas Canagarajah and Coulombe (1998) find that both the probability of working and the probability of attending school in rural areas increase with escalating education expenses. This odd result may reflect the fact that quality and costs are correlated, and quality has not been accounted for. For instance, it is a well-known fact that in Ghana the private schools are better and more expensive than the relatively cheap, low-quality public schools. Nielsen (1998) finds that decreasing school expenses by about U.S.$3 increases school attendance by a small margin, corresponding to an elasticity below 0.1, which is a relatively moderate effect.

Transportation costs are measured by an indicator for presence of a school in the community, distance to school, availability of a passable road, and availability of public transport. For rural areas in Côte d'Ivoire, Grootaert (1998) and Coulombe (1998) find some effect of the distance to schools. Grootaert finds that the distance to schools only matters in the second-stage decision of whether or not to combine work with school attendance. The absence of a school in the local community decreases the probability of combining work with school attendance by 18 percentage points. Coulombe finds a child labor elasticity of 0.2 with respect to distance, and he finds no effect on school attendance itself. Canagarajah and Coulombe (1998) find that decreasing the travel time to school by 10 minutes decreases school attendance by about 1 percentage point and labor force participation by half a percentage point. The latter may be explained by the fact that children who have to travel far to school do not have much time left to work. For rural areas, Nielsen (1998) finds large effects of the presence of a primary school in the community and the availability of a passable road and smaller effects of the other variables approximating transportation costs. The presence of a primary school increases school attendance by 10 percentage points in some cases, whereas the availability of a passable road decreases child labor by more than 10 percentage points and also increases school attendance significantly. Bhalotra and Heady (1998) find the expected signs on the variables to approximate transportation costs of schooling, although none are significant.

The study by Bhalotra and Heady (1998) is exceptional in that the authors use information on wages from child labor, and they find a significant effect of the daily wage for a child harvesting on the hours of work. Such measures are usually not available. Another example of a study that applies such a measure is the study by Mason and Khandker (1997) on Tanzania. They find a strong effect of opportunity costs on the probability to be enrolled in school.

Quality hypothesis

Only the study of Zambia includes indicators for the quality of schooling as reported by the community leaders. The condition of roofing is found to be a significant determinant of the probability of working, whereas both the conditions of roofing and furniture are important determinants for school attendance. In some cases, a school roof's poor condition increases the probability of working by 15 percentage points.

Earlier studies on related topics support the finding for Zambia that the physical conditions of schools are important. Glewwe and Jacoby (1994) analyze middle school education in Ghana. They find that school quality is more important for grade attainment than for school enrollment. Furthermore, they find that the relative effectiveness of repairing classrooms in schools with no usable classrooms when it rains is higher than that of providing instructional materials. Using an output-based quality measure, Hanushek and Lavy (1994) find that students attending higher-quality schools will tend to stay longer in school and complete higher grades.

Household composition hypothesis

All five studies carefully take into account household composition as an explanation for child labor and school attendance. One of the most important variables is the education of the parents or the household head. All but Bhalotra and Heady (1998) find a strong effect of this variable. Bhalotra and Heady find that only girls with mothers who have completed secondary education work less than other girls do. In the other studies, the education of the parents or the household head decreases the probability of working and increases the probability of school attendance significantly. Generally, the order of magnitude of this effect is 1-2 percentage points per year of education. However, Grootaert (1998) finds a larger effect of the education of the parents in his second-stage decision to combine work with school attendance. In rural areas, an extra year of education for the father increases the probability to combine work with schooling by 7 percentage points, whereas an extra year of education for the mother increases the probability by 3 percentage points.

The child's relationship to the household head might also have an effect. If the child is a son or daughter of the household head, the probability of working might be lower and the probability of attending school might be higher. Both Coulombe (1998) and Nielsen (1998) find that the effect is present for girls, although Nielsen only finds an effect in the school attendance equation and only for urban areas. Coulombe finds that the effect is less than 10 percentage points, whereas Nielsen finds an effect of about 10 percentage points. For Ghana, Canagarajah and Coulombe (1998) find no effect, and the other authors do not include variables to account for this effect.

Bhalotra and Heady (1998) find that the gender composition of the household is important. They find that boys work fewer hours if the female-to-male ratio is high. Coulombe (1998) finds that the presence of more female siblings in the 7-14 age group decreases the probability of working and increases the probability of attending school. Also, the presence of more females in the 15-59 age group decreases child labor and increases school attendance, indicating substitutability between child labor and the female labor supply.

Grootaert (1998) finds some importance of the presence of siblings, but not large effects. Nielsen (1998) finds that the higher the number of older siblings, the lower the probability of working and the higher the probability of attending school. The presence of children age 0-6 years only increases the probability of working, if housekeeping is included as a work activity (see Canagarajah and Coulombe 1998; Coulombe 1998). Canagarajah and Coulombe (1998) find that the presence of household members older than 60 increases the probability of working and decreases the probability of attending school. In Ghana, the effect varies from 1 to 4 percentage points. Coulombe (1998) finds no support for Côte d'Ivoire.

The results regarding the effect of the gender of the household head differ. For rural areas in Côte d'Ivoire (Grootaert 1998; Coulombe 1998) and for girls from rural parts of Ghana (Bhalotra and Heady 1998), it is found that the use of child labor is higher and the rate of school attendance lower in female-headed households. Canagarajah and Coulombe (1998) find the opposite in all cases except in the case of girls from rural areas.

Both of the two results makes sense. Female household heads might care more about the children and therefore use less child labor. Alternately, female heads might be forced to make use of child labor more often because they are under economic pressure because the husband is dead or has left either permanently or temporarily.

Some authors (Grootaert 1998; Nielsen 1998) find that the higher the age of the household head the lower the probability of working and the higher the probability of attending school; the latter effect is the strongest of the two. This means that children who are born at a later stage in the life cycle are less likely to work and more likely to attend school.

Owning a farm increases the probability of working and decreases the probability of school attendance; the latter effect is not always significant (Coulombe 1998; Grootaert 1998; Canagarajah and Coulombe 1998).

On the contrary, Nielsen (1998) finds that the fact that a household is involved in agriculture increases, rather than decreases, school attendance.

Different results are found regarding the effect of owning a nonfarm business; Canagarajah and Coulombe (1998) find that it decreases child labor and increases school attendance; hence it can be viewed as an asset. Grootaert (1998) finds that if the household owns a nonagricultural business, the children are more likely to participate in home care activities than in any other activity. This implies that their work is a substitute for the work of adults who participate in the business activities. Coulombe (1998) finds no effect of this variable.

Capital market hypothesis

The most obvious variables to account for the capital market effect would be indicators of credit availability. Bhalotra and Heady (1998) find a strong negative effect of an indicator for whether there is a commercial bank in the community on the hours worked. However, Nielsen (1998) includes an indicator for whether some sort of credit is available in the community, but this does not show a significant relationship for Zambia. However, an indicator for whether or not the household owns an asset has a significant effect on both the probability of working and the probability of attending school. The magnitude of the effect is as high as a 10-percentage-point change in the probabilities in some cases. Households that own assets are not constrained in the capital market, whereas households with no assets may have only the possibility of withdrawing children from school if the households experience a sudden shortfall in income due to a poor harvest or unemployment.

In Zambia, owning land has a similar effect in urban areas since children from households with land are more likely to attend school. However, in rural areas of Côte d'Ivoire, Coulombe (1998) finds that the probability of working increases and school attendance decreases proportionally to the number of acres of land owned by the household. The two counteracting results reflect that land is an asset but that land also needs labor.

As mentioned previously, owning a nonfarm business seems to account for the wealth effect in Ghana. When the household owns a business, it has assets in the business to sell instead of withdrawing children from school if it is economically stressed. This variable is also included in the studies of Côte d'Ivoire, and the results are different, reflecting a similar tendency as was seen for land: a business is an asset, but it also increases the demand for labor within the household.

The capital market hypothesis is closely related to the poverty hypothesis; poverty is a problem because the poor have no access to borrowing on the financial and physical capital markets, and hence they have no possibility of income smoothing. Therefore, Grootaert (1998) interprets his poverty variable as an indicator for lack of access to credit and insurance.

Other explanations

The five hypotheses represent an important set of explanations, although they are not exhaustive. Following research done in the fields of sociology and anthropology, traditions and attitudes toward child labor and education are also expected to be important. Traditions and attitudes are highly correlated with the religion and the ethnic group to which the individual belongs, and indicators for these are included in some of the surveyed studies. Bhalotra and Heady (1998) find that children from some ethnic groups work more hours than others, and the results differ across gender. Canagarajah and Coulombe (1998) find that in Ghana children from Protestant households are much more likely to attend school than those who practice traditional religion; in between are Catholics, other Christians, and Muslims. In rural areas, Protestants have a probability 22 percentage points higher of attending school than those who practice a traditional religion, whereas in urban areas, the similar number is 9 percentage points. In rural areas, Protestants seem to be most likely to use child labor, whereas in urban areas those who practice traditional religion are most likely to use child labor, although the differences are only a couple of percentage points and are not always significant. Coulombe (1998) finds for Côte d'Ivoire that Christians are more likely to attend school, and in rural areas they are also less likely to work than Muslims and those who practice traditional religion.

Traditions and attitudes are likely to be constant within a local community. Nielsen (1998) includes normally distributed community effects, and these effects are likely to account for the effect of traditions and attitudes, among other things. The community effects are found to be very important for the decision to use child labor. For instance, a 13-year-old who resides in a community that is one standard deviation below the average has a probability of working that is 30 percentage points higher than that of a similar individual who resides in an average community.

Of course, location effects reflect more than just traditions and attitudes. They also reflect measurement errors in included variables and other omitted variables describing, for instance, the educational system, infrastructure, demand for skilled and unskilled labor in the area, and credit constraints. All of the studies found some regions in which children are more exposed to child labor.

CONCLUDING REMARKS

Until now, the main argument on worldwide child labor has been rooted in an opposition to the violation of the human rights of children rather than a consideration of adverse economic incentives. Through the Convention on the Rights of the Child and the Minimum Age Convention, the United Nations advocates legislative action that bans harmful child labor and introduces policy measures to abolish child labor below the age of (preferably) 15. The World Bank has only recently begun to recognize the importance of addressing child labor. The World Bank is required to make its decisions on economic grounds, and it must respect the territorial jurisdiction of each sovereign nation. Therefore, it cannot enforce laws or morality, which have no bearing on specific operations.[6]

If politicians consider child labor the result of a rational economic decision rather than just a violation of human rights, they should be cautious about abolishing child labor through prohibition or compulsory schooling laws. Such laws would force households to choose suboptimal behavior. For instance, if laws forced a poor household that is living close to the subsistence level to send its children to school instead of work, an exogenous shock (for example, poor harvest) would have an unnecessarily harsh impact on the household's welfare. If the household were allowed to use child labor, it could take a child out of school if the harvest failed, or it could decide to let one child work permanently and use the income to smooth consumption. Another example in which the previously mentioned policy could lead to suboptimal behavior is the case of low-quality formal schooling. If this is the case, it may be more profitable to invest in informal education, such as learning by doing, on a farm. From an economist's point of view, policies that do not distort the economic incentives, such as subsidies, taxes, or even consumer boycott, would be preferred over legislation.

One way to guide households toward choosing school attendance and not child labor is to give an income subsidy and thereby reduce poverty. However, no matter whether poverty is the most important reason for child labor, it is difficult to reduce child labor through poverty elimination alone because that would require substantial subsidies to a large proportion of the school-age children. However, reducing child labor might be a beneficial side effect of poverty alleviation. Another problem is that targeting the poor might be difficult since information on household income is not readily available. A practical and viable policy would be to target characteristics that are closely related to poverty, such as geographical region.

The support for poverty as the dominant explanation of why children are working instead of attending school was limited in the surveyed studies. Some studies found no significant effect, others found a significant but moderate effect, and one found an effect that might be called substantial. As mentioned previously, even if the results are not interpreted as supporting the poverty hypothesis, the policy implication of that conclusion is debatable.

The capital market explanation, which is related to the poverty hypothesis, was confirmed in the studies. Households that own some sort of asset—either land, business, or other physical assets—were found to use less child labor than other households do. The reason may be that these households can sell the assets instead of withdrawing children from work if they experience a sudden drop in income. This result implies that one way to reduce child labor and increase incentives to keep the children in the educational system is to improve access to credit.

Another way of changing incentives for households to choose school attendance rather than child labor is to adjust school costs. The cost hypothesis found some support; many of the studies agreed that transportation costs were important. Some studies also found support for the importance of general education expenses, although the effect was small. The one study that accounted for the potential income from child labor found education expenses very important. The results would lead to a recommendation to decrease transportation costs and possibly supply education subsidies. One way to do this would be to give income subsidies that are conditional on school attendance. In practice, the subsidies could be implemented in terms of daily or weekly subsidies, food-for-school programs, or stipends for completing a grade.

Improving school quality would increase the returns to education and improve the incentives for education. Only the study for Zambia included measures to account for this hypothesis, and the results showed that it might be an effective tool for improving roofing and furniture.

Although the household composition hypothesis seems to be powerful, it is not directly useful when specifying a policy. However, it may be used to choose targets for policy. It was found that the education of parents and household heads was an important explanatory factor behind child labor and school attendance. Although this was expected, why this result is so strong is still an open question. It may be because the education of the head of the household and the parents approximates the household income potential or accounts for the effect of social heritage. No matter the explanation, the education of the head of the household might be a useful targeting device in confronting child labor.

One household characteristic that has a direct policy implication is whether the household owns a farm and whether it is involved in agricultural production. These factors make a difference for the use of child labor and school attendance. An obvious conclusion is that policymakers should accept this relationship and aim for facilitating the combination of school and farm work instead of eliminating child labor. One way to do this is to make school calendars flexible and adjust them to the slack and peak seasons in agriculture.

A similar conclusion is drawn by Grootaert (1998), who found that most significant effects were in the second-stage choice between combining work with schooling versus working only or performing home care activities only. He advocates a gradual policy approach toward child labor whereby the initial goal is to make the combination between working and school attendance possible instead of eliminating child labor immediately. He states that having no children work is not a viable policy for poor households in the short term.

The previously mentioned policy recommendations rely on the support for the five hypotheses, which are derived from economic theory. In addition to these economic explanations, sociological and anthropological explanations might be as important. In these fields, traditions and attitudes are emphasized, and confirmation of these explanations would imply that changing incentives might be completely ineffective. Instead of legislative action, such as enforced compulsory schooling or a ban on child labor, sensitization with the purpose of changing attitudes or traditions would be more effective.

Notes

1. This is consistent with the spirit of Article 32 of the U.N. Convention on the Rights of the Child, which concerns both hazardous work and work that interferes with education.

2. Examples are Patrinos and Psacharopoulos 1997; Jensen and Nielsen 1997; Grootaert and Kanbur 1995.

3. Alternatively, the household choice might be considered a bargaining model of multiple participants.

4. Retrenchment of civil servants and the shrinking public sector have reduced educated individuals' prospects for finding lucrative jobs. In the absence of private-sector growth, there are probably few good prospects for educated labor in Africa.

5. An elasticity of −0.3 means that a 1 percent income increase reduces child labor by 0.3 percent.

6. See Fallon and Tzannatos 1998 and Shihata 1996 for a discussion on the role of the World Bank in combating child labor.

References

Andvig, Jens. 1997. Child Labor in Sub-Saharan Africa: An Exploration. Working Paper No. 585, Norwegian Institute of Internal Affairs, Oct.

Becker, G. S. and H. G. Lewis. 1973. On the Interaction Between the Quantity and Quality of Children. *Journal of Political Fconomy* 81:S279-88.

Ben-Porath, Y. 1967. The Production of Human Capital and the Life Cycle of Earnings. *Journal of Political Economy* 75:352-65.

Bhalotra, S. and C. Heady. 1998. Child Labor in Rural Pakistan and Ghana: Myths and Data. Working paper, Department of Economics, University of Bristol.

Bonnet, M. 1993. Child Labor in Africa. *International Labor Review* 132: 371-89.

Canagarajah, S. and H. Coulombe. 1998. Child Labor and Schooling in Ghana. Policy Research Working Paper No. 1844, World Bank, Washington, DC.

Cartwright, K. 1998. Child Labor in Colombia. In *The Policy Analysis of Child Labor: A Comparative Study*, ed. C. Grootaert and H. A. Patrinos. Washington, DC: World Bank.

Coulombe, H. 1998. Child Labor and Education in Côte d'Ivoire. Background paper, World Bank, Washington, DC.

DeGraff, D. S., R. E. Bilsborrow, and A. N. Herriman. 1993. The Implications of High Fertility for Children's Time Use in the Philippines. In *Fertility, Family Size, and Structure: Consequences for Families and Children*, ed. C. B. Lloyd. New York: Population Council.

Fallon, P. and Z. Tzannatos. 1998. *Child Labor: Issues and Directions for the World Bank*. Human Development Network—Social Protection, World Bank, Washington, DC.

Gertler, P. and P. Glewwe. 1990. The Willingness to Pay for Education in Developing Countries: Evidence from Rural Peru. *Journal of Public Economics* 42:251-75.

Glewwe, P. 1996. The Relevance of Standard Estimates of Rates of Return to Schooling for Education Policy: A Critical Assessment. *Journal of Development Economics* 5:267-90.

Glewwe, P. and H. Jacoby. 1994. Student Achievement and Schooling Choice in Low-Income Countries: Evidence from

Ghana. *Journal of Human Resources* 29:843-64.

Grootaert, C. 1998. Child Labor in Côte d'Ivoire. In *The Policy Analysis of Child Labor: A Comparative Study*, ed. C. Grootaert and H. A. Patrinos. Washington, DC: World Bank.

Grootaert, C. and R. Kanbur. 1995. Child Labor: An Economic Perspective. *International Labour Review* 134: 187-203.

Hanushek, E. A. and V. Lavy. 1994. School Quality, Achievement Bias, and Dropout Behavior in Egypt. LSMS Working Paper No. 107, World Bank, Washington, DC.

Hiraoka, R. 1997. Child Labor in India. Ph.D. thesis, Cornell University.

International Labor Organization. 1997. *IPEC at a Glance*. Geneva: ILO.

Jensen, P. and H. S. Nielsen. 1997. Child Labour or School Attendance? Evidence from Zambia. *Journal of Population Economics* 10:407-24.

Lavy, V. 1996. School Supply Constraints and Children's Educational Outcomes in Rural Ghana. *Journal of Development Economics* 51:291-314.

Levison, D., R. Anker, S. Ashraf, and S. Barge. 1996. *Is Child Labor Really Necessary in India's Carpet Industry?* Labor Market Paper No. 15. Geneva: International Labor Organization.

Levy, V. 1985. Cropping Patterns, Mechanization, Child Labor and Fertility Behavior in a Farming Economy: Rural Egypt. *Economic Development and Cultural Change* 33:777-91.

Lloyd, C. B. 1994. Investing in the Next Generation: The Implication of High Fertility at the Level of the Family. Working Paper No. 63, New York Population Council.

Mason, A. and S. R. Khandker. 1997. Children's Work, Opportunity Costs, and Schooling in Tanzania. Background paper, World Bank, Washington, DC.

Mehra-Kerpelman, K. 1996. Children at Work: How Many and Where? *World of Work* 15:8-9.

Montgomery, M., A. Kouamé, and R. Oliver. 1995. The Tradeoff Between Number of Children and Child Schooling: Evidence from Côte d'Ivoire and Ghana. LSMS Working Paper No. 112, World Bank, Washington DC.

Nielsen, H. S. 1998. Child Labor and School Attendance in Zambia: Two Joint Decisions. Working Paper No. 98-15, Centre for Labour Market and Social Research, Aarhus, Denmark.

Parsons, D. O. and C. Goldin. 1989. Parental Altruism and Self-Interest: Child Labor Among Late Nineteenth-Century American Families. *Economic Inquiry* 27:637-59.

Patrinos, H. and G. Psacharopoulos. 1997. Family Size, Schooling and Child Labor in Peru: An Empirical Analysis. *Journal of Population Economics* 10:387-405.

Rosenzweig, M. R. 1977. Farm-Family Schooling Decisions: Determinants of the Quantity and Quality of Education in Agricultural Populations. *Journal of Human Resources* 12:71-92.

————. 1981. Household and Non-Household Activities of Youth: Issues of Modelling, Data and Estimation Strategies. In *Child Work, Poverty and Underdevelopment*, ed. G. Rodgers and G. Standing. Geneva: International Labor Organization.

Rosenzweig, M. R. and K. Wolpin. 1980. Testing the Quantity-Quality Fertility Model: The Use of Twins as a Natural Experiment. *Econometrica* 48:228-40.

Sakellariou, C. and A. Lall. 1998. Child Labor in the Philippines. In *The Policy Analysis of Child Labor: A Comparative Study*, ed. C. Grootaert and H. A. Patrinos. Washington, DC: World Bank.

Shihata, I.F.I. 1996. The World Bank's Protection and Promotion of Children's Rights. *International Journal of Children's Rights* 4:383-405.

Siebert, W. S. 1990. Developments in the Economics of Human Capital. In *Labour Economics*, ed. D. Carline et al. London: Longman.

UNICEF. 1997. *The State of the World's Children*. New York: UNICEF.

———. 1998. UNICEF's Emerging Response Towards Eliminating Child Labour. Paper presented at the seminar on child labor, World Bank, 21 Jan., Washington, DC.

U.S. Department of Labor. 1995. *By the Sweat and Toil of Children*, vol. 2. Washington, DC: U.S. Department of Labor.

World Bank. 1997. *World Development Indicators*. Washington, DC: World Bank.

World Health Organization. 1987. *Children at Work: Special Health Risks*. Technical Report Series No. 756. Geneva: World Health Organization.

ANNALS, *AAPSS*, **575**, May 2001

Child Soldiers and the Convention on the Rights of the Child

By JO DE BERRY

ABSTRACT: This article considers Article 38 of the U.N. Convention on the Rights of the Child (CRC), which concerns the prevention of children's active participation in armed hostilities as soldiers. It is argued that if this article is to move from ratification to practical implementation there should be consideration of the contexts that influence the phenomenon of child soldiers. Two contexts are identified: the first is state crisis, and the second is local influences on children's participation in armed conflict. The influence of both of these on the phenomenon of child soldiers is shown in the case of young fighters in the Teso region of Uganda. At both levels, there are global processes that undermine application of the CRC. It is argued that effective implementation of the CRC will be successful when it is considered less as a global charter and more as needing to be based in knowledge about the realities that frame children's lives.

Jo de Berry was, until recently, a research fellow in the Centre for Child-Focused Anthropological Research at Brunel University.

NOTE: This article is based on research funded by a Research Award (1995-99) from the Economic and Social Research Council of the United Kingdom and a Royal Anthropological Institute Research Fellowship (1999-2000) funded by the Diana, Princess of Wales Memorial Trust.

A RTICLE 38 of the 1989 U.N. Convention on the Rights of the Child (CRC) declares, "States Parties should take all feasible measure to ensure that persons who have not attained the age of fifteen years do not take a direct part in hostilities." Given that 191 states have, by the year 2000, ratified the convention, this clause provides a global agreement that persons under 15 should not bear the arms, perpetrate the violence, nor wear the uniform of any combative group in any form of political conflict in the world.[1] The reality, however, is far from this ideal. Brett and McCallin (1998, 9) have estimated that there are presently 300,000 child soldiers under the age of 15 involved in hostilities throughout the globe. There is, then, a large gulf between the lives of thousands of children who take part in armed conflict and the standard set for their protection in the CRC.

At its core, this gulf is created by the fact that the contexts in which young people under the age of 15 become fighters and live as soldiers is one not penetrated by the ideals of the CRC. Children become soldiers in light of the influences and pressures upon them, which they experience as part of their day-to-day environment. The global optimism of the CRC can seem a far cry from these local contexts. If the CRC is ever to move from a universal charter of idealism to a working and implemented agreement, there must be an account of the contexts and realities in which children come to fight.

There has been much discussion as to what it is that takes children to fight, what underwrites the context in which someone under the age of 15 will partake in armed hostilities. Some argue that the question of child soldiers is more a question of the contemporary nature of war. It has been noticed that what is common to collective violence in the contemporary world is that the proportion of intrastate civil conflict compared to interstate conflict has increased over the last century (Allen 2000, 168). There has been proliferation of situations where the legitimacy of the state is questioned and fragmented or has even collapsed through internal collective violence (Senghaas 1987, 6). These civil wars tend to be fought not so much with expensive and grandiose technology but with more easily available small arms (Allen 2000, 8). Small arms make the process of killing less expensive and more widely achievable—even children can handle many of the modern light weapons of war. In addition, a fundamental feature of these civil wars is the making of civilian communities into battlegrounds as a strategy of securing political control (De Waal 1997, 312-13; Kaldor 1997, 15). As the tide of civil war takes over people's lives and homes, young people may be forcibly conscripted and abducted into armed groups.

The phenomenon of child soldiers is thus inextricably linked to a crisis of the state as manifested in civil conflict. This is the argument Richards (1996) has made for Sierra Leone, where he records young men with real and reasonable hopes and desires being forcibly recruited into the Revolutionary United Front (RUF) rebel movement. The members of the RUF then become excluded from the wider national society through a crisis of patrimonialism in the state. Throughout postcolonial Africa, it has been shown that a crisis of the state—a crisis so often manifest in ethnic conflicts over power and access to resources—leads to the proliferation of child soldiers not only because of the prevalence of civil conflicts but also because, in failing to bolster education and employment opportunities for young people, children are rendered particularly vulnerable to recruitment by rebel movements and are offered comparable opportunity, protection, and gains by being members of armed groups (Honwana 1999, 5).

Child soldiers cannot, however, only be seen as victims of the wider political-economic context in which they live but must also be credited with agency and volition in the decisions that take them to fight (Cairns 1996, 131). Writing about young activists in South Africa, Dawes (1992) has stressed that children may grow up in situations where violence is legitimized, and they often devise their own violent strategies of political struggle. Again, working in South Africa, Reynolds (1995) suggests that young political activists might even go to the extent of renouncing ties with elders and relatives in order to pursue their cause. These cases suggest that we cannot assume that children and young people are "strangers to power and violence in the world" (Dawes 1992, 4). Even in the mire of war, children can be seen to make the decision to fight from the subjective appraisal of their options and safety. They might not

understand this in terms of state-level political processes but more in terms of how they understand their personal social relations and future (Cohn and Goodwin-Gill 1994, 35).

Here then are two contextual levels that appear to influence the phenomenon of child soldiers. The first operates at the level of the state, and the second through the personal agency and understanding of children themselves. In this article, I will give details of the working of these two levels in the particular situation of civil conflict in the Teso region of eastern Uganda between 1987 and 1992 in which many young people under the age of 15 fought as members of an antigovernment rebel army. By substantiating the influence of both the position of the state and the personal agency of children themselves in the reasons why young people joined this particular rebel army as combatants, I suggest the kinds of knowledge that are needed and the dynamics of conflict that need to be exposed and engaged with if the CRC is ever to be an active and implemented charter.

STATE-INSPIRED VIOLENCE
IN EASTERN UGANDA

The postindependence history of Uganda is one marked by the state's use of violence against political dissenters and reliance on the army for political power. The roots of this, no doubt, lie in British colonial policy for the Ugandan protectorate. Prior to independence, British influence served to foster ethnic and religious factionalism within the region (Kasozi 1994; Mutibura 1992). When the postindependence government was finally formed, it was constituted from an uneasy truce and coalition between different factions. It did not last long. Independence came in 1962; by 1966, the then president of Uganda, Milton Obote, leader of the Uganda People's Congress Party (UPC), had suspended the constitution and had had the army chase his political disputers from the country, leaving the UPC in absolute power but heavily dependent on the army.

In 1979, the army came to the forefront of politics in Uganda with the military coup led by General Idi Amin toppling the Obote government. Amin instigated the violent purge of all political opponents. He especially concentrated on eliminating supporters of Obote in the army. Obote originated from a northern ethnic group in Uganda called the Luo. Amin directed his supporters within the army to control and destroy all potential Luo opposition. This escalated into a general reign of terror for the Uganda population, as Amin became increasingly antagonistic both to suspected political opponents and to the Christian population. The State Research Bureau became infamous as a place of disappearance and torture. By 1978, Amnesty International claimed that Amin was responsible for the death of 300,000 people.

The precedent was set for military dictatorship of both political alliance and economic strategy in Uganda that continued throughout the 1970s and 1980s. Amin himself was deposed in 1979 by the Tanzanian-sponsored Uganda National Liberation Army (UNLA). UNLA was an army that included former UPC soldiers who had been in exile with Obote between 1971 and 1979. UNLA restored Obote to power in 1980. His second term of office was marked by military conflict. Between 1980 and 1985, Obote's army conducted campaigns against supporters of Amin. From 1982, Obote's military supporters also waged war against an Acholi ethnic faction of the army led in opposition to Obote by Tito and Bazilio Okello. In the southern Luwero Triangle region, Obote's forces were resisted by Youweri Museveni's National Resistance Army (NRA). The NRA was supported by the indigenous population in Luwero, and the conflict there escalated into full-scale civil war. Obote was eventually defeated in 1985 in a military coup by the Okellos. By this time, however, the NRA was in control of most of the south of Uganda, and it reached Kampala, the capital, in January 1986. Museveni implemented the National Resistance Movement (NRM) government, which remains in power at the time of writing.

Museveni came to power with the backing of much of the south of Uganda. His government brought widespread peace in these areas and the opportunity for rapid reconstruction and economic development. In the north of Uganda, however, the NRM and NRA met with widespread opposition and armed rebellion. This dissent is still to be resolved. As part of this dissent, in 1987, political leaders in Teso declared the Teso area and people at war with Museveni and the NRA. It was in this conflict that many young boys and men in Teso took up arms and went to the bush to fight.

The historical roots of the conflict in Teso lie in the nature of previous political alignment in the region and the impact on the Iteso of the events and politics of the preceding decades. At independence, the majority of the Iteso had been supporters of Obote's UPC. There were Iteso in Obote's police force and army. A number of Iteso had prominent positions in the first Obote government and had joined UPC supporters in exile in Tanzania between 1971 and 1979. People in Teso today see the period of UPC exile corresponding with the loss of much Iteso influence in national politics and the marginalization of Iteso as people of influence and power in Uganda. In addition, like the rest of the Uganda population, the Iteso were crippled by the impact of Amin's rule; with the expulsion of the Asians in 1972, trade and business collapsed. Today, people in Teso quite simply remember Amin's rule as "the time when there was no salt," when the most basic item of trade and cooking was totally unavailable.

The most direct impact of the political turmoil of the Amin period affected Teso in 1979. At that time, Karamojong cattle raiders from the north of Teso took the opportunity provided by a lack of law and order to loot an army arsenal in the north. Their acquisition of arms completely changed the character and balance of the cattle raiding that they had conducted against the Iteso for decades (Ocan 1994, 16). After the UNLA invasion of Uganda to restore Obote in 1979, Amin's army fled north, further arming the Karamojong who looted traded cattle for guns across the Sudanese border. Between 1979 and 1980, the Karamojong swept through Teso raiding cattle. These armed and vicious raids in which many were killed continued throughout the 1980s and left very few cattle in the area.

Under Obote's second regime, the Iteso once again enjoyed a degree of political and formal military power. The minister of state with responsibility for the army was the Itesot, and Iteso constituted the majority of Obote's Special Police Unit, a paramilitary body responsible for numerous human rights abuses between 1980 and 1985 (Amnesty International 1992, 15). Many Iteso had informally joined the UNLA as it pursued Amin's army northward, thus acquiring arms and uniforms from supplies abandoned by Amin's troops (Ingram 1994, 159). It was this state of armament, politico-military influence, and support for Obote that lay the foundations for the Iteso rebellion against Museveni and the NRA after Obote was deposed in 1985.

Museveni himself has analyzed the reasons why, after taking power in January 1986, the NRA faced military rebellion across the north and east of Uganda. He argues that such opposition came about through the Sudanese government backing of the remnant and subsequently resurgent armies of Obote and Okello (Museveni 1997, 176). Museveni states that, having fled into the Sudan, these armies regrouped and in August 1986 reentered Uganda to fight against the NRA.

In Teso, a more specific cause is cited for the rebellion. There people point to the fact that, during 1986, Museveni ordered the disarming of vigilante groups set up in Teso under the Obote II period to protect Iteso villages from cattle raiders (Brett 1995, 206; Pirouet 1991, 201). With such a situation, Karamojong raiding intensified. Excessive cattle raiding occurred in Teso between 1986 and 1987, with Karamojong taking advantage of the insecurity of Teso and causing widespread suffering and deprivation (Mudoola 1991, 244). When young men in Teso speak of their decision to "go to the bush" and join the Uganda People's Army (UPA) rebellion, they often cite their frustration and anger at this loss of cattle.

At the same time, former Iteso military and political leaders from the Obote II period had retreated to Teso. In late 1986 and throughout 1987, they visited trading centers, mobilizing supporters into an army called Fight Obote Back Again (FOBA). They argued that Museveni was in league with the Karamojong in a plan to raid all the cattle from Teso. FOBA units began campaigns of attack on NRA vehicles and barracks.

In 1987, FOBA regrouped as the Uganda People's Army. The UPA was allied with other factions opposed to Museveni across the north of Uganda.[2] All these factions held national political aims and have at varying times been sponsored by the Kenyan and the Sudanese governments.[3] The UPA had a political wing called the Uganda People's Front, headed by the former minister of Obote, Peter Otai, by then in exile in London. Otai argued for the need to war against the "totalitarianism and authoritarianism established by Museveni's ethnic dynasty" (Otai 1988, 6; 1991). The UPA waged a rebel insurgency against Museveni's NRA between 1987 and 1992 when the UPA was finally defeated and disbanded by NRA government forces.

On the ground, the UPA was led by a man now commonly known throughout Teso as Hitler Eregu. As with FOBA, leaders of the UPA held political meetings in centers throughout Teso asking for volunteers to join the ranks of the UPA and for support from villagers. A central corps of 300 men was formed around Hitler Eregu; many of these were young boys from rural areas who were trained in bush camps. There were three other mobile and regional columns consisting of former soldiers and recruited members. Beyond these columns, UPA organizations spread throughout Teso, where each village assigned 10 young men and boys to act as information carriers and potential activists if violence came into the area. The members of these groups were known as agwayo. They were equipped with knives, and the groups gave themselves names such as Panga Group, First Pangas, Speed Battalion, and Nuke Brigade.

The political history of postindependence Uganda makes it clear that these young boys came to fight as combatants in the UPA after a long period in which democratic political structures had collapsed, with influence and power being determined by military might and strategy. Factions, often ethnically aligned, competed for the state apparatus and in so doing undermined the state's ability to secure and cater to its people. Boys in rural villages, just as men, women, and other children, became part of this crisis of the state and went to fight for the grievances and possible gain of their people.

The government army, the NRA, responded to the UPA rebellion with ferocity. Indeed, there is evidence that in the course of the conflict a number of young boys joined the UPA rebel army in response to NRA violence and hostility. The NRA attacked rebel camps and civilian villages where there were suspected rebel sympathizers. NRA soldiers were involved in the extrajudiciary executions of suspected rebels and used terror as a deliberate counterinsurgency tactic. The army was responsible for looting, for attacks on homes and villages, and for raiding, rape, and unlawful detention (Amnesty International 1992, 23; Brett 1995, 147). Many former child soldiers of the UPA talk of joining the insurgency after the NRA's actions had left them homeless and, in some cases, parentless. The UPA, they say, offered their only security until the end of the conflict in 1992.

IMPLEMENTING THE
CRC IN A STATE CRISIS

The bloody history of Uganda, which resulted in boys under the age of 15 becoming child soldiers in Teso, was well entrenched before the CRC was formulated and ratified. Yet it gives an example of the kind of crisis of the state—such as those in Sri Lanka, Sierra Leone, Liberia, Sudan,

and Northern Ireland—that so often forms the contemporary context in which children become combatants in contravention to Article 38 of the convention. All the clauses of the CRC were designed so that together the aegis of the best interests of the child takes primary importance. Yet the context of conflict coming, as it did in Uganda, so often after the hijacking of the state processes into military brutality is a context where it is precisely the conceptualization of best interests that is at stake. Many child soldiers fight for a cause that is portrayed as being in their political and economic best interests. Indeed, it would be an anathema to fight for anything else. If people in Teso now regret that their boys went to the bush as fighters, it is only because they joined a cause that lost. If they had won, they argue, the UPA would have secured the interests of the Teso people in the national politics of Uganda. As it is, they still feel marginalized from the economic development that Museveni has brought to the south of the country. For those young men who joined the UPA as a result of NRA brutality, in that moment, at that time, they undoubtedly saw that it was in their best interests to join the UPA as fighters for their own protection.

It is these conditions with which the CRC must engage if Article 38, stipulating that no child under the age of 15 should take part in armed hostilities, is to be implemented. The CRC relies on state parties to be effected. In the case of child soldiers, it is often the state that is to blame. How is the implementation of the CRC, with its global remit, to make use of global processes to engage with the crisis of the state that takes so many young people to fight? The evidence is that global processes are more likely, in fact, to complicate rather than constructively work toward the implementation of the CRC. Take for example a recent article that appeared in May 2000 in the British press and promoted a wide media debate and outcry that resulted in embarrassment for the British government. The picture showed a 14-year-old boy in Sierra Leone, a member of the Sierra Leonian government army. He was dressed in a British-supplied uniform and carried a British-supplied gun.

The boy, Abu Kamara, is part of a conflict that the Sierra Leonian government is fighting against its armed rebel opposition who employs similar guerrilla and bush strategies as the UPA in Teso. That Abu carried a British-supplied gun shows the global connections of his being armed to fight. In the global arms trade, the guns that fall into the hands of children might well originate in Western countries like Britain and certainly come to war zones through global trade networks. In the case of Abu, he held a gun that had been supplied to the Sierra Leonian army through British support of progovernment forces against the RUF rebel movement after the perceived failure of the U.N. peacekeeping forces in the country. His gun thus came to him through the world of international politics, a world that is framed by the global history of colonialism and organizations, such as the United

Nations, of international intervention or nonintervention.

The contradiction of Abu's British gun and Abu's age was one well elaborated by the media at the time of the photograph. His gun came to him from the government of Britain, which has ratified the CRC, to the government of Sierra Leone, which has similarly ratified the convention. It came to him in the context of state crisis through global processes of international politics that undermined, rather than supported, the application of the CRC in that context. As the picture of Abu so clearly showed, the CRC is not to be implemented in a global vacuum, under global conditions that always facilitate the practical adoption of the terms within the convention. For the CRC exists in a context of global conditions and connections, some of which serve to undermine or complicate the implementation of the CRC.

What then are the global processes that can work to enhance the implementation of the CRC and prevent the use of child soldiers, even in the context of state crisis? Given that the phenomenon of child soldiers can be seen as part of the contemporary nature of war, with the prevalence of civil conflict, it might be said that only a global monitoring of arms and effective conflict prevention will be enough. Other perspectives more sensitive to the question of state sovereignty suggest that the role of the military in internal state politics must be neutralized from within to prevent children from feeling that their best political interests can only be achieved through recourse to violence. Indeed, Uganda has been cited as an effective example of how this might be achieved. Despite its brutal history, the country is now enjoying relative peace and economic development. Brett (1995) has argued that the settlement of independence in Uganda, with its expectation of Western-style parliaments and electoral systems, failed the country and led to the rule of force and conflict, of which the state, with the oppressive use of the army, was promoter rather than reconciler. In contrast, in recent years, Museveni's NRM has set up an inclusive form of democratic government.[4] The hope is that one day this form of government, bolstered by the economic success of foreign investment, will be enough to convince Museveni's opposition that the progress of the country can be best achieved through peaceful rather than armed politicking. If so, it will leave generations of children free from turning to violence to try to secure their best interests or being taken up into the ranks of those who fight for political recognition.

In Teso, it was the severity of Museveni's army in trying to quell the political dissent of the Teso people that drove many children into the UPA rebel army, seeking protection and action. As the army is separated from internal political control, such instances should diminish. In Uganda, Museveni has instituted a form of government that has the potential to do this. In other situations, governments themselves may fail children because of civil conflict and armed rebel groups that are beyond the control of law within their borders. As has been seen, there is a need to educate military personnel in

the terms of the CRC, to instill the knowledge that in their actions they may cause conditions antithetical to the terms of the human rights law to which their government has bound them. Also, there is a need to bind military personnel to legal recruitment processes (Kuper 1997, 234; Brett and McCallin 1998, 171). Only through knowledge of the CRC can its values permeate and hold resonance for those responsible for creating conditions under which clauses such as Article 38 might be violated.

LOCAL SOCIAL RELATIONS

So far, I have framed the phenomenon of child soldiers in the context of state crisis and modern warfare in which children can easily be forced into or make the decision to enter a situation where perceived political best interests are demanded with the use of a gun. Yet it is rare when talking with those who are or have made the decision to become child soldiers that they give the reasons for their fighting in hostilities in these terms. Often, how they subjectively perceive their local context and social relations are more salient in framing their participation (Brett and McCallin 1998, 57; Honwana 1999, 9).

In narratives from former child soldiers in Teso, it is evident that young men were motivated to enter the UPA bush forces through feelings of anger and frustration over the loss of their cattle at the hands of the Karamojong raiders. The Iteso are a pastoral people who practice settled agriculture. Cattle are integral to Iteso social reproduction; a man cannot marry a wife and set up a home without the use of cattle in a "bridewealth" transfer. Cattle are also vital to production since the ox plough has been part of agricultural practice in the area since the early 1900s. Cattle are, for the Iteso, a sign of social and material wealth and are integral to their sense of identity within the national context of Uganda.

The Karamojong raiding saw the number of cattle in Teso fall from about 1 million to just 10,000 by 1991. This was a loss with deep emotional resonance for it represented the loss of wealth, security, and a future. The loss of cattle proved one of the main rallying cries for the UPA military leadership as they sought recruits. It was a lament keenly felt by young boys and men who knew that without cattle they could not hope for marriage, a properly established home, rightfully held children, and the full requirements of what it is to be a mature man in Teso social life. They joined the UPA in anger and rebellion against their loss. They thus fought in the context of the state's failure to protect them from cattle raiding and in the context of how that loss felt to them in terms of their understanding of how maturity and masculinity is constituted in their society.

Given this context in Teso, it is tempting to suggest that being a child fighter had cultural backing. This, however, is misleading, for it suggests some kind of inevitability and tradition to the boys' behavior (de Berry 2000, 3). Instead, it is more helpful to see taking up arms and participating in hostilities as embedded in the social relations and priorities of a particular time and place. Other reasons cited by young men in Teso for becoming soldiers are the influence of their peers and male relations who persuaded them to fight; the opportunities afforded by carrying a gun, such as the ability to loot and to acquire food; and the excitement that they sensed from their peers already in the bush. All these reasons suggest that under certain historical conditions part of the social relations and makeup of what it was to be a young man in Teso took boys to join the UPA rebel army.

THE CRC AND LOCAL SOCIAL RELATIONS

How then can the values of the CRC permeate such particular influences in time and place? Indeed, one of the main criticisms of the convention has been its offer of universal solutions without recognition of the local complexities in which it is to be applied (Freeman and Veerman 1992, 109). This must be the first step: the knowledge of those social relations that during a time of conflict will take children to fight. There must be recognition of the local power, gender, and generational dynamics that are created in conflict. Some perspectives, especially prevalent in the international media, suggest an apocalyptic result of conflict and war on local social relations. Indeed, the picture of children carrying guns and being forced to fight as underage soldiers is the very image that is taken to confirm that war can be a travesty for the normal and propitious context of childhood, that war is a hell of unrestrained evil and moral breakdown. There is a feeling that war destroys and distorts all social relations so that those who are children during this time cannot help but be part of lost generations faced with the loss of innocence. Child soldiers are taken to be part and parcel of this apocalyptic nightmare. No one would wish an experience of war on anyone, let alone a child, but there is evidence that social relations during conflict are more nuanced than the prospect of being destroyed and undermined. Political conflict changes social relations, it changes the dynamics of gender, power, and generation, but it does not obliterate them (Zur 1993, 15; Green 1994, 228). The way that these social relations are changed and influenced by conflict is at the heart of children's subjective experience of war and what may take them to fight.

In Teso, the loss of cattle at the hands of the Karamojong caused a major shift in generational relations (de Berry 2000). Prior to the raiding, young boys and men would have looked to the herds of their fathers for the cattle they needed in order to marry and set up homes of their own. The Karamojong raiding took away these previous material certainties of being a young man in Iteso society. Indeed, fathers told their sons that gathering their bridewealth was now their own responsibility. Some young boys tell of joining the UPA precisely because they wanted to use the opportunity of fighting and looting to acquire the wealth and resources they could then use to marry. Others cite specific incidents of witnessing

and experiencing loss that gave them feelings of determination, with the backing of their fathers, to support the UPA cause and regain material prosperity for the Teso region. In the context of the conflict, the shift in generational relations represented by the loss of cattle framed many of the young boys' recruitment to the rebel group.

If state parties, bolstered by global parties such as international advocates, human rights organizations, and nongovernmental organizations, are to move the CRC from its position of universal idealism to practical implementation, there must be consideration of how the CRC can engage with local contexts. If Article 38 is fully operational, state parties can profit by creating and promoting conditions of peace based on the knowledge of how conflict affects local social relations. In Teso, for instance, the Karamojong raiding struck at the heart of young people's lives and community stability. Models for peace might have addressed and redressed this at the local, familial, and community levels with the backing of state-level security. Just as war will change and create social relations, so will peace. The creation of peace and security needs to be convincing at a local, community, and familial level so as to keep children from participating in conflict. It is at the local level of community, family, and children themselves that these social relations will be talked about and lived through, and thus knowledge of them can best start by taking on board people's own perspectives and subjective experiences as a knowledge base for the needs of peace and security. A global process—perhaps starting in the media—of recognizing and accepting what is unique and operational at a local level will bolster this.

CONCLUSION

There are two levels that appear to frame the phenomenon of child soldiers. The first is a crisis of the state as manifested in civil conflict; the second is the local social relationships that will influence the life of a child during a time of conflict. In the case of Teso, in East Uganda, it was the militarization of politics over the years after independence and the changes in social relations and institutions caused by the Karamojong cattle raiding that was at the heart of the young boys who took part in the UPA rebellion.

If the CRC is ever to be a working agreement, it must be applied in context at both of these levels by the state parties that have signed onto it. I have suggested that at both levels there are global processes that may serve to undermine the implementation of the CRC. The global arms trade, international interventions and noninterventions, and the portrayal of the effects of conflict in the media may both complicate and distort the actuality of fulfilling the articles of child protection in the convention. I suggest that implementation of Article 38, which protects children under the age of 15 from participating in armed conflict, can only take place from a basis of the dynamics, relationships, and particularities of

conflict. It is then that informed nonmilitarized politics, education, and peace initiatives that are used on a contextualized rather than idealized basis can be put into place.

Notes

1. On 25 May 2000, the U.N. General Assembly accepted an optional protocol for the CRC establishing 18 as the minimum age for recruitment of military personnel. To date, this protocol has been adopted by several countries.

2. The best documented of these is Alice Lakwena's Holy Spirit Movement (Allen 1991; Behrend 1999).

3. Some of these rebel factions are still in action. The most powerful is Joseph Kony's Lords Resistance Army, a group that descends from the Holy Sprit Movement.

4. The form of government in Uganda instituted in the 1995 constitution is a system of one-party rather than multiparty democracy. All Uganda citizens are held to be members of the Movement party. They vote democratically for leaders at every level of political representation, from the lowest Local Council One (LC1) level, consisting of 50-60 households, through to the LC5 level, to parliamentary wards. A referendum was held in July 2000 for the country to vote on whether to stay with this Movement system or to revert to multiparty democracy. The result was overwhelmingly in favor of the Movement system, although there were wide allegations of corruption in the voting system.

References

Allen, T. 1991. Understanding Alice: Uganda's Holy Spirit Movement in Context. *Africa* 61(3):370-99.

———. 2000. A World At War. In *Poverty and Development*, ed. T. Allen and A. Thomas. Oxford: Oxford University Press.

Amnesty International. 1992. *Uganda: The Failure to Safeguard Human*

Rights. London: Amnesty International.

Behrend, H. 1999. *Alice and the Spirits: War in Northern Uganda 1986-1998*. Chicago: University of Chicago Press.

Brett, E. 1995. Neutralising the Role of Force in Uganda: The Role of the Military in Politics. *Journal of Modern African Studies* 33(1):129-52.

Brett, R. and M. McCallin. 1998. *Children: The Invisible Soldiers*. Stockholm: Radda Barnen and Save the Children Sweden.

Cairns, E. 1996. *Children and Political Violence*. Oxford: Blackwell.

Cohn, I. and G. Goodwin-Gill. 1994. *Child Soldiers: The Role of Children in Armed Conflicts*. Oxford: Oxford University Press.

Dawes, A. 1992. Psychological Discourse About Political Violence and Its Effects on Children. Paper presented at Mental Health of Refugee Children Exposed to Violent Environments, Oxford Refugees Studies Programme.

de Berry, J. 2000a. The Impact of War on Generational Relations in Teso, Uganda. Paper presented at the 6th Biennial Conference of the European Association of Social Anthropologists, 26-29 July, Krakow, Poland.

———. 2000b. Understanding the Recruitment of Child Soldiers: An Anthropological Approach. Paper presented at the workshop Child Soldiers: An Anthropological Response, 2 June, Brunel University.

De Waal, A. 1997. Contemporary Warfare in Africa. In *New Wars: Restructuring the Global Military Sector*, vol. 1, ed. M. Kaldor and B. Vashee. London: Pinter.

Freeman, M. and P. Veerman, eds. 1992. *The Ideologies of Children's Rights*. Dordrecht: M. Nijhoff.

Green, L. 1994. Fear as a Way of Life. *Cultural Anthropology* 9(2):227-56.

Honwana, A. 1999. Negotiating Post-War Identities: Child Soldiers in Mozambique and Angola. *Codesria Bulletin*.

Ingram, K. 1994. *Obote: A Political Biography*. New York: Routledge.

Kaldor, M. 1997. Introduction. In *New Wars: Restructuring the Global Military Sector*, vol. 1, ed. M. Kaldor and B. Vashee. London: Pinter.

Kasozi, A. 1994. *The Social Origins of Violence in Uganda 1964-1985*. Montreal: McGill-Queen's University Press.

Kuper, J. 1997. *International Law Concerning Child Civilians in Armed Conflict*. Oxford: Clarendon Press.

Mudoola, D. 1991. Institution Building: The Case of the NRM and the Military in Uganda 1986-1989. In *Changing Uganda*, ed. H. Hansen and M. Twaddle. London: James Currey.

Museveni, Y. K. 1997. *Sowing the Mustard Seed: the Struggle for Freedom and Democracy in Uganda*. London: Macmillan.

Mutibura, M. 1992. *Uganda Since Independence: A Story of Unfulfilled Hopes*. London: Hurst.

Ocan, C. 1994. *Pastoral Crisis in North East Uganda: The Changing Significance of Cattle Raids*. Occasional Paper No. 21. Kampala: Centre for Basic Research.

Otai, P. 1988. *Notes Towards an Analysis of Lt. General Youweri Museveni's Dynasty*. London: Uganda People's Front.

———. 1991. *Uganda: The Hidden Tyranny*. London: Uganda People's Front.

Pirouet, L. 1991. Human Rights Abuses in Museveni's Uganda. In *Changing Uganda*, ed. H. Hansen and M. Twaddle. London: James Currey.

Reynolds, P. 1995. Youth and the Politics of Culture in South Africa. In *Children and the Politics of Culture*, ed. S. Stephens. Princeton, NJ: Princeton University Press.

Richards, P. 1996. *Fighting for the Rain Forest*. London: IAI/James Currey/Villiers.

Senghaas, D. 1987. Transcending Collective Violence, the Civilising Process and the Peace Problem. In *The Quest for Peace: Transcending Collective Violence and War Amongst Societies, Cultures and States*, ed. V. Varynen. London: Sage.

Zur, J. 1993. Violent Memories: Quiche War Widows in Northwest Highland Guatemala. Ph.D. thesis, University of London.

ANNALS, *AAPSS*, **575**, May 2001

The Political Economy
of War-Affected Children

By STEVEN HICK

ABSTRACT: The nature of armed conflict has changed since the rise of globalization and the end of the Cold War. Now wars predominantly take the lives of civilians, over half of whom are children. This article examines the effects of armed conflict on children. In particular, it discusses refugee and internally displaced children, child soldiers, the sexual assault and exploitation of girls, and children traumatized by war. How the international community should respond to protect children and prevent war is explored in relation to the political and economic context within which wars occur.

Steven Hick is an academic, author, and humanitarian activist. He teaches at Carleton University and is cofounder of War Child Canada. His recent works are a coedited book entitled Human Rights and the Internet *and several journal articles on the social implications of the Internet and its application for social activists. He is currently writing a social work textbook; implementing children's rights projects in Palestine, Sierra Leone, and Colombia; and researching the use of educational technologies with universities in Cuba.*

AN international policy shift is required to meet the challenges of growing and protracted armed conflicts. This is occurring in the context of increasingly global economic structures, sometimes called globalization. Globalization as it is currently discussed is often perceived largely in economic and political terms.[1] Here I examine globalization as the newest development in the expansion of global capitalism. It is a new manifestation of an old system of market liberalism, only this time it is occurring on an international, rather than national, level. Globalization has had numerous negative impacts on people worldwide, one of which is a quantitative shift in the nature of warfare. Increased poverty, weapons sales, new economic relations, and corporate intrusion have contributed to changes in the nature of warfare. All the major armed conflicts in the world are now protracted civil wars in which the primary victims are women and children.

Children's rights are affected by armed conflict in numerous ways. Due to armed conflicts, children are displaced and become refugees; children are recruited or abducted to become child soldiers; girls are sexually assaulted and exploited; wars disrupt the education of children; HIV/AIDS is spread by soldiers, who infect increasing numbers of women and children; and children going out to play are killed and maimed by land mines. The effects of war on children are multifaceted: economic sanctions to end wars deprive children of the necessities of life; the proliferation of light weapons makes communities dangerous; the experience of war traumatizes children, leaving lasting scars; and health care services are disrupted or are used to serve combatants and not citizens. Estimating the extent of these problems is not always straightforward. Graça Machel's report, *Impact of Armed Conflict on Children* (1996), provided the first comprehensive assessment. It found that armed conflict had displaced over 20 million children, had killed 2 million in the past decade, had 300,000 children fighting as soldiers, and had placed 60 million land mines in 87 countries. In short, modern wars are harming children in increasing numbers and in new ways.

GLOBALIZATION AND WAR

At the 2000 International Conference on War-Affected Children, in Winnipeg, Canada, Machel summed up the situation of the world's children caught up in wars:

Wars have always victimized children and other non-combatants, but modern wars are exploiting, maiming and killing children more callously and more systematically than ever. Children today find themselves caught up in complex and confusing conflicts that have multiple causes and that lack clear prospects for resolution. Children are being sucked into seemingly endless endemic struggles for power and resources.[2]

Machel identifies endemic struggles for power and resources as being at the core of modern wars. It was initially thought that the end of the Cold War would bring peace as the superpowers ceased to fight over control of different regions of the world. Instead, the number of wars has increased, and they have spread to all parts of the world. The wars, however, are different in nature. Instead of wars between nations, they are wars within nations. Mistakenly, these wars are often presented in the media as simply tribal conflicts or ethnic hostilities. But tribal and ethnic differences have always existed and cannot explain the rise of this new phenomenon. These new wars must be analyzed in the context of simultaneous changes that have occurred in the world's political and economic organization. The new wars should be examined within the changes taking place in the world economic organization.

These new wars—intranational wars—have recent and multiple roots, based primarily in the changing politics of economic globalization. Increased economic globalization has created important changes in the world that are resulting in new intranational wars. A review of the literature on recent trends in the global economy and analysis of the political and economic environment in new war-torn countries show three critical factors:

— free trade and direct foreign transnational corporation investment or incursion,
— forced structural adjustment, and
— diverging per capita incomes between countries.

Another factor, the end of the Cold War, has lent a hand in increasing international weapons sales as stockpiles of weapons are sold.

Part of the agenda of globalization is free trade. This aspect is embodied in the World Trade Organization's (WTO) 550-page document "Final Act of the 1986-1994 Uruguay Round."[3] This element of globalization is opening countries to the entry of transnational corporations that are exploiting both people and resources and selling products such as luxury items and weapons. Securing access to resources and cheap labor within countries has involved the use of armies to protect resource-laden land areas and corporate interests. For example, in Angola, Congo, Sierra Leone, and Sudan, competing oil prospectors, gold and diamond miners, and private armies and security firms hired by prospectors are at the root of war. Global businesses not only have created the conditions necessary for many of the current wars but are also directly involved in those wars. In addition, the existence of markets for these products in richer countries has created complicity on the part of developed countries.

As part of freer trade, global corporations are profiting from the new wars by selling the weapons that are used. The arms trade has flourished since the start of the 1990s, as corporations produce increased quantities of cheap assault rifles and small arms and as Cold War stockpiles of weapons are sold on the world market. Military spending globally in 1993 was estimated to be U.S.$790 billion, of which U.S.$121 billion was spent in developing countries (Sivard 1993, 20).

The institutions of globalization, such as the International Monetary Fund, fuel the new wars by forcing countries into structural adjustment programs that weaken national economies and create the conditions for conflict. Rigorous programs of structural adjustment promise long-term market-based economic growth, but demands for immediate cuts in budget deficits and public expenditure only weaken already fragile states, leaving them dependent on forces and relations over which they have little control (Machel 1996, 12). It is clear that poverty and lack of development fuel and escalate wars and that decreases in world inequality would go far to help reduce conflicts.

Another aspect is the increased wealth gap created by globalization. The neoliberal economic theory that international trade will result in an equalization of incomes between countries is not being borne out.[4] The adoption of trade liberalization policies and direct foreign investment, the two pillars of economic globalization, are having long-term social and economic impacts in the world. The number of children living in poverty continues to grow as globalization proceeds to expand markets across national boundaries and increase the incomes of a relative few.

The two-tiered world economy widens the gap between rich and poor countries and between rich and poor people within countries. Trends in income for the poorest 40 percent of countries have been "significantly downward since the mid-1960s" (Woodward 1998, 5). The increasing discrepancy between the rich and poor since the initiation of globalization illustrates this. In 1960, the richest 20 percent of the world's population had 70 percent of the world's wealth, and the poorest had 2.3 percent. Today, the richest have 85 percent of the wealth, and the poorest have just 1.1 percent. Individual billionaires, numbering 358, have more wealth today than the combined yearly income of 45 percent of the world's people. Poverty is not only persisting in the age of globalization; it is becoming more entrenched (Aristide 1997, 2). Woodward (1998, 4) found that the per capita income of countries during the period of globalization has diverged. For example, between 1965 and 1995, the gross domestic product per capita of the sub-Saharan African countries was halved, and Latin America's fell by 30 percent. Even a recent WTO study confirmed this, finding that "richer countries have been growing faster on average than poorer countries, thereby increasing the global income disparity" (WTO 2000, 5).[5] These are the very countries that are increasingly finding themselves in civil war. These levels of poverty and misery represent a massive denial of human rights that can generate only more violence and conflict.

Machel (2000, 4) has similarly identified several critical causes of the current wave of intranational wars:

1.   The fight over natural resources is one cause. Diamonds have financed long-running wars in Sierra Leone and Angola. In Sudan, oil fuels the civil conflict. The profits from

narcotics are at the heart of struggles in Afghanistan and Colombia.

2. None of these "economies of war" could flourish without markets in richer countries. Global businesses, some legal, some illegal, have spawned international complicity that makes war not just possible but highly profitable.

3. The wars themselves are perpetuated by international weapons sales, especially sales of small arms. Indeed, small arms are now so accessible that the poorest communities can gain access to deadly weapons capable of transforming any local conflict into a bloody slaughter.

4. Constrained by debt and structural adjustment programs, many developing countries have been forced to restructure their economies, cut basic services, and reduce the size of the public sector. In so doing, they have often weakened national economies and cleared the stage for other actors bent on power and profit.

THE IMPACT OF WAR ON CHILDREN

The impact of war on children has been devastating. Children are drawn into war as soldiers. They suffer from malnutrition, disease, sexual violence, and the depredations of forced flight. Sometimes they are deliberately killed. The new wars are particularly deadly for children because little distinction is made between combatants and civilians. In recent decades, the proportion of war victims who are civilians has increased from 5 percent to over 90

percent. During the 1990s, more than 2 million children died as a result of armed conflicts, and more than three times as many were permanently disabled or seriously injured (Machel 1996, 13).

Today's wars regularly involve horrifying levels of violence and brutality, from systematic rape, to the destruction of crops and the poisoning of wells, to ethnic cleansing and outright genocide. Increasingly, children are themselves drawn in as fighters, becoming not just the targets of warfare but also the perpetrators of atrocities.

The various Machel (1996) subreports have underscored the extent of the problem. The following is just a sample of the findings:

1. From 1985 to 1995, about 2 million children have been killed and 4-5 million have been disabled as a result of war and armed conflict.

2. War and armed conflict have left 1 million children orphaned and about 12 million homeless.

3. About 300,000 children under age 18 are currently participating in armed combat.

4. Of the 40 million refugees worldwide, 50 percent are children.

5. About 800 children are killed or maimed by land mines every month.

6. The number of child refugees increases by about 5000 per day.

7. Most child soldiers are between the ages of 15 and 18, but it is common for children as young as 10 to be actively recruited. (Existing international law, dating back to the end of World War II, sets 15 as

the minimum age for military recruitment.)

8. Children in 87 countries live amid the contamination of more than 60 million land mines.

9. Girls and women continue to be marginalized from mainstream humanitarian assistance and protection.

There are numerous impacts of armed conflict on children. The next four sections examine four of the effects of armed conflict on children. The coverage of the major issues is not exhaustive but instead highlights critical issues. The issues covered here include refugee and internally displaced children; child soldiers; sexual assault and exploitation of girls; and children traumatized by war. Other issues, such as land mines, sanctions, light weapons, education, and HIV/AIDS are not detailed here but are just as important.

The discussion strives to illustrate how children's well-being is best ensured both through family- and community-based solutions and through international action. Discussion of solutions is constructed within a framework that rests on the belief that action must be based on local cultures, must be drawn from an understanding of child development, and must include analysis that integrates personal, political, and structural elements. Too often, services directed at assisting war-affected children ignore the cultural specificity of the helping model and also fail to integrate, in a holistic fashion, the personal and structural elements of the problem or situation.

REFUGEE AND INTERNALLY DISPLACED CHILDREN

Approximately 1 in every 300 children on earth is displaced by armed conflict (1 in 150 of the general population is so displaced) (Machel 2000, 9). Armed conflict causes large numbers of people to flee their homes to escape danger. These people become either refugees or internally displaced persons (IDPs). People staying within their own countries are considered "internally displaced," while those who flee to other countries become "refugees." The majority of those fleeing armed conflicts become IDPs rather than refugees. Most refugee and displaced children travel with their families, but many lose their parents. Unaccompanied minors typically account for up to 5 percent of a refugee population and often more—as children are lost, separated, or orphaned in the panic of flight (Ressler, Tortorici, and Marcelino 1993, 142).

Today there are about 40 million refugees and displaced persons who are predominantly women and children (Machel 2000, 9). Children make up more than half of the refugee and IDP populations. Many die within the first days and weeks of displacement due to malnutrition and disease, especially measles, diarrheal diseases, respiratory infections, and malaria. Displaced children are also the most likely to be raped, tortured, murdered, or recruited as child soldiers. Girls and women are in constant danger of sexual attack and abuse, leading to pregnancy and HIV infection. The youngest children are also affected when they witness an attack on a mother or sister.

Refugees and IDPs are predominantly in Africa and Asia, although they can be found throughout the world. The greatest numbers of IDPs stemming from armed conflict are in Sudan (an estimated 4 million), Angola (1.5 million to 2 million), Colombia (1.8 million), Iraq (900,000), Afghanistan (540,000 to 750,000), Burma (500,000 to 1 million), Bosnia and Herzegovina (830,000), Azerbaijan (568,000), Sri Lanka (more than 500,000), and Burundi (800,000).

Camps for refugees and IDPs should be safe, but the violence, sexual assault, and alcohol and substance abuse there often reach high levels. Women in camps in Burundi told how they were forced to exchange sex for food or protection. Camps are also often highly militarized, and children are particularly vulnerable to recruitment by armed forces or other armed groups.

Many refugee and internally displaced children lose their chances of receiving an education, proper nutrition, and health care. In Colombia, for example, some 85 percent of refugee children do not receive primary education. Camps often lack adequate reproductive health care for women and girls.

Many children have lived their entire lives in a state of displacement, never knowing a normal, stable family environment. On top of that, many families have been displaced not only once but twice or three times, making them more

vulnerable each time. This is the case in many situations, including in Sierra Leone, Rwanda, Sri Lanka, Angola, Colombia, and Sudan. For example, in Rwanda, by the end of 1994, more than 100,000 children had been separated from their families—the highest number of such children registered by UNICEF since the agency was founded in 1946. In Angola in 1995, a UNICEF study found that 20 percent of the country's children had been separated from their parents and other relatives.

Although refugees are often in a desperate situation, IDPs are generally worse off. They may remain within or close to areas of conflict and have to move repeatedly. They are often more difficult to reach due to fighting or government policies. Unlike refugees, they have no specific agency or body of law to protect and assist them.

One of the most disturbing cases of lost children has emerged from the civil war in southern Sudan. Apart from the main government and opposition groups, there are also various militias that spread terror by pillaging villages and killing or seizing their inhabitants. Fearing capture or death, at least 20,000 Sudanese young people, mostly boys between the ages of 7 and 17, have fled their homes. Thousands of girls have also been killed or abducted by the raiders, but few have run away from their villages since it is more difficult for girls to envisage life outside their families. These "lost boys" of Sudan have been trekking enormous distances over a vast unforgiving wilderness, seeking refuge from the fighting. Hungry, frightened, and weakened by sleeplessness and disease, they have crossed from Sudan into Ethiopia and back. Many have died on the journey; most survivors are now in camps in the parched northwestern plains of Kenya (Zutt 1994, 1).

Though rebel forces are responsible for the displacement of many IDPs, in some countries large numbers of people have been forced to move by the government. In Burundi in 1996 and 1999, the government's "regroupement" policy forced over 300,000 people to leave their homes and live in guarded camps that lack adequate food, health care, shelter, and security.

Policies are necessary that discourage the separation of children from their parents during armed conflict. International principles and procedures must be sensitive to the particular needs of children. Also, family reunification programs must be a central part of emergency humanitarian work. The creation of institutional responses or camps for unaccompanied children should be a last resort as such centers may actually encourage parents to leave their children where they think they can get proper food and care.

The treatment of IDPs is covered by the Guiding Principles for Internally Displaced Persons, a set of 30 principles introduced in 1998 by the United Nations. The principles address the special needs of internally displaced children, especially unaccompanied children. They prohibit the sale into marriage, sexual exploitation, and forced labor of children, as well as the military recruitment of children.

In the absence of their parents, children, usually adolescent girls, often assume responsibility for their younger siblings. In September 1995, UNICEF and the Rwandan government identified 1939 children living in child-headed households. Armed conflict is not the only reason children have to assume such responsibility: in many African countries, AIDS has cut a swath through an entire generation of young parents. Child-headed households have an acute need for social and legal protection. While some communities are supportive, all too many neighbors and relations are ready to exploit orphans and steal their property. "The principle of family unity, as safeguarded in the Convention of the Rights of the Child, must be the basis of all support for these children" (Machel 1996, sec. 89).

Machel (2000, 11) recommends that the survival and protection of unaccompanied and separated children be ensured, with priority given to family tracing and reunification. To accomplish this, tighter procedures are required to guarantee that each child has a continuous caregiver, preferably from his or her own family or extended family or, failing that, neighbors, friends, or other substitutes. One innovative alternative has been tried effectively in Sudanese refugee camps in Ethiopia: villages have been created, with three to five children living together in each traditional hut under the supervision of a caregiver from their own people.

CHILD SOLDIERS

One of the most alarming trends in armed conflict is the participation of children as soldiers or in supporting roles for armies. A child soldier is a boy or girl under the age of 18 who is compulsorily or voluntarily recruited or otherwise used in hostilities by armed forces, paramilitaries, civil defense units, or other armed groups (Machel 2000, 6).

In the new wars, armies, rebels, paramilitary groups, and militia groups have abducted or recruited over 300,000 child soldiers. While the majority are adolescents, many are 10 years of age or younger. Increasingly, however, adults are deliberately conscripting or taking children as combatants or soldiers. Some commanders have even noted the desirability of child soldiers because they are "more obedient, do not question orders and are easier to manipulate than adult soldiers" (Brett, McCallin, and O'Shea 1996, 88). Beyond their use as soldiers, armies are using children for sexual services, as forced "wives," and also as spies, messengers, porters, and cooks. The number of children used to support and service armies (as opposed to being used as soldiers) is unknown.

The number of children used as soldiers is known. It has remained constant over time, while the cumulative impact has increased steadily. The estimated figure of 300,000 child soldiers reflects the number of children being used in combat at any one time. As new conflicts begin and

children are killed or wounded, grow older, and are replaced by other children, the cumulative total is much higher and the destruction carries over from one generation to the next. Poorer children are particularly vulnerable. Adolescent boys working in the informal sector, selling cigarettes, gum, or lottery tickets on the streets, are a particular target. For example, in Myanmar, groups of 15- to 17-year-old children have been surrounded in their school yards and conscripted as soldiers against their will (Brett, McCallin, and O'Shea 1996, 23).

One reason for the growing problem of child soldiers is the proliferation of inexpensive and light weapons. Previous weapons were too heavy and cumbersome for children to use. The lighter and cheaper assault rifles, such as the Soviet-made AK-47 or the American M-16, are light and simple to use. The rifles have also become much cheaper and more widely available. Their availability has steadily increased in war zones. Since their introduction in 1947, around 55 million AK-47s have been sold; in one African country, for example, they cost no more than U.S.$6 each (United Nations Research Institute for Social Development 1995, 113).

While most child soldiers are recruited by conscription, abduction, or coercion, some also volunteer. For them, joining an army may be the only way to escape starvation and death, and a military unit may serve as a refuge, providing a kind of surrogate family. In Uganda in 1986, the National Resistance Army had an estimated 3000 children, many under age 16, including 500 girls. Most of these children had been orphaned and looked on the army as a replacement for their parents (Dodge 1991, 55). Hunger, poverty, and lack of opportunities not only drive children to volunteer but may also compel parents to offer their children for service. Children volunteer when they believe that this is the only way to guarantee regular meals, clothing, or medical attention (Brett, McCallin, and O'Shea 1996, 33).

Many children joined armed groups in Cambodia in the 1980s as the best way to secure food and protection. Similarly, in Liberia in 1990, children as young as 7 were seen in combat because, according to the director of the Liberian Red Cross, "those with guns could survive." In Myanmar, parents volunteer their children for the rebel Karen army because the guerrillas provide clothes and two square meals a day; in 1990, an estimated 900 of the 5000-strong Karen army were under the age of 15 (Dodge 1991, 11).

Girls abducted into armed groups are mainly forced into sexual slavery, subjected to physical and emotional violence, and forced to provide other personal services. The majority become infected with sexually transmitted diseases and, increasingly, with HIV/AIDS.

In 2000, the United Nations adopted the Optional Protocol to the Convention on the Rights of the Child, establishing 18 as the minimum age for the participation of children in hostilities. Although the protocol prohibits nongovernmental forces from recruiting children below the age of 18, it allows states to establish a minimum age for voluntary recruitment that is not necessarily 18. The research conducted for Machel 1996 (see sec. 58) found a variety of methods to prevent the future recruitment of children as combatants.

First, Governments should work for the finalization and rapid adoption of the draft optional protocol to the Convention on the Rights of the Child on involvement of children in armed conflicts. Next, Governments must pay much closer attention to their methods of recruitment, and in particular, they must renounce the practice of forced recruitment. They should ensure that all children are registered at birth and receive documentation of age. To be certain that these measures succeed, Governments must establish effective monitoring systems and back them up with legal remedies and institutions that are sufficiently strong to tackle abuses.

All peace agreements should include specific measures to demobilize and reintegrate child soldiers into society. There is an urgent need for the international community to support programmes, including advocacy and social services programmes, for the demobilization and re-integration into the community of child soldiers. Such measures must address the family's economic security and include educational, life-skills and vocational opportunities.

Peace agreements and minimum age protocols will help lessen the problem, but they will not address the international structures that propagate and encourage the new wars in the first place. The warfare of globalization increasingly involves paramilitary, rebel, and corporate private armies. In many cases, the warfare is part of a campaign to clear people off the land for resource extraction or agribusiness. In addition, extreme poverty is pushing children into situations where they are susceptible to local armed groups—the children see these groups as their only option for survival. Until such activity is stopped, children will continue to be recruited and abducted into combatant service.

SEXUAL VIOLENCE
AGAINST CHILDREN
DURING ARMED CONFLICT

Sexual attacks and exploitation are used methodically during armed conflict to humiliate and terrorize. Women and girls are continually threatened by rape, assault, sexual exploitation, trafficking, sexual humiliation, and mutilation. The main perpetrators of sexual attacks and exploitation are male combatants or soldiers, whether from government military groups, rebel groups, paramilitary groups, or private armies. Sexual violence against girls has traumatic long-term damaging effects on their psychological and physical development. The spread of HIV/AIDS from sexually active soldiers to girls is another growing problem.

Those who authorize or perpetrate sexual brutality during armed conflict are committing crimes against humanity and are violating international law. For example, a statute of the International Criminal Court explicitly recognizes sexual violence as a war crime. The International Criminal Tribunals for the former Yugoslavia and for Rwanda have highlighted the use of rape during those conflicts and brought gender-based charges against the instigators of war crimes. In the former Yugoslavia, the International Tribunal attempted to prosecute people on specific charges of rape and sexual assault. Despite estimates of up to 20,000 victims, the tribunals were able to indict only eight people. Even with this dismal result, the judgments represent a historic precedent in prosecuting sexual violence within armed conflicts. For the first time, perpetrators of sexual violence were charged and brought to justice.

Armed conflict often leaves women and children vulnerable to commercial sexual trafficking and sexual exploitation. Despite the fact that the commercial sexual exploitation of women and girls is a well-documented result of armed conflict, the 1996 Congress Against Commercial Sexual Exploitation and the Optional Protocol on the Sale of Children, Child Prostitution and Child Pornography failed to address the link between war and the commercial sexual exploitation of women and girls. This is a large problem, and countries that have adopted the 1996 Congress Declaration and Agenda for Action and that have signed the Optional Protocol on the Sale of Children, Child Prostitution and Child Pornography should examine their relevance to situations of armed conflict (Machel 2000, 16).

The rape of women and girls is a widespread instrument of war. Machel (1996) argues that "the failure to denounce and prosecute wartime rape is partly a result of its mischaracterization as an assault against honour or a personal attack rather than a crime against the physical integrity of the victim" (sec. 103). Machel goes on to recommend that

national and international law must codify rape as a crime against the physical integrity of the individual, national Governments must hold those who commit rape in internal conflicts accountable and must reform their national laws to address the substantive nature of the abuse. Unwanted pregnancy resulting from forced impregnation should be recognized as a distinct harm and appropriate remedies provided. (sec. 104)

In her latest report, Machel (2000, 16) emphasizes the importance of the International Criminal Court in ending the impunity for crimes against women and girls.

CHILDREN TRAUMATIZED BY WAR

During every conflict, children witness and experience terrible atrocities. They witness the torture, murder, or rape of a loved one; they see dead bodies; they see people being beaten or being in situations where they thought they would die. All these events leave children with some degree of trauma. In many cases, they are left in a state of shock. For example, in a survey of 1505 children in Sarajevo, where almost 1 child in 4 has been wounded in the conflict, UNICEF found that 97 percent of the children had experienced shelling nearby, 29 percent felt "unbearable sorrow," and 20 percent had terrifying dreams. Some 55 percent had been shot at by snipers, and 66 percent had been in a situation where they thought they would die

(UNICEF 1993, 3-4). In a 1993 study in Angola, UNICEF found that 66 percent of the children had seen people being murdered, 91 percent had seen dead bodies, and 67 percent had seen people being tortured, beaten, or hurt. In all, more than two-thirds of children had lived through events in which they had defied death (UNICEF 1993, 3-4).

The physical, sexual, and emotional violence to which children are exposed undermines the very foundations of their lives. It causes painful psychosocial damage and erodes their trust in adults. The word "psychosocial" highlights the dialectic relationship between psychological and social elements. Psychological elements are those that affect emotion, behavior, thoughts, memory, learning ability, perceptions, and understanding. Social elements include altered relationships due to death, separation, estrangement, and other losses; family and community breakdown; damage to social values and customary practices; and the destruction of social facilities and services. Social effects also extend to economic aspects as people become impoverished.

Armed conflict causes a variety of reactions in each child. The response depends on the child's age, gender, personality, personal and family history, cultural background and experience, as well as the character and length of the incident. A traumatized child has a range of symptoms, including increased separation anxiety, developmental delays, sleep disturbances, nightmares, decreased appetite, withdrawn behavior, and a lack of interest in play (Machel 2000,

19). Younger children can have learning difficulties; older children and adolescents can show anxious or aggressive behavior and depression.

INTERNATIONAL EFFORTS TO PROTECT WAR-AFFECTED CHILDREN

Since the 1990 World Summit for Children, the United Nations has increasingly sought to draw international attention to the horrendous plight of children affected by armed conflict. At that time, the U.N. General Assembly adopted an international instrument: the Convention on the Rights of the Child (CRC). The convention has been endorsed by 191 states, making it the most widely ratified international instrument in history. The principles and provisions of the CRC set out explicitly the obligations of countries to ensure the security, rights, and welfare of children everywhere and under all circumstances.

The CRC speaks very directly to the situation of millions of children who are exposed to the impact of armed conflicts: "Every child has the inherent right to life, and States shall ensure to the maximum extent possible the survival and development of the child." It specifies that "children exposed to armed conflict shall receive special protection" and that "no child shall take part in any hostilities."

In 1994, the United Nations appointed Graça Machel, former minister of education of Mozambique, to study the impact of armed conflict on children. The 1996 final report, *Impact of Armed Conflict on Children*, was a milestone in our understanding of the problem of war-affected children and provided the first comprehensive and most compelling assessment of the many ways in which children are abused and brutalized in the context of armed conflict.

In 1997, in response to the Machel report, the United Nations appointed Olara A. Otunnu as Special Representative for Children and Armed Conflict. Otunnu was to be a public advocate and moral voice on behalf of children whose rights and welfare have been and are being violated in armed conflicts.

The world has progressed on this topic since the Machel report. In January 2000, consensus was attained on the text of the Optional Protocol on the Involvement of Children in Armed Conflict. Since its adoption by the U.N. General Assembly, 69 states have signed the protocol. In addition, there was the initiative of the Rome Statute of the International Criminal Court, which makes the violation of children's rights a war crime.

For the first time in history, there appears to be real movement toward a legal framework and international infrastructure concerning the promotion and protection of children's rights. This general development is essential in shaping the search for concrete action on the issue of war-affected children.

The central question then becomes, How do we build on these foundations? How do we ensure that the framework for the protection of children is implemented? In order to have a real impact, the world must abide by and enforce the ample laws and conventions that exist today. The world must find ways to mobilize people and states to enforce the conventions. The International Criminal Court also has the potential to be an innovative and effectual tool to protect the rights of children.

First and foremost, the Convention on the Rights of the Child must be followed by all states. In over 50 countries in which either war is raging or recovery from war is just beginning, the CRC's aspirations are being ignored with impunity. The convention is clear in setting out the responsibilities of all states. It has been ratified by all but two countries, but respecting the word and spirit of this document means more than a signature on a piece of paper. It means actively safeguarding and advancing the rights of all children and youths at home and abroad. It is only through guaranteeing the safety of the next generation that the reinforcing cycles of violence and poverty can be broken.

The Save the Children Alliance, in its recent publication *Children's Rights: Reality or Rhetoric* (n.d., 3), states that there has been a general lack of political will to make a reality of the radical vision of the CRC. The alliance believes that there is little or no coordination between government departments at a national level and between national government and local government and that few countries have even begun to develop an explicit strategy for its implementation.

PREVENTION IS THE BEST MEDICINE

The best way to protect children from wars is to stop wars from happening. Movement toward this goal could be attained by promoting equitable development, reducing the wealth gap between countries and within countries, stopping the proliferation of weapons sales from the developed to the developing countries, controlling the unchecked exploitation of resources of war-torn countries by transnational corporations, and finding peaceful ways to resolve conflict. While it is crucial to protect children from today's armed conflicts, it is just as important to prevent the outbreak of future wars. The only way of truly protecting children from the impact of armed conflict is to stop the conflicts from occurring. Once a war has started, children's suffering can only be mitigated.

The international community can lower the likelihood of intranational war by addressing these root causes. Corporations must be held accountable for their actions. Governments must lower the risk of armed conflict by demilitarizing their societies and reducing the percentage of their gross domestic product spent on military expenditures. Tighter controls need to be placed on the international flow of weapons, and a halt must be put to the illicit trafficking in diamonds, narcotics, and other products that fuels so many conflicts. As a start, the International Labor Organization and other U.N. bodies need to strengthen enforcement of international labor rights as well as establish an enforceable corporate code of conduct. The operations of transnational corporations must be open to more effective citizen, governmental, and multilateral regulation.

CONCLUSION

The rights of children are being trampled in the new warfare. Millions of youngsters are killed, violated, displaced, maimed, and traumatized. International organizations (such as the United Nations and UNICEF), national governments, and a range of nongovernmental organizations are involved in efforts to raise public awareness and mobilize international action on the plight of children affected by armed conflict. While rapid and important progress is being made to protect children and to ameliorate the effects of war on them, little attention is given to addressing the root causes of today's wars. Until the economic and political effects of globalization are seriously addressed, this new kind of warfare and its effusive effects on children will continue.

Poor countries are being pushed further toward the margins. Income inequality between countries and within countries is increasing, weapons sales to poor countries are increasing, and free trade and corporate control of national economies are increasing. In many cases, exploitation of people and natural resources by transnational corporations is increasing poverty and other social problems. Even the WTO (2000, 1), the architect of global economic integration, finds that 1.2 bil-

lion people—at least half of them children—live in absolute poverty, on less than $1 per day, and a further 1.6 billion, more than a quarter of the world's population, live on $1-$2 a day. Equitable and sustainable development, at an international level, is a prerequisite for reducing global conflict. Unfortunately, the international community has not been prepared to take the necessary steps to enable poor countries to control their destiny and develop their economies.

Notes

1. This article does not intend to discuss the issues and debates underlying the concept of globalization. Further discussion is contained in the articles in this issue; see also Beck 2000 and Hutton and Giddens 2000.

2. The remarks by Graça Machel at the Winnipeg conference are available online as text at http://www.waraffectedchildren.gc. ca/machel-e.asp and as video at http://www. waraffectedchildren.gc.ca/menu-e.asp.

3. The text of the WTO's trade agreements and the "Final Act of the 1986-1994 Uruguay Round" are available online at http://www. wto.org.

4. There is not space here to detail neoliberal trade and economic theories. The theory of international trade that predominates among economists today is that international trade initiates a tendency toward a gradual equalization of incomes between different countries. The criticism is that the assumptions that underlie the theory are unrealistic and against all experience. Also, actual per capita income data are contrary to the theory.

5. The WTO study goes on trying to show that the apparent correlation between declining growth rates in developed countries and reductions in trade barriers is a "statistical fallacy." The study then goes on to state in theoretical terms that trade should lead to the "potentially faster alleviation of poverty" (WTO 2000, 5).

References

Aristide, J. 1997. The Persistence of Poverty in the Age of Globalization. Speech delivered at the University of North Carolina, Chapel Hill.

Beck, U. 2000. *What Is Globalization?* Cambridge: Polity Press.

Brett, Rachel, Margaret McCallin, and Rhonda O'Shea. 1996. *Children: The Invisible Soldiers*. Geneva: Quaker U.N. Office and the International Catholic Child Bureau.

Dodge, Cole P. 1991. Child Soldiers of Uganda and Mozambique. In *Reaching Children in War: Sudan, Uganda and Mozambique*, ed. C. P. Dodge and M. Raundalen. Uppsala: Sigma Forlag.

Hutton, W. and A. Giddens, eds. 2000. *On the Edge: Living with Global Capitalism*. London: Jonathan Cape.

Machel, Graça. 1996. *Impact of Armed Conflict on Children*. United Nations Report No. A/51/306. Available at http://www.unicef.org/graca.

———. 2000. *The Impact of Armed Conflict on Children: A Critical Review of Progress Made and Obstacles Encountered in Increasing Protection for War-Affected Children*. Winnipeg: Government of Canada. Available at http://www.waraffectedchildren.gc.ca/machel-e.asp.

Ressler, Everett M., J. M. Tortorici, and A. Marcelino. 1993. *Children in War: A Guide to the Provision of Services*. New York: UNICEF.

Save the Children Alliance. n.d. *Children's Rights: Reality or Rhetoric?* Available at http://www.savethechildren.net/newstc.

Sivard, Ruth Leger. 1993. *World Military and Social Expenditures 1993*. Washington, DC: World Priorities.

UNICEF. 1993. Psychosocial Programme. Emergency Operations in Former Yugoslavia Kit. New York: UNICEF.

United Nations Research Institute for Social Development. 1995. *States of Disarray: The Social Effects of globalization*. Geneva: UNRISD.

Woodward, David. 1998. Globalization, Uneven Development and Poverty. Working paper series, United Nations Development Programme, Geneva.

World Trade Organization. 2000. *Special Study No. 5: Trade, Income Disparity and Poverty*. Geneva: WTO.

Zutt, Johannes. 1994. *Children of War: Wandering Alone in Southern Sudan*. New York: UNICEF.

ANNALS, *AAPSS*, **575**, May 2001

From Street to Stage with Children in Brazil and Ghana

By KATHLEEN MCCREERY

ABSTRACT: Children have lived and worked on city streets since time immemorial. But in recent years, free-market policies have led to a growing gap between rich and poor, unprecedented urbanization, and the fracturing of traditional social structures. One result has been the development of entire subcultures made up of children, including many whose family ties have been cruelly cut. Childhood is supposed to be a time of safety, laughter, and learning. But these children lead stunted lives characterized by fear, shame, and discrimination. That they succeed in organizing and fighting back, as they have in Brazil, that they doggedly strive to realize their dreams of betterment, as they do in Ghana, is a wonder. The author's play, *When I Meet My Mother*, offers a glimpse into the lives of a gang of Brazilian street children in one 24-hour period.

Kathleen McCreery has worked as a playwright, director, actor, journalist, lecturer, and enabler in the United States, Britain, Austria, and Germany. A founder-member of Red Ladder and Broadside theater companies, she coauthored the book Theatre as a Weapon *(1986). Northern Arts has awarded her two international writers' bursaries to work in Zimbabwe. She is currently an artist in residence with the National Health Service in the north of England.*

THE CAUSES AND
THE CASUALTIES

On 26 September 2000, in Managua, Nicaragua, Harold José Orozco, age 16, was shot twice in the back and left to die. He had tried to steal a chain from a man who refused him money for food. On 15 June, in Mexico City, Bernardino Garcia Cruz, age 12, drowned in the flooded basement of an abandoned building where he had been sleeping. On 16 May, in Tegucigalpa, Honduras, Gerson Noé Ramirez Salgado, age 17, hung himself in the bathroom of the Casa Alianza refuge. He had been shot several weeks earlier and was on the run.

These deaths have been recorded on the Internet on the Street Children Memorial Page maintained by Joe Walenciak. They give an indication of the harshness and brevity of life on the streets. They are also a reminder that the statistics represent individuals, each with a name and a history, each struggling to survive in circumstances that are, in the end, unique to them.

In 1994, the United Nations estimated the number of the world's street children at 100 million (Judson 1994, 2). Today, that figure is 300 million. Most are in those nations described as "developing" (Beauchemin 1999, 5). This extraordinary growth is a consequence of neoliberal economic policies that have increased poverty and migration to urban areas and accelerated the destruction of nuclear and extended families. But generalizations do not help us tackle the problem. Just as each child is different, in each country particular conditions lead to specific manifestations of the phenomenon.

BRAZIL

In terms of gross national product, Brazil is the world's eighth economic power (U.S. Department of State 1998). However, the vast wealth from agriculture, timber, mining, manufacturing, and tourism is distributed unevenly. A tenth of the population controls half of it; the poorest fifth receives only 2 percent (U.S. Department of State 1995). Between 1960 and 1980, 40 million rural families either abandoned or were expelled from their land. Powerful landowners, developers, and mining and logging companies forced them out, often at gunpoint. The population had been 75 percent rural; in a few decades, it became 75 percent urban (Swift 1991, 5).

Meanwhile, the government, which until 1985 was a military regime, was overextending itself with large-scale capital projects. Heavy borrowing, soaring interest rates, and the rising cost of oil led to debt, inflation, and recession. The International Monetary Fund stepped in, demanding structural adjustment. In 1990, President Fernando Collor announced the new Brazil plan: liberalization of trade, privatization, cuts in public spending, and public service employment (Save the Children 1992, 4). Collor's successor, Fernando Henrique Cardoso, a moderate right-winger, has been pursuing similar policies (U.S. Department of State 1999).

The dispossessed families who had earned their living by farming, fishing, and rubber tapping arrived in the cities and found no work and nowhere to live. They built their shanties in the *favelas*, or slums, and took their children out to sell newspapers, shine shoes, carry shopping, watch cars, scavenge, or beg. If the parents were lucky enough to have jobs, the older girls looked after their younger siblings and kept house. School was a luxury.

Initially, at least the family was together, cooperating in generating income so that all its members could survive. But gradually the stresses and strains took their toll: with little or no education, fathers were often underemployed or unemployed. If they did work, it was in the insecure and badly paid informal sector. Often, both parents would have to travel considerable distances and work long hours. The children had to fend for themselves. As their traditional status diminished, many fathers deserted their families (Swift 1991, 7). Parents and stepparents frequently turned to alcohol; some abused their children.

Most of the 8 million children on the streets of Brazil (Save the Children 1992, 6) return to their families at night and hand over a good part of their earnings. But many others have left home for good. They sleep on the streets and join gangs for protection. It is easy to slide into petty crime, drugs, and prostitution. The abuse of glue and other solvents is ubiquitous.

In the 1960s, the popular perception of a street child was of a clever, mischievous urchin. Street children could be a nuisance, but they were regarded with tolerant amusement,

even affection. As their numbers grew, as family ties disintegrated, as they grew too old to beg successfully and resorted to theft to get by, street children were no longer cute. They became pests, criminals, and *desechables* ("disposables") (Scheper-Hughes and Hoffman 1994).

The logical next step was that merchants began to pay vigilantes, including off-duty policemen, to exterminate street children like vermin. Brazil, a country whose children's rights legislation is among the world's most progressive, was unable or unwilling to stop the execution of thousands of its children. Eventually, after a particularly gruesome massacre of eight young children in front of the Candelaria Church in Rio de Janeiro in 1993 (Scheper-Hughes and Hoffman 1994), the international media got hold of the story. There was an outcry.

But Brazilian street children continue to die at the rate of 1000 a year, or 4 a day (Butcher 1996). Whether or not they are shot, like the 16-year-old boy known as Pelopar who had been sleeping in a doorway in the Copacabano beach area of Rio (Walenciak 2000), their deaths are an indictment of an economic system that breeds violence and the abuse of children's rights.

GHANA

The official Information Services' handy booklet, *Ghana at a Glance* (n.d.), boasts of "market-driven economic policies designed to ensure a welcoming investment climate" (3). The World Bank, International Monetary Fund, European Investment

Bank, and U.N. Development Bank have commended the government of Ghana for its "success in implementing its courageous and comprehensive reform programme" (13). This has included disciplined payment of debt interest, liberalization of trade, abolition of foreign exchange controls, a range of investment incentives, and privatization. "Skilled and inexpensive labour" is offered as a further inducement to investors (16). The government's Vision 2020 program anticipates Ghana becoming a middle-income nation in 20 years' time (Beauchemin 1999, 5).

However, kudos from the International Monetary Fund have not improved life for the rural population, according to a timely report by Eric Beauchemin (1999) for Catholic Action for Street Children and UNICEF. His work, *The Exodus*, is the result of a four-month study in 5 of Ghana's 10 regions. Researchers learned that market-driven policies have led to price instability. In the Ashanti region, for example, a bag of maize that had earned the farmer 50,000 cedis brought in just 20,000 cedis six months later. Government annexation of land for forests and takeovers by large-scale rubber and palm oil producers have resulted in a shortage of viable land for farmers who lease their plots. Subsidies for fertilizers and insecticides are a thing of the past (Beauchemin 1999, 10-11).

Climate changes are also taking their toll. The dry, or "hunger," season used to last six months. Now, it lasts closer to eight months (Wheat 2000). The vicious cycle of deforestation, soil erosion, and decreasing fertility means smaller harvests. St. Paul's Disease has devastated coconut trees and the communities that rely on them, including the fishermen who traditionally worked on the plantations in the rainy season (Beauchemin 1999, 13).

Many people have given up and migrated to the cities. Accra, the capital, now covers 10 times the area it did in 1960 (Ensor 2000). The population explosion has contributed to the swollen cities. Nevertheless, roughly 70 percent of Ghanaians still live on the land (Vidal 1999). But the young are turning their backs on their parents' hand-to-mouth existence. They are leaving for the cities in droves, sometimes under pressure from their families. According to Beauchemin's survey (1999), 64 percent were between 12 and 18 years of age, while 14 percent were under the age of 10 when they left home or were sent to live with urban relatives (45).

Poverty was the reason given by 35 percent of the street children registered with Catholic Action for Street Children (CAS) in Accra for coming to the city. But, as in Brazil, even close-knit families are vulnerable when survival requires a constant struggle. The children also cited divorce, death of one or more parent, neglect, violence, and sexual abuse as reasons for leaving (Beauchemin 1999, 15). These problems are complicated by the fracturing of traditional customs as they collide with Western and urban attitudes, values, and behavior. The result can be children in limbo.

Educational reform and the building of new schools have led to a significant rise in school enrollment rates in Ghana. Education is supposed to be free and compulsory for all children under age 16. In reality, fees are still charged in one form or another, and the cost of school uniforms and materials can be prohibitive for large families. Attending senior secondary school means traveling long distances and boarding at school, so even fewer children manage to attend (Beauchemin 1999, 19-25). "My father could not pay school fees" was the most common explanation given to me by street children for their departure.

The schools themselves are scarcely inviting. In one, 20 pupils have to share a single textbook; in another, 137 students jostle for space on six benches, and blackboards are so worn that pupils cannot read the teacher's writing. Qualified teachers are reluctant to work in rural schools that have no electricity, running water, toilets, or libraries (Beauchemin 1999, 21-22).

Ironically, when electricity does arrive in a village, it results in more children leaving. Television whets their appetite for the bright lights of Accra or Kumasi. When their peers return wearing the latest fashions, the pressure to leave becomes enormous.

The returnees do not tell other children how hard life can be: about the bullying; about sleeping in doorways in the rainy season, standing up "like horses"; about the long hours of exhausting labor in the pollution and heat for a pittance; about the pressure on the girls to accept a minder who will look after them in exchange

for sexual favors; about giving birth alone at a rubbish dump; about the babies that die of cholera and malaria; about the growing risk of contracting HIV/AIDS, with 200 new cases reported daily. But returning to the village would be an admission of failure. Very few street children come back to stay. They might drop off their babies if the taboo is not too great, visit for a few days, and then go back to the city and a life to which they have become accustomed, a life they claim is preferable to the hopelessness and grinding poverty on the land.

The numbers are not as great as in Brazil. CAS estimates that there are 15,000 street children and perhaps 4000 street babies in Accra. Most of the children are eager to work, they do not sniff glue, they are less likely to take to drugs, they are not as involved in crime and prostitution, and nobody is shooting at them. But what kind of childhood is this? And what kind of future can they give their children? We are beginning to see not just second- but third-generation street children. And still they come.

I am a playwright. My response to these issues has been to use my skills to try to raise awareness and to share those skills with the children so they can tell their own stories. The play *When I Meet My Mother* is an attempt to give Brazilian street children a platform. They have voices, loud ones, and they can be formidably articulate. The challenge is to persuade people to listen.[1]

WHEN I MEET MY MOTHER

It is the hour just before dawn in a large city in Brazil. In the distance, we hear traffic, an ambulance, or police sirens. Dogs bark, someone is running. A baby wakes and cries insistently; its weary mother tries to hush it. A drunk staggers home, singing, arguing with the people in his head. A bus pulls into the station. A sleepy peasant family emerges slowly, clutching their possessions: cardboard boxes tied with string, cloth bags, bundles wrapped in blankets, cheap plaid plastic shopping bags.

The narration can be taken by an individual or by several voices, even a chorus. It could be set to music.

Narrator: Can you see their eyes in the darkness
        shining with hope and with fear?
        They come from Pará, Maranhao, Mato Grosso do Sul.
        Bid them welcome,
        The new arrivals.
        Cattle graze where they once grew cassava.
        Hotels take root on white beaches
        where they spread their nets.
        Look, their feet are still wet:
        a dam has swallowed their village.
        In their ears the saws of the loggers still whine,
        in their dreams giant rubber trees
        crash to the floor of the forest
        over and over again
        and they wake up trembling.
        Greet them.
        The newcomers.
        The first of the day.
        But sure as the sun in the sky
        not the last.

A taxi driver lounges nearby. The family pushes one of the older children forward.

Child: Senhor. Please, can you tell us how far it is to São Bartolomeu?
Driver: In my taxi, 45 minutes.
Child: And on foot?
Driver: Aaaaaaah! *(He makes a dismissive gesture and turns away.)*
Narrator: Welcome them. The swollen city will not. *(The family members pick up their bundles, help each other load them on their backs, and looking uncertainly around, prepare to walk. If there are musicians, they might surround them. The narrator speaks to them in passing.)* It's that

way. Hold tight to your children's hands. *(They look at him in surprise, and exit.)*

The dawn is breaking. The city is waking up. We become aware of what looks like a large pile of cardboard and rags. It moves, just a little. A shopkeeper is opening for business, bringing out boxes of fruit and other foodstuffs. He kicks the heap, or pokes it with a broom or with the long stick he uses to open his shutters.

Shopkeeper: Wake up, scum. Go on, disappear.

The cardboard and cloth begin to shift. Seven young people, 12- to 17-years-old, girls and boys, emerge slowly from the pile. They shiver, yawn, blink, stretch, and scratch and begin to fold up their cardboard and blankets. One of the boys, Luis, goes hurriedly to urinate against a wall. The shopkeeper sees him.

Shopkeeper: Hey! Isn't it enough that you stink to high heaven?! Do you have to leave a trail behind you like a dog?! Animals! Do you think I work my fingers to the bone to pay rent and taxes so garbage like you can foul the streets and drive away my customers?!
One of the girls confronts him boldly.
Cristiane: So we're garbage, are we?
Shopkeeper: Filthy little—
Cristiane: Garbage belongs on the street, right? Well, then this is where we belong! On the street! *(She begins to dance and sing around the shopkeeper, maybe one [or more] of the others dances with her, drums or juggles or does acrobatics, whatever the skills of the cast.)*
Shopkeeper: *(waving his broom or stick)* Get out of here—
Cristiane: *(extending an open palm)* Give me one real and you won't see us all day!
Shopkeeper: I'll give you the *justiceiros* [vigilantes] that's what I'll—
Luis: *(a little nervously)* Let's go.

They make as though to leave, the shopkeeper returns to his shop. The gang dart back, and quickly fill pockets, skirts, t-shirts, and hands with fruit from the box he has left out front. The shopkeeper sees them, yells "Thieves! Police!" They might tip over a box to trip him up or distract him, then run away laughing. He chases them, furious, but is unsuccessful, and returns to his spilt fruit, defeated.

Shopkeeper: *(to himself, or to a neighbor, passer-by, or his wife, who might have emerged from the back)* Ai, ai, ai! They are like a cloud of mosquitoes! You crush one, and another takes its place, sucking out your life-blood. And what does the government do? *(He makes a contemptuous gesture indicating "nothing!")* They should bulldoze the *favelas* [shanty towns]. They're nothing but swamps, breeding more and more parasites.

The gang, all except Cesar, regroups and settles down for breakfast.

Renata: Quick! I am so hungry!
Marco: What did you get?
Cristiane: *(distributing the food, making sure everyone receives an equal amount)* Oranges, tomatoes . . .
Antonio: I wish we had some bread.

Cesar appears, panting, with a loaf of bread.

Cesar: *(trumpet noise)* Daa Daaa!

Cheering, they clap him on the back.

Antonio: *(trying to break off a bit)* It's hard as a rock!
Cesar: What do you want me to do, take it back to the bakery and complain?! *(He makes a gesture to Antonio, indicating that he is thick, Antonio starts pelting him with bits of bread; they begin a play fight, rolling over and over each other like puppies.)*
Priscilla: *(saving the food)* Hey! Watch out!
Narrator: See how we swim through the city
              slippery as eels.
              Whatever you want is here,
              if you're tough enough, you can take it.
              Some kids say the water's too cold,
              they're afraid of the fish with big teeth.
              But if you follow the rules
              you'll do fine:
              First. Sleep with one eye always open.
              Second. Moving targets are harder to hit.
              Third. A grownup who says he's your friend
              wants something, buried deep in the bait is a hook.
              Fourth. You won't last long on your own.
              Join a gang, stick together like glue.
Cesar: *(lazily)* It's going to be hot today. We should go to the beach.
Antonio: We don't have money.
Cesar: Luis does.
Renata: He's saving it.
Cesar: What for? Come on, Luis, let's go to the beach.

Luis: It's Friday. My mother is expecting me. *(Cesar makes pleading gestures or moves to rifle Luis' pockets or the purse he wears on a string around his neck.)* NO! I always give her half.

Cesar: You never do!

Luis: Well, this week my sister needs shoes. Anyway, the bus drivers won't let us on if we all go together, whether we have money or not.

Cristiane: We can catch a lift on the back.

Luis: And end up like Roberto? No thanks.

Marco: Roberto does all right. When he sticks his arm under the noses of the tourists, they'll give him anything just so they don't have to look at it. *(He grabs Antonio's hand and does an impression of a faint-hearted, guilt-ridden tourist faced with Roberto's mangled arm.)* "Oh! How dreadful! The POOR child! Here! . . . More money? Of course, just . . . take it away, PLEASE!"

Luis: I have to go to work.

Cesar: Luis is turning into a home boy. Ever since the police got him.

Priscilla: Leave him alone. They gave him a very bad time. I think that's why he has to pee so often. *(She catches sight of someone.)* Ana? . . . it's Ana! *(runs to embrace her)*

Cristiane: Hey, where you been?

Renata: New clothes, she's got new clothes.

Marco: *(turning away)* Looks like that pimp Ze finally got to her.

Renata: *(checking the labels)* No, Ze said he'd buy her designer clothes, these are "false goods." *(politely, in case she hurts Ana's feelings)* Nice, though.

Ana: Hello, Luis. You OK?

Luis: Sure. You look good. I mean, it's good to see you. We thought . . .

Ana: Yeah, I know. Sorry. I missed you. I missed you all.

Antonio: *(embarrassed)* Well, you're back now. We should celebrate. Have a party. We'll have to get some funds. Cesar?

Cesar: No problem! *(They go through a complex handshaking routine.)*

During the following narration, the gang's "employers" or "clients" appear. The scenes should melt in and out, continuing over, around and under each other, as the focus shifts.

Narrator: It's easy.
Wherever you look, there's money,
moving from one hand to another.
Sometimes all you have to do
is stretch out yours
and, still talking about the World Cup,
French fashions
or the war between Pepsi and Coke
and the $2 billion

they're going to invest in Brazil,
the people with clean fingernails, rings and Rolexes,
they drop coins in your palm.
They don't stop to count them.
They don't stop to look at you.
But sometimes
you have to work a little harder.

Marco: Hey, Senhor, over here, here's a space! S'cuse me, but see those two kids, they're crazy, high all the time, they don't care, they'll do anything! Nice new Merc like that, be a real shame if it was scratched or the tires got slashed, but hey, I could watch it for you, make sure nothing happens to it.

Businessman: *(giving him money)* If anybody touches this car, I'll come looking for you.

Marco: You want me to wash it for you, too? I can do it for . . .

Businessman: *(calling back over his shoulder)* I want you to leave it alone!

Marco: I'll be here when you get back, you can trust me!

Cristiane: Lady, let me carry your shopping, fine lady like you shouldn't have to carry so much, mess up your nice clothes, you want me to get you a taxi, here, give me that—

Well-to-do shopper: But you are a girl!

Cristiane: So?! I'm strong, stronger than all of them boys put together, I can carry anything, me!

Woman: You should be at home with your mother! *(She brushes past, sighing and muttering, Cristiane pursues her.)*

Cristiane: Come on, just 20 cents a bag, why should the boys get all the good jobs—

Luis: Shine your shoes, senhor? . . . Shine, senhor? Shine?

Priscilla: Chiclets . . . chewing gum . . . *(She tentatively stretches out a hand to a smiling student talking to a friend. S/he turns and spits in her face, the friend laughs, they turn their backs. She wipes it off, continues, as though nothing has happened.)* Chiclets . . . chewing gum . . .

Antonio: You finished with that bottle, Madam? Can I have it? Thanks, Madam.

Renata: Hey, senhor! Want some fun?

Middle-aged man *(could be a tourist)*: How old are you?

Renata: *(trying to look grown up)* Almost 16.

Man: I'm looking for something fresher. You got a little sister?

Felix *(a drug dealer)*: Cesar! Job for you. *(He passes a small packet over.)* Largo do Pelourinho. Outside the Acropole Fitness Centre. Red Ferrari. *(smiles)* Very Important Customer. Daddy's loaded. So be polite, be discreet and don't keep her waiting. Her minder will take delivery.

Cesar: No problem, Senhor Felix.

Felix: No problem, no problem, that's what I like to hear. *(to his mate)* Cesar is one of my best "little airplanes." And he keeps his mouth shut. *(grabs*

Cesar by the nape of the neck) He's smart, he knows a file of information that lets the wrong people have a peek, well, it gets burnt, eh, Cesar?! Stick with me, kid, and who knows, I might promote you. Just don't get any smart ideas about sampling the merchandise. You want a taste, you ask me first, I'll take care of you. Hurry back now. And wash your neck sometimes! *(He wipes his hands on a silk handkerchief.)*

Narrator: The sun is high in the heavens
       and yesterday is already buried.
       Don't think of the father who beat you
       while the television blared in the corner.
       This is the moment that matters.
       Don't think of the mother who ran off,
       she was only 13 when she married.
       Just keep your mind on the present.
       Every day is a gift, an adventure.
       Tomorrow is too much to hope for.

Two policemen (could be out of uniform) meet a businessman who is finishing a meal.

Joao: Senhor Alves . . .

Sr. Alves: Joao, Nei . . . A coffee? Or something stronger?

Joao: No thanks, Sr. Alves. We're on our way to work. *(OR if in uniform)* We're on our break, we have to get back to work.

Alves: Well, then. *(He pushes back his plate, gets out an envelope. The men's eyes fix on it greedily.)* I mustn't keep you. *(He opens the envelope. They look around nervously. There is cash inside.)* Wonderful, isn't it? *(He spreads out the money on the table.)* Yet it's only paper. Just like this serviette. *(He wipes his mouth fastidiously with a note, crumples it, disposes of it in the ash tray.)* But because it has a picture of some Portuguese explorer on it—you can pay your rent with it. Buy your kid a confirmation outfit. How is your daughter, by the way, Nei?

Nei: She—she's fine, sir.

Alves: Good. Very good. *(He takes out a lighter and, selecting a note, sets it alight. The men's eyes widen. The hand of one makes an involuntary move to rescue the burning note, then draws back.)* My fellow businessmen and I are very conscious of the value of these pretty bits of paper. Especially now, with inflation down to less than 2 percent. I trust you voted for him, our President Fernando Henrique Cardoso. *(They clear their throats nervously.)* Oh, surely, gentlemen! He's brought us stability, foreign investment. No longer do we have to hoard rice or coffee or toilet paper for fear the price will go up in an hour's time. My wife and I are planning a trip to the States for Christmas, did I tell you? *(He lights another note from the pile in front of him.)* Of course, I realize the salaries of public servants are still lagging behind. That must be hard for men with young families, men with pretty girlfriends. Eh, Joao? *(He winks suggestively, smiles, lights another note.)*

Joao: *(swallowing, sweating)* Senhor—

Alves: Toilet paper. Every time I opened a wardrobe, rolls of the stuff, falling down on my head. I used to look at it sometimes and think "There can't be this much shit in the whole world!" My wife likes the fancy stuff with the patterns. I used to tell her we should use banknotes to wipe our arses, the toilet paper was probably worth more than cash. *(He laughs, selects a note but does not ignite it.)*

Nei: *(laughing)* Senhor Alves—you have a good sense of humor. You are joking, of course. It's not—the money *(gesturing to the ashes)*—is it?

Alves: Real? Oh, yes, Nei. It's real, all right. *(quietly angry)* You see, I'm beginning to think I might as well burn it as give it to you and your incompetent friends. When we invest good money, my colleagues and I, money that's finally worth something, we expect results. *(He might get up, go to look out the window.)* Out there! There's shit all over the streets, in the parks, on the beaches, outside the Opera, the Municipal Theatre, the Fine Arts Museum, the Cathedral, in front of our shops and businesses! I pay you to mop it up. Just like toilet paper. It's not a pleasant job, so I pay you well. But when I leave my building, first thing you know, I've stepped in it. And that means my customers, and our foreign visitors, are also walking knee-deep in filth, and then they go home and they call us a Third World country. You'd like the rest of the money, wouldn't you? *(Joao and Nei nod miserably.)* Then earn it. Or your wretched jobs will go up in smoke. You'll have to live on your policemen's salaries. *(He pockets the envelope.)* I trust I've made myself clear. Give my regards to the Colonel. *(He exits.)*

The following narration should be divided between different voices. Could be done as if by reporters or foreign correspondents or human rights investigators phoning and faxing their head offices or taping a broadcast. If done this way, the actors should give the appearance of continuing underneath the next voice, each report is followed by another and another.

Voice: In the city of Belem, Carlos Alberto Rodrigues, 17, was charged with stealing a paint brush. He was taken to the police station and beaten to death . . .

Voice: In São Paulo, four children were killed when acid was poured on them as they slept . . .

Voice: In Nova Ituaca the bodies of three boys, aged 15 to 17, were pulled out of the Sarpui River. Fragments of teeth and pools of blood were discovered nearby . . .

Voice: In Caxias, Rio de Taneiro, 9-year-old Alexandre Silva was raped at the bus station. He was found dead in another town . . .

Voice: In the Nova Jerusalem favela of Rio de Janeiro, Flavio, aged 9, Erivaldo, Marcio, and Andreia, all 16, Edson, 17, Cristiano, 15, and Rose, 14, were accused of stealing a pair of tennis shoes and carrying weapons. They were beaten, forced to lie face down on the ground, and shot in the back of the head at point-blank range. Andreia was the only survivor . . .

Voice: In the fashionable neighborhood of Ipanema, Rio de Janeiro, the body of 9-year-old Patricio Hilario da Silva was left wrapped in a rug. He had been strangled. A note was found near the body: "I killed you because you do not study, you do not work and you have no future." . . .

Voice: In 1995 three children a day were murdered in the state of Rio de Janeiro . . .

Narrator: Today it is the turn of Ana. Ana Isabel Amados.

PAUSE. Those on stage turn and look at the last speaker.
A chorus of protest. Some may be characters we have seen before.

Taxi driver: Hey, don't make them out to be heroes, OK? They're not exactly sweet little flowers.

Tourist 1: Well, it's not very nice, you'll be sitting down to a beautiful meal by the sea and then there's this grubby little hand right across your plate and this skinny little face with big pleading eyes. It kind of takes away your appetite.

Tourist 2: And of course we were told not to give them anything because it just encourages them and they only use it for drugs and anyway there's so *many* . . .

Shopkeeper 1: They piss in public, pester you for money and if you don't give them anything, they pick your pocket!

Shopkeeper 2: I've had to employ a full-time guard at the front of my shop. They're costing me a fortune! It's got to stop.

Unemployed man: Operation Santa Claus! Funny name for a raid, huh? Well, I thought so. It was like a big vacuum cleaner *(makes sucking noise)*, they went right through the city sucking up kids. Me? I cheered! The police are always picking on the wrong people, for once they got tough with the side that deserves it! So for a little while we had nice clean streets. Didn't last, though. It's like they come out of the cracks in the concrete.

Woman shopper: "Human rights!" That's the privilege of bandits and muggers! What about *my* right to walk down the street in safety?

Woman holding baby: You call them kids, they're not kids, they may be 13, but they've killed people! They deserve to die themselves.

There is the sound of laughter. The gang spills onto the stage, all except for Luis. They swig from a bottle of cheap wine, sniff from plastic bags or bottles containing glue or a can or jar containing petrol. Marco, Cesar, Antonio, and

Cristiane are playing football, it may be brand new and they have stolen it, or it may be a can or other substitute.

Marco: *(to Cesar)* Hey! Pele! To me! To me!

Cristiane intercepts, passes to Antonio, who misses, perhaps because he has stopped to sniff or swig.

Cristiane: 'Tonio, you are hopeless!

Antonio: *(looking up)* What? *(He weaves a little, and suddenly his legs buckle and he sits down.)*

The others pile on him laughing.

Cristiane: *(knocking on his head)* Hello? Anybody home?

Priscilla: *(taking away the glue, sniffing some herself)* He's been at the glue too long. He told me, years ago he used to work in a shoe factory.

Ana: Our 'Tonio, a shoemaker?

Priscilla: No, no, he just stuck the soles on.

Antonio: With glue. *(He laughs, takes off his broken shoes and pretends to inhale, passes his shoe to one of the others, who makes a face and groans at the smell.)*

Renata: Give me some more, I'm getting hungry again. *(They pass the bag, she inhales.)*

Cesar: What a brilliant job! You'd get paid for being high all day. Hey, 'Tonio, how old do you have to be, to work in your factory?

Antonio: Dunno. There were some little kids. They put them in the boxes . . .

Cesar: What, the little kids?!

Priscilla: No, stupid, the *shoes*! *(laughter)*

Antonio: . . . They went to America . . . England . . . Portugal . . .

Marco: *(dreamily)* America . . .

Cesar grabs the shoe, turns it into an airplane, demonstrates a plane taking off and landing underneath his next speech which he illustrates with appropriate noises and action.

Cesar: America! Disneyland! Cowboys! Baseball! New York, Hollywood! Mickey Mouse! Madonna! Michael Jackson!

Marco: One day . . .

Cristiane: You? No way!

Priscilla: Neli's baby went to America. Some rich people adopted him. Neli wanted to go too, but they said 13 was too old.

Cristiane: How do you know he was adopted? How do you know he wasn't kidnapped and killed and his heart and his lungs and his kidneys and his brain cut out and transplanted into a rich American?

Ana: Those are just stories!

Cristiane: It's true! It was in the newspapers! I can read! The child stealers are in it together with the people who run the children's homes. Why do you think they built the cemetery so close to the one at Carioca? They will never get me into one of those places. And if I have a baby, I will never give it away.

Renata: Shut up, Cristiane. *(She gestures to Ana.)*

Priscilla: Neli got some money. But I don't know what happened, 'cause last time I saw her, she was back on the streets. She didn't look too good.

Renata: *(snorting derisively)* And men think if they go with the younger ones they're not going to get sick! Serves them right.

Cristiane: Tell us about the house you worked in, Priscilla.

Priscilla: I've told you a hundred times.

Cristiane: I don't care, I like to hear it.

Priscilla: Well, it had a big garden and—

Cristiane: Tell about the bathroom. With the bath in the floor you could swim in and the hot water and the gold taps and the mirrors and the soft towels . . .

Renata: Tell about the kitchen. I would never leave a house with a fridge like that.

Priscilla: You would if you had to work like a slave. They promised my mother I could go to night school but by the time I finished all the cooking and cleaning and shopping and washing and ironing I was so tired, I couldn't see the words. I never had time to do homework. The Senhora would shout at me when I got home. And then the master—he had no respect.

Marco: I could have been a lawyer if I'd stayed at school.

Cesar: They wouldn't let me in. I didn't have a birth certificate.

Marco: They don't criticize lawyers . . . the way they do parking boys . . .

Renata: I was always hungry at school . . .

Priscilla: Ssssh. I'm dreaming . . . of a school where you can learn ballet . . . and reading and writing . . .

Cesar: . . . and capoeira . . . *(He makes a few moves.)*

Priscilla: It must be the best thing . . . in the world . . .

Cristiane: . . . a bicycle . . .

Marco: . . . a machine gun . . . to destroy the police . . . *(makes soft machine gun noises)*

They are half asleep, eyes closed. Esther, a street educator, walks towards them. She sees Ana and stops. Marco notices. He half sits up, pokes the others, they stir drowsily. Esther approaches slowly.

Esther: Ana? It's me, Esther.

Ana gets up unsteadily. She moves away from the group. Esther follows her.

Ana: *(defiantly)* What do you want?

Esther: I think I should ask you that. You're the one who disappeared without a word to anyone.

Ana: So?

Esther: So people were worried. And you left Luciana to clean up the dirty dishes you smashed on the floor.

Ana: I've cleared up after her lots of times! She wets the bed, you know. Fifteen and she wets the bed!

Esther: And now you're sniffing glue. The shelter rules—

Ana: I'm sick of rules! Nobody tells *me* what to do!

Esther: If you don't like them, call a meeting. Talk to the other girls. See if you can persuade them to change them. You make the rules. All of you.

Ana: *(pause, and then an outburst)* It's easy for you.

Esther: *(dryly)* Yeah, sure. I know nothing about it, I never been on the streets, right?

Ana: Well then, you must be better than me.

Esther: No. I was definitely worse.

Ana: For me it's hard! It's too hard. "Go here, go there!" "What time is it?" "Do this, don't do that!" I miss my friends.

Esther: I know. And you are scared.

Ana: WHY?

Esther: Nobody beats you. Nobody yells at you. The police and the pimps and the pushers and the death squads don't come in the shelter.

Ana: But sometimes . . . I'm more afraid in there . . . than I am out here.

Esther: You already know this life. You know what to expect.

Ana: I'm no good. I'm dirty. I'm going to go to hell. What's the point? That's my fate.

Esther: Who told you that?

Ana: Look! If I was worth anything, my mother wouldn't have left me! All right?!

Esther: Ana. It's not your fault.

Ana: Then why did she go and do it, huh? Why did she leave me? She's my mother. A mother is supposed to look after you, it doesn't matter if you're hungry or cold, but if you're near your mother you're protected, the police and the street boys don't touch you! But when I woke up she was gone. I HATE HER! I HATE HER!

Esther: It's OK. It's OK. Just don't hate yourself.

Ana: I used to think . . . if I died . . . and they put my picture in the paper . . . real big . . . then she'd see it . . . and she'd be ashamed and sorry . . . she didn't help me.

Esther: She was sorry, believe me.

Ana: You don't know.
Esther: I know . . . and you know it too. *(pause)*
Ana: Can I still . . . come back?
Esther: Yes. But you start all over again.
Ana: I'll try.
Esther: Good.
Ana: Tonight. I'll come back tonight. I have to say goodbye . . . to my friends.

Esther looks at her, concerned, but accepts what she says.

Narrator: Pick up the chalk, the crayon, the pencil.
Draw a house on the pavement, the paper, the blackboard.
Add flowers and green grass and windows with curtains.
Some birds in the sky and the sun always shining.
And there at the door put the Mother, smiling.
This mother never gave birth on the streets.
This mother never was stabbed in a fight.
This mother never gets drunk, drops her baby.
This mother never takes her kids begging.
One day you will find her, your own real mother.
And then you will know, you will know who you are.

The focus shifts to the favela where Luis' mother lives. He has gone to bring her some money. Desperate to stop him leaving she has chained him or locked him in. She is probably doing some kind of work during the dialogue.

Luis: Ma!
Mother: No.
Luis: Come on, Ma, let me go.
Mother: I can't hear you, Luis.
Luis: I'll come back more often. *(silence)* OK, I'll come back every night.
Mother: You said that last time.
Luis: Ma. How am I supposed to earn money for you and Regina?
Mother: We'll manage.
Luis: We'll starve.
Mother: *(almost crying)* I don't care. I can't let you go. You are my son. They almost killed you.
Luis: I'm more careful now. Please, Ma.
Mother: When your father comes back—
Luis: He's not coming back.
Mother: He's looking for work, he'll come back and he'll be angry . . .
Luis: He'll be glad I'm gone. He only took his head out of the bottle to nag me. *(begins hammering in frustration)* Ma! What am I supposed to do all day in this stinking slum? I can't sit around doing nothing.

Mother: You can look after your little sister.

Luis: That's not a man's job.

Mother: You aren't a man. You're only a boy! You were such a good boy. You've just got into bad company. That gang comes and they whistle and you go with them.

Luis: Ma. I have to pee.

Mother: Use the can. I'm going to get your sister.

She exits quickly. There is silence for a moment. Then, a long low distinctive whistle. The sound of struggling with fastenings, a lock. Luis escapes. His mother has heard the whistle, comes running back. She sees that he is gone. She stands still for a moment. Then she sits down, slowly, gingerly. She wipes her eyes. Helplessly, she opens her hands, makes an aimless gesture. She has lost him.

Luis has rejoined the gang. They are wandering through the city in the early evening. Antonio is supported by Cristiane and Marco. Cesar joins them. He has a radio, either pocketsize or larger and in a carrier bag.

Cesar: Let's go round the restaurants.

Renata: Too early. They don't throw out the best stuff till a lot later.

Luis: 'Tonio doesn't look too good.

Cesar: It was Carlos' gang. Punks!

Priscilla: They said we were on their turf. Rambo here wanted to take them on. We tried to shut him up but—

Cesar: We could have beat them, easy.

Marco: He sniffs a little glue, he thinks he's the Hulk.

Cristiane: 'Tonio? You want some cola?

Antonio: Mmmmm.

Priscilla: We had to run. 'Tonio's breathing went funny. He should be better by now, that was hours ago. Maybe we should take him to the hospital.

Renata: *(scornfully)* Yeah, sure. *(pretending to be a hospital receptionist)* "Where's your papers? Got any money? No money, no medicine. Don't think you can come in here and fake it just to steal drugs, they're all under lock and key, and I've called security, they're on their way!"

Cesar: He'll be all right. He's tough. *(He strokes his face, might even kiss his forehead.)* Hey, 'Tonio! Look! Look what I got! *(He pulls out a stolen radio, either from his pocket or the bag he is carrying, depending on its size. He turns it on, fiddles with the dial, finds some music, begins to dance.)*

Ana and Luis have drawn apart from the others. They are shy with each other. They speak at the same time.

Ana: Your mother really locked you up?—

Luis: When you came back this morning I—

Luis: *(smiling)* You first.
Ana: No, you . . .

They are tongue-tied. Luis takes Ana's hand. Marco turns and sees them. He is jealous. He grabs the radio away from Cesar who has been dancing with it on his shoulder or in his hand or dancing around it on the ground.

Cesar: Hey! What are you doing? This is my music!
Marco: It's rubbish, man. *(He moves the dials. Cesar tries to grab it back, they begin to wrestle. Cristiane rescues the radio, which transmits the sounds of a demonstration.)*
Radio announcer: . . . Our reporter Raul Reyes was in the nation's capital, Brazilia, to witness the invasion of street children . . .
Cristiane: Listen. Hey, shut up! Listen.

She turns up the volume, gradually the others stop whatever they are doing and listen. A demonstration of street children and educators has taken place in the capital, Brasilia. The gang huddles together over the radio, the demonstration takes place around them, but there must be a sense in the way it is staged of them being separate from it. They can't see it, they hear it. The rest of the cast become demonstrators (M/F), senators and other government officials (M/F), policemen and security guards (M), and journalists (M/F). There is mayhem. The demonstrators have invaded the Congress. Depending on the skills and resources of the company, we might see street children on stilts and unicycles, beating drums or using other noisemakers, dressed as clowns, wearing carnival and folk costumes and masks and pouring onto the stage. They shout slogans and carry banners calling for justice, education, and an end to violence. The politicians are bemused, upset, or angry depending on their point of view. The police and security guards are outnumbered; no sooner do they succeed in grabbing a child when another scuttles between their legs or under their arms. They can't be too rough because the media are present.

Reporter: The National Congress Building is surrounded by an army of children. I have never seen anything like it, and neither have most of the senators. Earlier today, a fleet of buses arrived from all over the country. Some have been travelling for days. There must be at least a thousand, some as young as 7 years old—
Demonstrator 1: *(grabbing mike, yelling above the commotion)* They murdered six of my cousins in Recife!
Journalist: Who did?
Demonstrator 1: The death squads!
Demonstrator 2: Once they put a gun to my head. They pressed so hard I thought they were going to shove it through my skull to save on bullets!
Journalist: So you're saying you've been tortured?

Demonstrator 2: Yes, of course, what else?! They burn us with cigarettes and boiling water, they beat us, they cut us. They say we're criminals, so nobody's going to care.

Demonstrator 1: Most of us are workers. If we steal it's only to survive. It's either that or starve!

Speaker of the House: Order, order . . . we must have order! This is a democracy! You must go through the proper channels. You cannot disrupt the—

Demonstrator 3: (S / he has got to the floor of the chamber, managed to grab the Speaker's mike.) A democracy is supposed to listen to its citizens. We are citizens too, but nobody listens to us because we are young and because we are poor!

Senator 1: Let them speak.

Senator 2: This is intolerable, eject them.

Senator 3: Give them the floor.

(The cries for the demonstrators outweigh their opponents, a representative of the children is given the mike.)

Demonstrator 4: My name is Theresa da Costa. I come from São Paulo. I am an elected representative of the National Movement for Street Children. We are here to protest. All over the country children are dying, so many that we can't keep track. And yet Brazil has one of the most progressive Child and Adolescent Statutes in the world. In spite of this, our rights are still not respected. We are angry, angry that the government is doing so little to implement its own laws. They have passed the responsibility on to the municipalities. Some are taking action, but others do nothing. We are angry with the press. They maintain the lie about the "mysterious death squads." The truth is, the authorities often know the identity of the vigilantes. We are angry with the police. They routinely harass us, extort money from us, or force us to steal for them. Some join the so-called justice committees and rape, torture, mutilate, and kill us! They do this because we know too much about their involvement in drugs and other criminal activities, or because they are paid by the business community to exterminate us. They are rarely prosecuted. Of course not, how can the police investigate themselves? Witnesses, too, are threatened and assassinated. We want an end to the violence against street children and those who work with us! We want the guilty punished! *We want justice! (cheers)* But this will not solve the problem. We must have the right to an education. We need more schools in the neighborhoods where we live, and the teachers must understand that we are hungry and tired after long hours of work. And finally, we want employment for our families. Yes, most of us have families, just like you. If our parents had the means to support us, very few children would end up on the streets! Thank you for giving me a chance to speak! I was very nervous, but now I feel strong! *(cheers)*

The demonstration ends. The participants leave the stage, the slogans fade out.

Announcer: Representatives of the street children went on to meet the Minister for Sport, former soccer star Pele, and education ministers. World news now, in London Prime Minister Tony Blair . . . *(This could be changed according to the news of the day.)*

Luis switches off the radio. The gang doesn't move. They stand or sit around the radio in silence for a few minutes. Then, Priscilla begins to clap. One by one the others join in, applauding the radio. It has grown dark.

Narrator: For a moment they dare to imagine,
　　　　　imagine the world could be different,
　　　　　imagine that they could help change it.
　　　　　For a moment eyes shine in the darkness.
　　　　　For a moment they touch tomorrow.
　　　　　And this
　　　　　is the moment that matters.
Antonio: *(a little weak, but recovered)* Hey, Cesar. Good radio.
Cesar: *(hugging Antonio)* What did I tell you? He's tough!
Marco: Let's go get something to eat. How about sleeping at the railway station tonight?
Cesar: *(finds music on the radio, dances)* You know what? We should organize our own samba block. For Carnival. We could think of a theme . . . to teach the people about us. Show them how good we can dance . . . People would throw money at us. We might even win a prize.
Priscilla: *(sarcastically)* Sure. And Michael Jackson will see us and ask us to be in his next video!
Cesar: He might! This kid I know said his uncle was in the Santa Marta one. *(He sings a refrain from "They Don't Care About Us.")*
Cristiane: Michael Jackson's *been* to Brazil. He's not going to come back, is he? Anyway, where we going to get costumes? *(They walk along arguing.)*

Ana walks with Renata.

Renata: You want to work with me tonight? At the station?
Ana: No. Thanks. I'm not doing it anymore. *(Renata shrugs.)* Renata. Are you careful?
Renata: *(laughs)* Why worry about what might happen in a year? We could be dead tonight. *(calling)* Cristiane!

Ana: She's only a kid.

Renata: They're going to take it off her anyway, she might as well get paid. Cristiane— *(She moves to speak to her.)*

Ana: *(stopping)* I'm going back! *(They turn and look at her.)* To the shelter. To stay. I have a bed there.

Priscilla: You been at the girls' house?

Ana: Yes. It's a good place. I want . . . to be someone. That sounds bad, I don't mean . . . If I had known before . . . about the shelter . . . maybe I wouldn't have given my daughter up. *(She moves to them, almost formal, awkwardly hugging, touching, kissing. They are aware that something momentous is happening.)* Last time I went away . . . I didn't say goodbye. But I'll—I'll see you. I will!

Luis: I'll walk with you.

They start walking. Cesar breaks away from the gang and runs up to Ana. He gives her the radio.

Cesar: I was only going to sell it. *(He dances away from her, making his own music.)*

The gang exits. Ana and Luis walk hand in hand, absorbed in each other. They don't see the man who appears behind them, another who moves in from the right, a third from the left. Only when a man blocks their path from the front do they stop. They look round. They are surrounded.

Man in front: Where did you get that radio? *Pivetes* [thieves].

Man behind them: *Prosuntos* [ham, meat—term used by death squads for their victims].

The lights dim.

Narrator: As soon as the sun comes up
the Lourenço family go as usual to the municipal dump
scavenging for things to eat, wear, and sell.
The youngest son, a boy of 5, hears a noise.
It is Luis. The bullet with which he was shot deflected.
He is alive.
Ana is dead.

The lights come up on the gang on another part of the stage. They are standing as if at a graveside.

Cristiane: Maybe if she'd met her mother . . .

They lay flowers, then move away. The other cast members gradually create a street scene, and the gang are absorbed into it. A child is following them. It might be the child from the peasant family which had asked directions at the bus station. Eventually, they notice.

Marco: *(to the child)* Well, come on then.
The child joins the gang.

THE END

When I Meet My Mother was commissioned by Cheshire Drama Education Services for Cheshire Youth Theatre. No portion of the play When I Meet My Mother may be reprinted, adapted, or performed without the permission of the author.

PLAYMAKING IN GHANA

In 1999 and again in 2000, I ran drama and playmaking workshops for street children in Accra. The campaigning organization Street Child Africa initiated the project; my hosts on the ground were local NGOs Street Girls' Aid and Catholic Action for Street Children. Together we have produced five plays based entirely on the participants' own experiences.

At first they were doubtful: "Why should we tell our stories?" was the response at the CAS refuge. But as they unwrapped their particular sorrows and gave them breath, as they heard their pain acknowledged, as their skills and confidence grew, they reached out and grasped the opportunity with both hands.

At SAID, I worked with young women who have been sponsored to learn dressmaking and hairdressing, and with the mothers: heavily pregnant or with brand-new babies, they are the most vulnerable group on the streets.

In the second year, with the assistance of my daughter Rosa, a student of performing arts at the University of Middlesex, we were able to extend the workshops to the crèches set up by SAID for street and shanty town dwellers, and offer training to the staff.

The CAS group was mixed, boys and girls who attended the refuge regularly for education, medical care, crafts, table tennis, and television. We also journeyed to the outskirts of Accra to the rural training center where boys and girls tend crops and livestock, and learn to read and write and to make pottery.

We began with games and exercises. I rely heavily on the methods developed by Brazilian theater practitioner Augusto Boal. There are thirty or so languages current in Ghana, and few street children speak English. Social workers translated for us, but a Eurocentric approach would have been doomed.

An exploration of power relationships led to the recreation of a Ghanaian village structure, with a king, queen mother, and elders, all represented by chairs. A young man called Kwesi got up and turned over the king's stool. The room went quiet. I asked what it meant. He said simply, "The king is dead."

In small groups they shared their problems, decided what to dramatize, presented their frozen pictures. These were the seeds for the plays that explained why they were on the streets, how hard it was to survive there, plays about poverty and problems with parents and stepparents and pregnancy, about hygiene and HIV/AIDS.

Given the weight of fighting for such basic needs, and the complexity of the histories and personalities of the individuals they work with, it sometimes amazes me that SAID and CAS have made room for drama in their program. They have recognized its value in engaging and stimulating children and young people, helping them develop their creativity, their concentration, and confidence. Through drama they have learned to listen, to think about others' feelings, to work in a team. They have gained in articulacy and practiced problem solving, handled abstractions. They have told their stories truthfully, and with artistry, and understood that their predicament is not the result of inferiority or unworthiness. They have won respect from others and they have achieved a measure of self-respect. They have played. They have laughed. They have had fun, become children again.

Note

1. An exhibition of photographs of Ghanaian street children by Rik Walton, with text by Kathleen McCreery, is available for viewing at www.snaps.free-online.co.uk/ghana/ghana.html.

References

Beauchemin, Eric. 1999. *The Exodus, the Growing Migration of Children from Ghana's Rural Areas to the Urban Centres*. Accra, Ghana: Catholic Action for Street Children and UNICEF.

Butcher, Andy. 1996. *Street Children*. Milton Keynes: Nelson Word Ltd.

Ensor, Patrick. 2000. Remains of the Day. *The Guardian*, 12 Feb.

Information Services. n.d. *Ghana at a Glance*. Accra, Ghana: Information Services.

Judson, Keith, ed. 1994. *Streetlife: An Educational Resource for Secondary Schools About Street Children*. Guildford: Jubilee Action.

Save the Children. 1992. *Country Report, Brazil*. London: Save the Children.

Scheper-Hughes, Nancy and Daniel Hoffman. 1994. *Kids out of Place*. New York: North American Congress on Latin America Report.

Swift, Anthony. 1991. *Brazil: The Fight for Childhood in the City*. Florence: UNICEF.

U.S. Department of State. 1995. *Brazil Human Rights Practices, 1994*. Available at http://www.cpsr.org/cpsr/privacy/privacy_international/country_reports/State_Department_1994/Brazil.txt.

———. 1998. *Background Notes: Brazil, March 1998*. Available at http://www.state.gov/www/background_notes/brazil_0398_bgn.html.

————. 1999. *Country Commercial Guides, FY 1999: Brazil*. Available at http://www.state.gov/www/background_notes/brazil_0398_bgn.html.

Vidal, John. 1999. The Rising Tide That Nobody Can Hold Back. *The Guardian*, 22 Sept.

Walenciak, Joe. 2000. *Street Children Memorial Page*. Available at http://www.jbu.edu/business/sk-mem.html.

Wheat, Sue. 2000. Well Wishers. *The Guardian*, 22 Mar.

ANNALS, *AAPSS*, **575**, May 2001

The Sex Trade Industry's
Worldwide Exploitation of Children

By R. BARRI FLOWERS

ABSTRACT: The twenty-first century brings with it some of the dark realities of the last century with respect to the commercial sexual exploitation of children. Worldwide, untold numbers of children are being systematically deprived of their human rights, dignity, and childhood through child prostitution, child pornography, and other sexploitation. Many of these children are routinely subjected to rape, beatings, displacement, drug addiction, psychological abuse, and other trauma, including exposure to the AIDS virus and a life with no future. This study examines the current state of international trafficking of children and other child sexual exploitation. Child sex tourism plays a major role in the child sex trade as prostituted youths are routinely lured or abducted into sexual slavery and sex-for-profit. Other prostitution-involved girls and boys are at the whim of pimps, pornographers, and other sexual exploiters. The global exploitation of children continues to plague society, in spite of international efforts to combat the proliferation of the child sex trade industry. Organizations such as ECPAT remain committed to addressing the central issues pertaining to the prostituting and sexual exploitation of children.

R. Barri Flowers is a research criminologist and author. He has published 22 books, including Runaway Kids and Teenage Prostitution *(2001),* Sex Crimes, Predators, Perpetrators, Prostitutes, and Victims *(2001),* Domestic Crimes, Family Violence and Child Abuse *(2000),* The Prostitution of Women and Girls *(1998), and* The Victimization and Exploitation of Women and Children *(1994).*

I N the early part of the twenty-first century, the ongoing issue of worldwide commercial child sexploitation through child prostitution, child pornography, and a flourishing sex trade industry shows little sign of abating. The literature is replete with research addressing various aspects of this tragedy (Bracey 1979; ECPAT 1996; Ennew et al. 1996; Flowers forthcoming; Truong 1982; Weisberg 1985). Much of the focus has been on child sexual exploitation in Southeast Asia, especially Thailand and the Philippines (Ennew 1986; Leuchtag 1995), South Asia, and countries such as India, Nepal, and Sri Lanka (Barry 1995; Flowers 1998; Hodgson 1994), and in the West, including Australia, Canada, the United States, and Western Europe (Densen-Gerber and Hutchinson 1978; Flowers 1994; James 1980; Johnson 1992). Less attention has been paid to the significant sex trade industry and exploited children in other parts of the world, such as Latin America, Africa, and Eastern Europe (Ennew et al. 1996; Hornblower 1993; U.S. Department of Justice 1999). For example, recent years have seen an explosion in the child sex-for-sale market in Russia and other countries of the former Soviet bloc with the fall of Communism and rise of organized crime and poverty (Flowers 1998; Hornblower 1993; Leuchtag 1995).

In reality, there is still much that we do not know about the dimensions and dynamics of the world marketplace for child prostitution and child pornography. The very nature of the child sex trade, with its flesh peddling of minors by adults—sometimes in cooperation with the government or powerful organizations—makes it one that in many respects remains secretive, seedy, and hard to get accurate, conclusive information on. Yet there has been enough research and documentation to know that

the proliferation of the sex trade industry globally has resulted in an increase in the prostitution and sexual exploitation of children. Millions of children . . . are being targeted by flesh traders, pimps, gangs, organized crime syndicates, and promoters of tourism worldwide for a lucrative sex tourism business. . . . The growth of international prostitution is not only robbing its victims of innocence and any semblance of a normal life during or after prostitution but is also putting them at greater risk for exposure to crime, criminals, unfamiliar foreign countries and languages, and health problems, including the AIDS virus. (Flowers 1998, 176)

The gross violation of children's fundamental rights through commercial international sexual exploitation can be seen in every aspect of a sex industry that insists on profiting and benefiting through sexual gratification against those most vulnerable and least able to protect themselves (Melton 1991; Seng 1989; World Health Organization 1996). Only in continuing to address the crisis of prostituted children and other forms of child sexploitation and its impact on victims and society at large can we hope to avert an even greater tragedy.

INTERNATIONAL SCOPE OF CHILD SEXUAL EXPLOITATION

How big is the problem of child sexploitation globally? Many sources—including government and nongovernment organizations, researchers, and experts in the commercial sexual exploitation of children—have produced figures estimating its incidence and prevalence from country to country and internationally (Campagna and Poffenberger 1988; ECPAT 1996; Ennew et al. 1996; Flowers 1998; Smolenski 1995; U.S. Department of Justice 1999).

The clear indications are that the worldwide exploitation of children by the sex trade industry has reached numbers that merit serious attention and action, if not epidemic proportions. According to UNICEF, there are over 1 million child prostitutes in Asia alone (Flowers 1998). End Child Prostitution, Child Pornography and Trafficking of Children for Sexual Purposes (ECPAT) estimated that there are 800,000 child prostitutes in Thailand, 400,000 in India, and 60,000 in the Philippines (ECPAT 1996; Smolenski 1995). A 1991 conference of Southeast Asia women's groups reported that 30 million women and girls had been forced into prostitution since the mid-1970s (Leuchtag 1995).

Other figures on child prostitution are just as notable. Up to 500,000 children are being exploited in the sex trade industry in Brazil, while as many as 200,000 teenage prostitutes are plying their trade in Canada (Flowers 1998; Kotash 1994). In the United States, estimates of juvenile prostitutes range from the hundreds of thousands to 2 million selling their bodies on the streets (Flowers 1986, forthcoming; Smolenski 1995). Child sexual exploitation is also believed to be flourishing in Western Europe, Eastern Europe, and Africa (Flowers 1998; U.S. Department of Justice 1999).

Further examples of the global sexual exploitation of children were described in the ECPAT *Country Reports* (1996) and in the U.S. Department of Justice's *Prostitution of Children and Child Sex Tourism* (1999):

— In Cambodia, the Human Rights Vigilance reported that more than 3 in 10 sex workers in the country were between 13 and 17 years of age.
— In China, the *Peking People's Daily* reported that in Sichuan alone over 10,000 children and women are sold into sexual slavery annually.
— In Columbia, the Bogotá Chamber of Commerce recently reported that child prostitution had increased five times in the preceding seven years.
— In Sri Lanka, an estimated 100,000 minors age 6 to 14 are being prostituted in child brothels, with 5,000 other children selling sexual favors in child sex tourism areas of the country.
— In Johannesburg, South Africa, black and white juveniles are reported to be prostitution-

involved, while brothel prostitutes are often young females from Russia, Thailand, and Taiwan.

— In a 1995 *Asia Watch Report*, it was reported that around half of the 100,000 girl prostitutes working in Bombay came from Nepal. In Nepal, the number of girls under the age of 15 working for pimps or as brothel prostitutes was on the increase.

— In the 1995 *Human Rights Watch Report*, one in five brothel prostitutes in Bombay was reported to be a female under the age of 18.

— In Vietnam, as many as one in five prostitutes are under the age of 18. The rise in juvenile prostitution is attributed to a growing sex tourism industry in the country.

Given the wildly varying estimates, serious definitional and methodological differences, and a lack of worldwide studies, it is virtually impossible to measure the true global extent of the sexual exploitation of children (Ennew 1986; Flowers 1998; U.S. Department of Justice 1999). Many studies, for example, focus only on sexually exploited girls (James 1972; Newman and Caplan 1981); others focus on boy prostitutes (Cates 1989; Lloyd 1976; Snell 1995). There are other studies that do not sufficiently explain the differences between child prostitution and child sexual abuse (Joseph 1995). There are also differences in defining what constitutes a child or minor by age and in separating figures on children

from figures on adults in the sex trade industry (Ennew et al. 1996).

Most studies of child sexploitation focus mainly on child prostitution without adequately accounting for the global danger of child pornography and the correlation between the two through child sex rings and the trafficking of children (Flowers 1994; Smolenski 1995; U. S. Department of Justice 1999). There is also the issue of illegal versus legal use of children for purposes of sexual exploitation. For example, in some countries, child prostitution is technically legal, making it difficult to separate what is outlawed from what is tolerated (Flowers 1998; Goodall 1995; Leuchtag 1995; Miller 1995). Perhaps the greatest limitation in assessing the true measure of international child sexual exploitation is the lack of cooperation between countries and researchers in gathering and quantifying data.

CHILD SEX TOURISM

A major component of the international sexual exploitation of children is the child sex tourism industry, defined by the United Nations as "tourism organized with the primary purpose of facilitating the effecting of a commercial-sexual relationship with a child" (U.S. Department of Justice 1999, 32). Child sex tourism is particularly prominent in Thailand, the Philippines, and other countries in Southeast Asia. Between 6.2 percent and 8.7 percent of Thai females, for example, are estimated to be sex workers (Robinson 1993). Many of these prostitutes can earn up to 25 times the salaries of other occupations in Thailand. However, some are recruited from poor rural areas and become indentured sex slaves, supporting their entire families (Flowers 1998). In the Philippines, sex tourism and the trafficking of Filipino girls and women continue to be used to spur economic development, in spite of efforts to curb the practice (Smolenski 1995).

According to a report on child sex tourism in Southeast Asia, Americans account for the largest group of foreign tourists (*ECPAT Newsletter*, 1996). In data gathered from 1991 to 1996, of 240 tourists who sexually abused and exploited children in Asia in the prior seven years and faced arrest, imprisonment, deportation, or fled the country, around one-fourth were American child sex tourists. Other tourists came from Germany, Britain, Australia, France, and Japan. Most foreign tourists who sexually exploit children tend to travel from wealthy, economically developed Western nations to impoverished countries such as those in Southeast Asia with well-established and commercialized sex tourism industries (Smolenski 1995; U.S. Department of Justice 1999).

Aside from such notoriously recognized child sex tourism marketplaces as Thailand and the Philippines, other countries have also entered the sex tourism industry in recent years as a means to generate revenue, stimulate the economy, and exploit women and children by flesh peddling them to foreign or local businessmen with deep pockets. These include China, Vietnam, Cambodia, Indonesia, Brazil, the Dominican Republic (Flowers 1998), and countries in Africa, such as Zimbabwe, Nigeria, Kenya, and Ghana (ECPAT 1996; U.S. Department of Justice 1999).

GLOBAL CHILD PORNOGRAPHY

Untold numbers of children around the world are being sexually exploited through child pornography (Burgess 1984; Flowers 1998; Johnson 1992; O'Brien 1983; Smolenski 1995). Often referred to as "kiddie porn" and "child porn," child pornography includes photographs, magazines, books, videotapes, audiotapes, motion pictures, and images on Web sites on the Internet that depict children in sexually explicit acts with other children, adults, animals, and/or foreign objects (Flowers 1994; Tannahill 1980). Victims of child pornographers are subjected to many forms of sexual abuse, perversions, and exploitation such as rape, sadism, pedophilia, triolism, torture, and even murder (Flowers 1998). In many instances, child prostitutes are initiated into the sex trade by being coerced into performing pornographic sexual acts as a way to normalize prostitution and lower the child's resistance (Rickel and Hendren 1993). Other prostituted youths are enticed into entering the kiddie porn business as a way to make extra money or support drug habits (Flowers 1998; Johnson 1992). Some children are forced into child pornography by pimps and operators of child sex rings or child sex tourism, where they are turned into sex slaves (Burgess 1984; Burgess and Grant 1988; Flowers 2001).

Child pornography is, by most accounts, a multi-billion-dollar global enterprise. In Germany alone, estimated sales of child porn exceed $250 million, with the number of consumers ranging from 30,000 to 40,000 (Serrill 1993). The biggest market for child pornography is the United States, where an estimated $6 billion is generated annually (Flowers 1998). Eighty-five percent of the worldwide sales of child pornography comes from America. Each year, an estimated 30,000 children are sexually exploited by child pornographers in Los Angeles alone (Flowers 1990).

Many of the kiddie porn magazines and films are created outside the United States in countries such as Switzerland, Germany, Denmark, and Sweden. At least 264 different magazines depicting children in sexually explicit acts are produced and distributed in the United States each month (Flowers 1998; Freeman-Longo and Blanchard 1998). These can be produced for as little as 50 cents and are sold for 20 times as much (Flowers 1990).

The consumers of child pornography are predominantly male child molesters, pedophiles, and others with an abnormal sexual interest in children (Flowers 1994). Many of these child exploiters are involved in child sex rings. These can involve individual or multiple offenders and often multiple victims in child prostitution and child pornography (Burgess 1984). Syndicated child sex rings are in many cases international

in scope and highly organized in recruiting children, producing child pornography, delivering other sexual services, and maintaining a large customer base (Flowers 2001; Lanning 1992).

The use of the Internet by pornographers and other sexual exploiters of children has increased the globalization of child pornography and the child sex tourism industry, while making it more difficult for law enforcement authorities to track down perpetrators (Flowers 1998).

AIDS AND THE GLOBAL
CHILD SEX TRADE MARKET

Perhaps the most devastating and deadly risk that sexually exploited children face worldwide is exposure to the acquired immunodeficiency syndrome virus, known as AIDS (Flowers 1998; Plant 1990; U.S. Department of Justice 1999). It is unknown just how many prostituted children have been infected with HIV (the human immunodeficiency virus), the precursor to AIDS, but estimates suggest that the figure may well be in the millions. In Thailand, an estimated 50 percent of the girl prostitutes are HIV-positive (Robinson 1993). Young female prostitutes in Bombay are seen as the primary carrier of the AIDS virus and, as such, the most responsible for its spread throughout India (Friedman 1996). In Brazil, the correlation between underage prostitution, intravenous drug use, and poverty are blamed on the high rate of AIDS; Brazil ranks fourth in the world (Black, Collins, and Boroughs 1992). In Africa, which has the highest

AIDS rate, infection rates among young prostitutes are particularly high and are primarily related to unsafe sexual practices (Neequaye 1990; Rosenberg and Weiner 1988). By comparison, the high rate of HIV infection among underage prostitutes in Western Europe and the United States is thought to be the result of a combination of high-risk activities such as multiple partners, unprotected sex, substance abuse, and intravenous drug use (Flowers 1998; Rosenberg and Weiner 1988).

With the threat of AIDS, many international tourists and other johns favor young child prostitutes over adult prostitutes, believing the risk of infection is lower (Flowers 1998). Conversely, young girls and boys are actually more likely to become infected with AIDS due to their underdeveloped bodies, weaker immune systems, and greater susceptibility to injuries and lesions incurred during sexual relations (Hodgson 1994; Serrill 1993). Young prostitutes are also less likely than older prostitutes to be in a bargaining position to practice safe sex with resistant customers, thereby further increasing the risk to them and those they are having sex with for exposure to the AIDS virus (U.S. Department of Justice 1999). In some countries, sex with a minor is actually and fatally seen as a cure for AIDS (Ennew et al. 1996; Lee-Wright 1990).

OTHER CONSEQUENCES OF SEXUAL EXPLOITATION

Children who are victims of commercial sexual exploitation face a number of health and psychological hazards in addition to AIDS. The rate of sexually transmitted diseases such as herpes, chlamydia, crabs, gonorrhea, and syphilis is high among prostituted children worldwide (Flowers 1998; World Health Organization 1996). This is attributed in great measure to the limited or nonuse of condoms among underage prostitutes. Many girls involved in prostitution are at increased risk for other infectious diseases such as pelvic inflammatory disease (U.S. Department of Justice 1999). Pregnancy is also common among young female prostitutes, as is developing complications in giving birth (Widom and Kuhns 1996; World Health Organization 1996). In poorer countries, sexually exploited girls—including those abducted from other countries—are especially vulnerable to pregnancy and disease, due to lack of birth control or safe sex practices, language barriers, and poverty.

Sexually exploited children worldwide are prone to being raped, assaulted, robbed, and even killed (Flowers 1998; Volkonsky 1995). Many are runaways or have been thrown out of sexually, physically, or mentally abusive homes; they become dependent on alcohol or drugs as prostitutes, sex slaves, or other victims of the child sex trade (Flowers 1994, 1998; Harlan, Rodgers, and Slattery 1981; James 1980).

Child prostitutes and other sexually exploited children are also susceptible to a number of psychological effects such as severe depression, low self-esteem, post-traumatic stress disorder, and attempted suicide

(Flowers 2001; World Health Organization 1996).

FIGHTING FOR SEXUALLY EXPLOITED CHILDREN'S RIGHTS

In spite of the existing laws against the sexual exploitation of children in many countries, most countries fall far short in adequately reducing the problem. In fact, the global sex trade industry continues to flourish, and innocent young victims are brought into the marketplace every day. In some cases, the government either encourages the sexual exploitation of its children or looks the other way. There have been many efforts to address and respond to the issue of child sexploitation, some more successful than others. ECPAT was one of the first organizations formed to combat the international child sex trade industry. It began with three Asian-based Christian groups and has since become a worldwide leader in attempting to end child prostitution and sexual exploitation with an extensive network of connections with other influential organizations. ECPAT has played an important role in strengthening the prostitution laws in many countries (ECPAT 1996; Smolenski 1995).

One of the more prominent international responses in recent years to protecting children from sexual exploitation and misuse has been the 1989 U.N. Convention on the Rights of the Child (CRC). Currently ratified by 191 countries, including the United States, the CRC strongly condemns the sexual exploitation of children through prostitution or other illegal sexual practices (Flowers 1998; U.S. Department of Justice 1999).

Another important initiative in developing global strategies to fight child sex tourism and other child sexploitation came in 1996 when the First World Congress Against Commercial Sexual Exploitation of Children took place in Stockholm, Sweden. The congress called on governments worldwide to coordinate efforts to stop the commercial sexual exploitation of children in all capacities. Delegates from more than 120 countries vowed to cooperate in stiffening criminal sanctions against child sexual exploiters—including pimps, child sex tourist operators, pedophiles, and customers—while assisting sexually exploited child victims (Flowers 1998).

Other notable efforts at attacking the sexual exploitation of children include the Task Force to End Sexual Exploitation in Thailand, which represents 24 government and private agencies, and the Programme for Action for the Prevention of the Sale of Children, Child Prostitution, and Child Pornography, which was adopted in 1992 by the U.N. Commission on Human Rights (U.S. Department of Justice 1999).

These actions notwithstanding, global commercial child sexual exploitation by the sex trade industry continues to proliferate almost unabated. Flesh peddlers, pornographers, and promoters of child sex—along with an insatiable market of child tourists and international clients—are taking away the freedom and violating the rights of those children victimized. Aside from the fundamental issues, many sexually exploited children face diseases such as AIDS and numerous other health problems that they are ill equipped to deal with. Prostituted youth are routinely raped and abused and sometimes killed. Many sexually exploited children are kept drugged as sex slaves or dependent on alcohol or drugs as a means of physical and psychological control. Most prostitution-involved girls are at high risk for pregnancy, inflammatory disease, and other complications related directly to their sexual exploitation.

While we cannot know for certain precisely how many children are currently being exploited by the international sex trade industry, even conservative estimates from many countries suggest that the problem is one that is likely affecting hundreds of thousands and, quite possibly, millions of children around the world.

Much of this can be attributed to the global child sex tourism industry and its ability to lure vulnerable children into its web of commercial sexual exploitation and a steady clientele attracted to the pool of young, obedient children. Contributing to the problem is the worldwide child pornography business and its peddling of children through syndicated child sex rings, kiddie porn, prostitution services, and the Internet.

However, as bleak as this may seem, the problem of child sexual exploitation is not a lost cause. Organizations such as ECPAT continue to be dedicated to combating such commercial sexual misuse of children. Further, today there is greater recognition across the spectrum that the problem exists on a global basis, encouraging more cooperation between nations in addressing the issues pertaining to the sexual exploitation of children as part of the overall discussion on human rights.

References

Barry, Kathleen. 1995. *The Prostitution of Sexuality.* New York: New York University Press.

Black, Robert F., Sara Collins, and Don L. Boroughs. 1992. Shooting Up the Future. *U.S. News & World Report* 113(27 July):55.

Bracey, Dorothy H. 1979. *"Baby-Pros": Preliminary Profiles of Juvenile Prostitutes.* New York: John Jay Press.

Burgess, Ann W. 1984. *Child Pornography and Sex Rings.* Lexington, MA: Lexington Books.

Burgess, Ann W. and Christine A. Grant. 1988. *Children Traumatized in Sex Rings.* Arlington, VA: National Center for Missing & Exploited Children.

Campagna, Daniel and Donald Poffenberger. 1988. *The Sexual Trafficking in Children.* Westport, CT: Auburn House.

Cates, Jim A. 1989. Adolescent Male Prostitution by Choice. *Child and Adolescent Social Work* 6:151-55.

Densen-Gerber, Judianne and S. F. Hutchinson. 1978. Medical-Legal and Societal Problems Involving Children— Child Prostitution, Child Pornography, and Drug-Related Abuse: Recommended Legislation. In *The Maltreatment of Children*, ed. Selwyn M. Smith. Baltimore, MD: University Park Press.

ECPAT Newsletter. 1996. The Paedo File. Presented at ECPAT International, Aug., Bangkok, Thailand.

End Child Prostitution, Child Pornography and Trafficking of Children for Sexual Purposes (ECPAT). 1996. *Country Reports,* Aug. Available at http://www.rb.selecpat/country.htm.

Ennew, Judith. 1986. *The Sexual Exploitation of Children*. Cambridge: Polity Press.

Ennew, Judith, Kusum Gopal, Janet Heeran, and Heather Montgomery. 1996. *Children and Prostitution: How Can We Measure and Monitor the Commercial Sexual Exploitation of Children?* 2d ed. New York: UNICEF.

Flowers, R. Barri. 1986. *Children and Criminality: The Child as Victim and Perpetrator*. Westport, CT: Greenwood Press.

———. 1990. *The Adolescent Criminal: An Examination of Today's Juvenile Offender*. Jefferson, NC: McFarland.

———. 1994. *The Victimization and Exploitation of Women and Children: A Study of Physical, Mental and Sexual Maltreatment in the United States*. Jefferson, NC: McFarland.

———. 1998. *The Prostitution of Women and Girls*. Jefferson, NC: McFarland.

———. 2001. *Sex Crimes, Predators, Perpetrators, Prostitution, and Victims: An Examination of Sexual Criminality in America*. Springfield, IL: Charles C Thomas.

———. Forthcoming. *Runaway Kids and Teenage Prostitution*. Westport, CT: Greenwood.

Freeman-Longo, Robert E. and Geral T. Blanchard. 1998. *Sexual Abuse in America: Epidemic of the 21st Century*. Brandon, VT: Safer Society Press.

Friedman, Robert I. 1996. India's Shame: Sexual Slavery and Political Corruption Are Leading to an AIDS Catastrophe. *The Nation* 262:12.

Goodall, Richard. 1995. *The Comfort of Sin: Prostitutes and Prostitution in the 1990s*. Kent: Renaissance Books.

Harlan, Sparky, Luanne L. Rodgers, and Brian Slattery. 1981. *Male and Female Adolescent Prostitution: Huckleberry House Sexual Minority Youth Services Project*. Washington, DC: U.S. Department of Health and Human Services.

Hodgson, Douglas. 1994. Sex Tourism and Child Prostitution in Asia: Legal Responses and Strategies. *Melbourne University Law Review* 19:512-15.

Hornblower, Margaret. 1993. The Skin Trade. *Time* 141(21 June):44-45.

James, Jennifer. 1972. Two Domains of Streetwalker Argot. *Anthropological Linguistics* 14:174-75.

———. 1980. *Entrance into Juvenile Prostitution*. Washington, DC: National Institute of Mental Health.

Johnson, Joan J. 1992. *Teen Prostitution*. Danbury, CT: Franklin Watts.

Joseph, Cathy. 1995. Scarlet Wounding: Issues of Child Prostitution. *Journal of Psychohistory* 23(1):2-17.

Kotash, Myrna. 1994. Surviving the Streets. *Chatelaine* 67:103-7.

Lanning, Kenneth V. 1992. *Child Sex Rings: A Behavioral Analysis*. Alexandria, VA: National Center for Missing & Exploited Children.

Lee-Wright, Peter. 1990. *Child Slaves*. London: Earthscan.

Leuchtag, Alice. 1995. Merchants of Flesh: International Prostitution and the War on Women's Rights. *The Humanist* 55(2):11-16.

Lloyd, Robin. 1976. *For Money or Love: Boy Prostitution in America*. New York: Vanguard.

Melton, G. B. 1991. Preserving the Dignity of Children Around the World. *Child Abuse and Neglect* 15:343-50.

Miller, Laura. 1995. Prostitution. *Harper's Bazaar* 3400(March):208-10.

Neequaye, Alfred. 1990. Prostitution in Accra. In *AIDS, Drugs, and Prostitution*, ed. Martin A. Plant. London: Routledge.

Newman, Frances and Paula J. Caplan. 1981. Juvenile Female prostitution as a Gender Consistent Response to Early Deprivation. *International Journal of Women's Studies* 5(2): 128-37.

O'Brien, Shirley. 1983. *Child Pornography*. Dubuque, IA: Kendall/Hunt.

Plant, Martin A. 1990. *AIDS, Drugs, and Prostitution*. London: Routledge.

Rickel, Annette U. and Marie C. Hendren. 1993. Aberrant Sexual Experiences. In *Adolsecent Sexuality*, ed. Thomas P. Gullotta, Gerald R. Adams, and Raymond Montemayor. Newbury Park, CA: Sage.

Robinson, Lillian S. 1993. Touring Thailand's Sex Industry. *The Nation* 257:494-96.

Rosenberg, M. J. and J. M. Weiner. 1988. Prostitutes and AIDS: A Health Department Priority. *American Journal of Public Health* 78:418-23.

Seng, Magnus J. 1989. Child Sexual Abuse and Adolescent Prostitution: A Comparative Analysis. *Adolescence* 24:665-71.

Serrill, Michael S. 1993. Defiling the Children. *Time* 141:52-54.

Smolenski, Carol. 1995. Sex Tourism and the Sexual Exploitation of Children. *Christian Century* 112:1079-80.

Snell, C. L. 1995. *Young Men in the Street: Help-Seeking Behavior of Young Male Prostitutes*. Westport, CT: Praeger.

Tannahill, Reay. 1980. *Sex in History*. New York: Stein and Day.

Truong, T. D. 1982. The Dynamics of Sex Tourism. *Development and Change* 14(4):533-53.

U.S. Department of Justice. 1999. *Prostitution of Children and Child Sex Tourism: An Analysis of Domestic and International Responses*. Alexandria, VA: National Center for Missing & Exploited Children.

Volkonsky, Anastasia. 1995. Legalizing the "Profession" Would Sanction the Abuse. *Insight on the News* 11:20-22.

Weisberg, D. Kelly. 1985. *Children of the Night: A Study of Adolescent Prostitution*. Lexington, MA: Lexington Books.

Widom, Cathy S. and Joseph B. Kuhns. 1996. Childhood Victimization and Subsequent Risk for Promiscuity, Prostitution and Teenage Pregnancy: A Prospective Study. *American Journal of Public Health* 86:1607-10.

World Health Organization. 1996. Commercial Sexual Exploitation of Children: The Health and Psychological Dimensions. Paper presented at the World Congress Against Commercial Sexual Exploitation of Children, Aug., Stockholm.

ANNALS, *AAPSS*, **575**, May 2001

Challenging Child Labor: Transnational Activism and India's Carpet Industry

By GEETA CHOWDHRY and MARK BEEMAN

ABSTRACT: Transnational movements have become an important component of an emerging and relatively recently theorized transnational civil society in the field of international relations. Nongovernmental organizations, social movements, and social activists concerned with the global issues of poverty, environment, and human rights have created an intellectual and political global space outside the national territorial space to give voice to their concerns on issues of transnational importance. This article examines transnational human rights movement around the issue of child labor in the carpet industry in India. Although the intersection of child labor with the carpet trade from India was utilized effectively by Indian and German activists to bring about changes in child labor use, the more foundational impact has been the creation of Rugmark, a label that certifies child-labor-free carpets and provides services for the rehabilitation and education of children involved in the carpet industry.

Geeta Chowdhry is associate professor in the Department of Political Science and co-ordinator of Asian Studies at Northern Arizona University.

Mark Beeman is associate professor in the Department of Sociology and Social Work at Northern Arizona University.

ALTHOUGH the discourse on universal human rights has claimed universal appeal and applicability, it is only as recently as 1989 that the Convention on the Rights of the Child was adopted by the United Nations.[1] However, the enforceability of this convention, like many other U.N. conventions, remains problematic as evidenced by the prevalence of child labor in many parts of the world. Transnational human rights groups have been active in their efforts to eradicate child labor and have recently sought to bring publicity to the continued use of child labor through a number of tactics, including exposing the practices of multinational corporations using child labor in other countries and organizing a global march against child labor in June 1998. In addition, many domestic social activists have worked with transnational human rights groups to eradicate child labor in their home countries.[2] For example, transnational social activists from India and Germany have made a concerted effort against the use of child labor in the carpet industry in South Asia. This effort has culminated in Rugmark, a label that identifies child-labor-free carpets. This article seeks to examine the role played by transnational social movements and international trade in the creation of Rugmark and the successes and failures that have marked this effort.

Much of the popular discourse on human rights focuses on the West pressuring developing countries to accept its interpretation of human rights. Indeed, the idea of human rights has been used as a tool to enforce the competitive advantage of Western-based corporations. This article focuses on two themes. First, we will examine a case study where the human rights initiative comes from activists in a developing society, after which coalitions are formed with Western activists, each realizing their own societies share some responsibility in addressing child labor. Second, this case illuminates how child labor intersects with trade and how social movements can utilize international trade to bring about changes in child labor use.

TRANSNATIONAL ACTIVISM
AND SOCIAL CHANGE

Transnational movements have proliferated in recent years, with more than 60 percent of active organizations being formed after 1970 and a large percentage having a human rights focus (Smith 1997). Although transnational movements can be traced to the latter half of the nineteenth century (Keck and Sikkink 1998; Boulding 1997), transnational social movements have only recently become an important component of an emerging and relatively recently theorized transnational civil society in the field of international relations. The preoccupation of mainstream international relations theorists, particularly realists, with traditional notions of security reifies the state as the dominant actor in international relations. In addition, the arbitrary separation of the international from the domestic has created artificial dichotomies of outside and inside, with the outside focusing only on international relations and the inside focusing only on domestic ones. However, as pointed out by many scholars, domestic and international relations are often interconnected, and a substantial literature has developed on the domestic influences of foreign policy and vice versa (Walker 1993). In the past, relatively few scholars have explored the "liminal space that cuts across inside/outside, a space that is neither within the state nor an aspect of the international state system but [that] animates both" (Rudolph 1997, 1).[3] More recent scholarship on transboundary activism has attempted to fill this vacuum and occupy what Rudolph has called the "cross-cutting arena" of the inside/outside (Haas 1992; Brysk 1993; Sikkink 1993; Smith, Chatfield, and Pagnucco 1997; Keck and Sikkink 1998; Smith, Pagnucco, and Lopez 1998).

Despite the nuanced differences in the scholarly understandings of this phenomenon, as evidenced by the range of terms used—epistemic communities (Haas 1992), transnational social movements (Smith, Chatfield, and Pagnucco 1997), and transnational advocacy networks (Keck and Sikkink 1998)—there is much in common between them. In general, these scholars agree that nongovernmental organizations, social movements, and social activists concerned with global issues of democratization, poverty, environment, and human rights have created an intellectual and political global space, outside the national territorial space, to give voice to their concerns on issues of transnational importance. They have also organized across national borders to lobby and

pressure nations and intergovernmental organizations like the United Nations to put an end to abusive practices. However, Smith, Chatfield, and Pagnucco (1997) caution us from including all types of international nongovernmental organizations (INGOs) in this category. For these authors, the distinction between most INGOs and ones that are transnational social movements is telling. Whereas the former, like the Trilateral Commission, are status quo organizations seeking to preserve the current distribution of power in the international state system, the latter, like Greenpeace, "seek to bring about change in the status quo" (12) and work toward changing "some elements of the social structure and/or reward distribution of society" (McCarthy and Zald, quoted in Smith, Chatfield, and Pagnucco 1997, 12). This definition implies that transnational social movements are those INGOs that have a progressively radical agenda. However, not all the changes sought by transnational social movements are progressive, as evidenced by some stances of groups like Greenpeace or various transnational religious movements.[4]

Keck and Sikkink (1998) also distinguish between different types of transnational activity. They use a motivation criteria to distinguish between three categories of transnationalism: the instrumental motivations of actors promoting transnational capital flows, such as multinational corporations and banks; those that are motivated by "shared causal ideas, such as scientific groups or epistemic communities";[5] and transnational advocacy networks that are motivated by agreed-on norms, "shared principled ideas or values" (30).[6] For Keck and Sikkink, transnational advocacy networks are distinct from international financial institutions and other similar organizations whose goal is linked to the internationalization of capital. Transnational advocacy networks are also distinct from epistemic communities that rely extensively on scientific truths to guide their work. On the contrary, transnational social movements are norm driven; that is, they converge around shared understandings of values and issues. A related premise is that these shared norms and their subsequent advocacy and practice by transnational social movements challenge state action and may lead to state initiatives for policy change.

Practices do not simply echo norms—they make them real. Without the disruptive activity of these actors neither normative change nor changes in practice is likely to occur. States and other targets of network activity resist making explicit definitions of "right" and "wrong," and overcoming this resistance is central to network strategies. (Keck and Sikkink 1998, 35)

However, implicit in this literature is that human rights violations become associated with norm-violating states. Risse, Ropp, and Sikkink (1999) explicitly make this observation. They argue that transnational networks "put norm-violating states on the international agenda in terms of moral consciousness-raising. In doing so, they also remind liberal states of their own identity as promoters of human rights" (5). Indeed, none of the case studies of human rights violations presented by Risse, Ropp, and Sikkink are Western countries; African, Latin American, Southeast Asian, and Eastern European countries are examined. Unfortunately, the notion that human rights is an issue of a liberal state versus a norm-violating state reinforces the stereotypical division of the world into modern (Western) and traditional (non-Western) societies. Indeed, Risse, Ropp, and Sikkink define the global human rights polity as human rights regimes, human rights INGOs, and Western states.[7]

While we agree with Risse, Ropp, and Sikkink (1999) that the role of transnational networks in advancing human rights is crucial, it is too simplistic to present human rights violations as a problem confined to norm-violating states. First, this approach ignores the complicity of Western states in some human rights violations. Second, by defining norm violation solely in terms of states, one underestimates the role of the private sector in human rights violations. Third, the liberal/norm-violating dichotomy essentially overlooks developing societies that may enact significant human rights legislation without arm twisting by Western powers.[8]

In this article, we focus on the case of child labor in the Indian carpet industry and the development of Rugmark. In this case, the state's failure to enact anti-child-labor legislation was not the issue. Norm compliance was a significant factor, but more relevant than changing the norms of the state was to bring an industry into compliance with existing state law. Transnational activism was the crucial element in bringing about significant change, but it had less to do with pressure from Western states than from grassroots organizations that affected economic trade.

OUTLAWING CHILD LABOR

Both international legislation and Indian law have contributed to changes in the use of child labor in India.

International legislation on child labor

The International Labor Organization (ILO) and the United Nations have played a critical role in the development of international law regarding children. International child labor laws have been developed under the umbrella of human rights. The ILO was the first international institution to develop and adopt a convention regarding child labor; Convention No. 5 was adopted by the ILO in 1919. It established 14 years as the minimum age for working in an industry (Byrne 1998). Since then, the ILO has adopted nine additional conventions regarding minimum age for work in different sectors. The following are a few critical landmarks regarding child labor laws in the ILO. The Minimum Age Convention adopted by the ILO in 1973, formally known as ILO Convention No. 138, replaces previous conventions on minimum age and requires member states to establish minimum age laws for various sectors of the economy. It sets the general minimum age at 15 years but provides an exception clause for countries with "insufficiently developed economies" that can set the minimum age at 14 years. However, children under the age of 18 are prohibited from working in industries that are deemed hazardous to the "health, safety and morals of young persons" (Cox 1999). A global technical program called the International Program for the Elimination of Child Labor was established by the ILO in 1992. It assists member states in eliminating child labor worldwide (Mishra 2000). On 17 June 1999, the ILO adopted Convention No. 182, the "Recommendation Concerning the Prohibition and Immediate Action for the Elimination of the Worst Forms of Child Labor." This instrument has raised the minimum age limit for child labor to 18 years. It seeks to prohibit bonded child labor; sexual abuse, pornography, and prostitution of children; child drug trafficking; and child labor in other hazardous industries. It also targets parental poverty, the special problems of female children, and resource availability in the struggle to eradicate child labor.

The 1948 U.N. Universal Declaration of Human Rights (UDHR) is the broad umbrella under which legislation regarding specific human rights is developed in international law. Two international covenants, collectively called the International Bill of Rights, emerged from UDHR, focusing on civil and political rights as well as on economic, social, and cultural rights. It is under the latter covenant that children's rights get recognition in the United Nations. The

International Covenant on Economic, Social and Cultural Rights adopted by the United Nations in 1966 has several articles that are relevant to child labor: the right to an education, the right to be free from hunger, and the right to protection from economic and social exploitation. In addition, Article 10 also recommends that states should set minimum age laws that prevent children from working in industries that are hazardous to their health, safety, and morality. However, it is not a legally binding document. The 1989 Convention on the Rights of a Child is the first legally binding international convention to encompass the full range of human rights for children; "child" is defined here as every human being under the age of 18. This convention seeks to protect the economic, political, social, and cultural rights of children. Of particular importance is Article 32.1, which seeks to protect children from economic exploitation through the provision of minimum age(s) of employment (Article 32.2.a), through the regulation of hours and conditions of employment (Article 32.2.b), and through the provision by nations for appropriate penalties or other sanctions to ensure the effective enforcement of this article (Article 32.2.c). Children are also protected under this convention from sexual exploitation (Article 34); from abduction, sale, and trafficking (Article 35); and from all other forms of exploitation prejudicial to the child's welfare (Article 36) (United Nations 1989).

The success of international law in promoting national law in a type of norm-osmosis cannot be denied. For example, the 1989 Convention on the Rights of the Child is the most signed and ratified convention in the history of human rights; only two nations, the United States and Somalia, have not ratified the convention, and Somalia is not a signatory as well. However, despite the success of the numerous conventions that address children's human rights, poor children around the world continue to be exploited and are becoming a dominant part of the world's poor and displaced, pointing to the limits of legislative influence. Hence it is argued that even though international law seeks to legislate child labor out of the international political economy, the silence of international law on the amelioration of poverty, corporate behavior, and its imbrication in child labor practices limits its ability to ban child labor.

Child labor legislation and carpet industry in India

Child labor legislation in independent India is grounded in the constitution enacted in 1949.[9] Article 24 of the Indian Constitution prohibits the employment of children in factories and mines and in other hazardous occupations.[10] Article 39 of the Indian Constitution directs the state to protect the safety and morals of workers and children. Article 23 bans bonded labor or any other form of slavery or traffic in human beings. In addition, the Bonded Labor System Abolition Act (1976) outlawed bonded labor, and the Child Labor (Prohibition and Regulation) Act of 1986 provides further restrictions on the use of child labor, including regulating the hours and conditions of work for children under the age of 14 years. However, it does prohibit the use of child labor in 25 hazardous industries (Tucker 1997; Mishra 2000).[11] The carpet industry is listed as one in which the use of child labor is prohibited by the Indian government.

In this case, unlike the formula of developing nations being pressured by Western societies to adopt more progressive human rights legislation, child protective legislation was adopted in India's first independent constitution. Other legislation, for example, the 1989 Convention on the Rights of a Child, has been signed and ratified by India but has yet to be ratified by the United States. In addition, some significant child labor legislation in India preceded similar international legislation. For example, Indian legislation banning the worst forms of child labor in hazardous industries predates similar legislation in the ILO. However, similar to the international legislation on child labor, Indian legislation on child labor fails to legislate child labor out of the Indian economy and society, including the carpet industry. Consequently, although the incidence of child labor in the Indian carpet industry is on the decline, in the 1990s there were still over 300,000 children employed in the handwoven carpet industry in India (Dutt 1995; McDonald 1992; Mehta 1994; Juyal 1993).

BACKGROUND OF THE
CARPET INDUSTRY IN INDIA

Most historians' and popular accounts of the carpet industry in India date the beginning of the industry to the sixteenth century when the Mughal emperor brought Persian carpet weavers to India and set up a carpet workshop in the royal palace.[12] Although the Mughal King Akbar is credited with the introduction of pile carpets into India, his son Jehangir and grandson Shah Jehan are hailed as the Mughal emperors who brought the art of Indian carpet making to its current prominence (Waziri 1986; Saraf 1986; Juyal 1993). Many of the carpets produced during the reign of Shah Jehan are housed in the Victoria and Albert Museum in London and in other museums across Europe, including a few in the Jaipur museum in India (Saraf 1986).

It is said that during the first war of Indian independence, listed as the Indian Mutiny of 1857 by the British, a number of carpet weavers fled Akbarabad, now known as Agra, in the state of Uttar Pradesh, and sought refuge in the villages of Madhosingh-Ghosia, which are located between Mirzapur and Badohi, in eastern Uttar Pradesh, on the Grand Trunk road.[13] To survive, the weavers started carpet manufacturing on a very small scale in this area. In the late nineteenth century, this industry came to the attention of a Mr. Brownford, a Britisher, who established E. Hill and Company in the village of Khamaria. It was soon followed by the creation of H. Tellary in Badohi and Obeetee in Mirzapur (Waziri 1986).[14] It is important to note that other British firms, like the East India Company, Mitchel and Company, and Hadow and Company, were also involved in the procuring and trading of carpets in the states of Uttar Pradesh, Punjab, and Kashmir.[15] However, Mirzapur-Badohi soon acquired a prominent position in the handmade carpet industry both nationally and internationally. Currently, according to Juyal (1993),

if India shares about 14-18 percent of the global market in carpet/rugs, with a turnover of US, \$2000 million annually, Mirzapur Badohi alone accounts for about 85-90% of the total value exported from India and nearly 75% of the loomage. . . . the Indian carpet industry has become almost synonymous with what is commonly known as the Mirzapur-Badohi carpet belt. (13)

International trade
and the carpet industry

Although the carpet industry traditionally used family labor, using children as apprentices in the making of carpets, the nature of the industry has changed dramatically since colonization. A successful exposition of Indian carpets at the Great London Exposition of 1851 made the Indian carpet industry attractive to British companies. Subsequently, as noted previously, many British companies invested in the carpet industry in India. Not only did the discovery of the carpet industry by British companies integrate carpet making in India with international trade, but in so doing, it changed the nature of the carpet industry. Although commercialization and internationalization of the carpet industry invigorated carpet production, it also led to a transfer of control in the making of carpets from local artisans and weavers to British merchant traders.

Western markets and Western tastes became increasingly influential in carpet production, leading to the decline in quality of Indian carpets (Juyal 1993). Further, this increased the exploitation of carpet weavers. Since then, the carpet industry has been one of the major sources of export from India, and control of carpet production continues to remain in the hands of merchant traders, who are now mostly Indians (Juyal 1993).

The carpet industry is one of the most lucrative export industries in India. The Indian carpet export industry cornered a large chunk of the export market in 1974 when the Iranian carpet industry was facing a crisis.[16] The Iranian revolution of 1979, which increased the regulation of exports combined with the closure of U.S. markets to Iranian carpets, further increased the proportion of the global market held by Indian carpets. Although Iran retains the largest share in the world markets, China and India are competing to secure the next largest share. Table 1 shows the major suppliers of hand-knotted carpets in the world and their market shares.

The carpet industry is one of the main sources of Indian exports. Export earnings from the sale of Indian carpets has been increasing from U.S.\$316.13 million in 1993-94 to U.S.\$478.68 million in 1998-99, an increase of about 51 percent. Germany and the United States accounted for approximately 68 percent of these exports. In 1980 and 1986, Germany accounted for 37.3 percent and 36.1 percent and the United States accounted for 20.7

TABLE 1
MAJOR SUPPLIERS OF HAND-KNOTTED CARPETS
AND THEIR SHARE IN THE WORLD MARKET

Country	1980	1994	1995	1996	1997	1998
World	2,137.30	2,214.30	2,181.11	2,169.56	2,164.76	2,126.88
	(100)	(100)	(100)	(100)	(100)	(100)
Iran	592.90	631.07	599.80	582.31	577.10	580.18
	(27.7)	(28.5)	(27.0)	(26.9)	(26.6)	(26.8)
China	397.60	414.07	412.23	400.48	399.19	393.34
	(18.6)	(18.9)	(18.9)	(18.5)	(18.4)	(18.4)
India	395.50	431.78	405.69	389.65	381.73	380.37
	(18.5)	(19.5)	(18.6)	(18.0)	(17.59)	(17.5)
Nepal	228.20	274.78	239.92	233.79	227.80	212.16
	(10.7)	(12.5)	(11.0)	(10.8)	(10.5)	(9.8)
Pakistan	157.70	163.85	150.50	147.20	141.20	136.39
	(7.3)	(7.4)	(6.9)	(6.8)	(6.5)	(6.4)
Turkey	119.80	115.14	130.87	109.58	108.98	108.46
	(5.6)	(5.2)	(6.0)	(5.06)	(5.02)	(5.01)

SOURCE: Carpet Export Promotion Council.
NOTE: In millions of U.S. dollars and percentage share (in parentheses).

percent and 21.0 percent, respectively, of the total value of Indian exports. However, in 1998-99, the United States accounted for 40.95 percent and Germany accounted for 27.73 percent of the total value of exports (Juyal 1993; Chadha 2000).[17]

Child labor in the carpet industry

In India, the use of child labor is banned in 25 hazardous industries, including the carpet industry. However, child labor continues to be utilized in the carpet industry in India. Official statistics citing an independent survey taken by the National Council of Applied and Economic Research, as shown in Table 2, claim that child labor is on the decline. However, unofficial statistics state that about 300,000 children continue to be employed in the carpet industry in India (Tucker 1997). Child labor includes local and migrant child labor. Local and migrant child labor can be family child labor, wage labor, or bonded labor. Based on some village studies, it appears that child labor in the carpet industry largely comes from the lower castes and that severely impoverished districts provide a large share of the migrant and bonded child labor (Juyal 1993).

Child labor in the carpet industry is used in preprocessing, weaving, finishing activities, washing, and dyeing.[18] However, nearly 80 percent of children are used for weaving (Juyal 1987). The argument of children's "nimble fingers" has often been used to explain the demand for child labor for weaving carpets. Proclaiming the mythical nature of this argument, activists have argued that the small wages—or no wages—paid to children better account for their demand in the carpet industry.

TABLE 2
CHILD LABOR (CL) IN THE CARPET INDUSTRY

Year	CL as a Percentage of Total Weavers	Legal Family CL as a Percentage of Total CL	Illegally Hired CL as a Percentage of Total CL
1992	8	4.4	3.6
1994	7.5	4.8	2.7
1997	5.1	3.9	1.2

SOURCE: National Council of Applied and Economic Research cited in Misra 1999.

Many carpet manufacturers argue that the decentralized and cottage nature of the carpet industry prevents any kind of monitoring by them; loom owners in the villages and in their own houses can use child labor without the knowledge of manufacturers and traders. However, according to Juyal (1993), this picture is seriously misleading. First, the carpet industry has always had an organized sector in which processes other than weaving have occurred, and recently, factories have also incorporated weaving itself. Second, since the process of production is based on export market demand, the process is highly controlled, with contractors, subcontractors, and intermediaries being hired to deliver the goods. Third, Juyal suggests that the unorganized sector of the carpet industry was introduced by merchant traders to undercut the demands of organized labor in the industry.

TRANSNATIONAL ACTIVISM
AND THE CREATION
OF RUGMARK

The use of child labor in the carpet industry was challenged initially by social activists in India. Subsequently, recognizing the export nature of this industry, these activists worked with human rights groups from Germany and the United States to launch a consumer campaign against the use of child labor in the carpet industry.

In India, Bandhua Mukti Morcha (Bonded Labor Liberation Front, or the BLLF) was initially involved in the campaign to free bonded labor from the Indian carpet industry. Kailash Satyarthi and Swami Agnivesh were two of the prominent social activists involved with the BLLF. On 30 March 1984, 30 bonded children were rescued by the BLLF from the village of Bilwaria in Mirzapur district. Interviews with the children revealed that labor suppliers had obtained these children from village Chichori in the Palamau district in Bihar, which is extremely poor and often serves as the labor catchment area for bonded labor. Many more such raids were conducted by the BLLF, and these raids were brought to the attention of the media and the Indian legal system. Subsequently, Prembhai, a social activist, was appointed by the Supreme Court of India as the commissioner to investigate the incidence of child labor in the carpet industry. Prembhai's interviews with child laborers established that after the initial payment of 500 rupees, many children had not received any money and were coerced into doing free work. Although the work of the BLLF was invaluable in the freeing children in bonded labor, Satyarthi (1999) said that it was also disheartening to see other children take the place of those who were freed.[19]

In 1986, Satyarthi and others founded the South Asian Coalition on Child Servitude (SACCS), a coalition of 65 South Asian organizations, including the BLLF, dedicated to the eradication of child labor in South Asia. Currently, SACCS has over 400 organizations as its members and has been involved in the Global March Against Child Labor and the Liberation for Education, Education for Liberation campaign.

Given the prevalence of child labor and the growing demand for Indian carpets in the West, particularly in Germany, Satyarthi sought the help of German nongovernmental organizations to launch a consumer campaign in Germany against the employment of child labor in the carpet industry in India. In May 1990, Satyarthi addressed human rights organizations in Germany seeking to build transnational coalitions for the eradication of child labor in the carpet industry in India (Satyarthi 1992). Subsequently, Satyarthi, with the church-based human rights groups Bread for the World, Terre des Hommes, and Misereor, launched the Campaign Against Child Labor. Terre des Hommes in Germany, like its international body, had been involved with child labor issues for 30 years (Kuppers 2000, 1). Bread for

the World is a Protestant agency that works toward the eradication of poverty and hunger in the world. Misereor is a Catholic agency involved in international aid work. In addition, the Federal Association of Oriental Carpet Importers (Germany), the German Trade Union Association, and the Association for the Protection of Children (Kinderschutzbund) also assisted in advocacy work (Brandstater 1991).

In some cases, the activism of the Campaign Against Child Labor necessitated a significant change of position by major players in the coalition. For example, according to Satyarthi, the initial response of Bread for the World was not encouraging. Bread for the World had defined its goals as eradicating poverty and hunger as an international donor agency. Its initial assessment of the grassroots strategy for addressing child labor was a reluctance to become involved in political causes. Ultimately, the coalition realized that to be effective it must also pursue a political strategy. Armed with data about the prevalence of child labor in the carpet industry, Satyarthi met with national organizations that then mobilized their local church groups. As consumers, church group members asked carpet dealers, including department stores, for child-labor-free carpets, and they refused to buy the merchandise on hand (Puetter 2000). Further, these groups invited journalists to their meetings, and "as small children in slavery is bad enough to be news," the media responded with extensive coverage of child labor in the carpet industry in India (Kuppers 2000, 1).

Initially, many Indian carpet manufacturers and German importers denied that child labor was used in the carpet industry. However, the threat of a consumer boycott from its main importer, Germany; the German government's expressions of concern to the Indian government; a marginal decline in the import of carpets to Germany; and the spread of the child labor campaign to Holland, Sweden, the United Kingdom, and the United States forced the All India Carpet Manufacturers Association (AICMA) and Carpet Export Promotion Council (CEPC) to begin a dialogue with SACCS to resolve the problem. AICMA membership was divided. Some members claimed that child labor was necessary to keep prices low, some claimed that no child labor was being used, and some felt Satyarthi's strategy should be pursued. In December 1991, AICMA declared that it would ensure that all child laborers would be sent back to their homes (Kruijtbosch 1995). More important, the carpet manufacturers most concerned about the child labor issue severed their ties with AICMA to form the Carpet Manufacturers Association Without Child Labor (CMAWCL). These manufacturers remained steadfast in their commitment to work against the use of child labor in the carpet industry.

Further, in 1991, Satyarthi spoke at the U.N. Human Rights Commission's (UNHRC) subgroup on the contemporary form of slavery. In 1991, UNHRC passed a resolution supporting the creation of a special mark indicating that child labor was not used in the production of the carpet. In addition, the resolution advocated an information campaign promoting the boycotting of all goods manufactured with child labor.

By developing a transnational network of social activists in India and in Germany and by developing global sentiment against the use of child labor, as evidenced by the UNHRC's endorsement of a label, Satyarthi was able to foster the conditions for the creation of Rugmark. After several years of negotiations with CMAWCL, the Indo-German export Promotion Council, Gessellschaft fur Technische Zussammenarbeit, other nongovernmental organizations, and carpet exporters and importers, the Rugmark Foundation was incorporated in September 1994 as "a private, voluntary, non-profit entity" under Section 25 of the Indian Companies Act of 1956 (Rugmark n.d.). The label provided by the Rugmark Foundation in New Delhi indicates that a hand-knotted carpet is child labor free. It also guarantees that the adult carpet weaver has been paid minimum wage (Williamson 1995; Kruijtbosch 1995).

In carpet-producing countries, Rugmark licenses carpet exporters, collects the license fees of 0.25 percent of the export value of the carpet, and carries out surprise inspections on the registered looms of registered carpet exporters.[20] Further, Rugmark is also engaged in social and rehabilitation programs with children whom it has discovered at the looms. Currently, there are Rugmark Foundations in the carpet-producing countries of India, Nepal, and Pakistan.

In carpet-importing countries, Rugmark seeks to educate consumers about child-labor-free carpets, promote Rugmark-labeled carpets among importers, collect the license fee of 1 percent of the import value of the labeled carpet, and transfer funds to the respective Rugmark organizations in the producing countries. Licensed Rugmark importers are now located in Germany, the Netherlands, Belgium, Luxembourg, Sweden, Switzerland, and the United States, with licenses pending in several other countries (Rugmark 2000b).

In Germany, where the international headquarters of Rugmark is based, Rugmark-Germany is "attending to marketing, promotion, public relations and educational work as well as the label administration for Europe and the international coordination" (Rugmark 1999). Recently, in the United States, Rugmark carpets became available through the advocacy of the New York–based Robert F. Kennedy Memorial Center for Human Rights, the Washington, D.C.–based Child Labor Coalition, the AFL-CIO, the National Consumer League, several political and religious leaders, and the Rugmark Foundation.

CONCLUSION

The success of transnational activism and Rugmark can be measured on several fronts: (1) the number of licensees, both importers and exporters, with Rugmark; (2) the number of

Rugmark carpets exported; and (3) the norm-creating effect it might have. In India, there are 218 licensed exporters registered with Rugmark. As mentioned previously, many former members of AICMA broke away and formed CMAWCL, whose members became licensed by Rugmark. In addition, many of the remaining AICMA members also registered with Rugmark. Currently, 27,968 looms are registered and under inspection (Rugmark 2000a). Rugmark continually monitors looms to ensure that child labor is not being used. Of the 54,416 Rugmark inspections during 1998-99, only 794 looms were found employing child labor (Rugmark-India 1998-99). In India, nine Rugmark schools provide education and social care for approximately 1300 children. Rugmark has also established a rehabilitation center, Rugmark Balashrya, for children rescued from the industry. Upon the initiative from weavers themselves, Rugmark has established four adult education centers that provide education for 120 weavers. In terms of its presence in the market, in 1999 the 1.5 millionth Rugmark carpet was imported into Germany, with Rugmark sales reaching DM 118 million (Rugmark 1999).

Although Rugmark has not succeeded in banning child labor, nor has it been accepted by all importers and exporters, it has succeeded in diffusing the norms surrounding human rights and child labor in the Mirzapur-Badohi carpet belt in India. In the 1980s and the early 1990s, carpet manufacturers justified the existence of child labor in the carpet industry on the basis of poverty, the welfare of the industry, and so on. They claimed,

The government rather than realizing the gravity of the situation [faced by the industry], is proposing to bring up measures to raise the minimum wages on the pretext of regulating the wages of bonded child workers, which shall prove suicidal to the development of the industry. (Sridhar Mishra, quoted in Juyal 1987, 7)

Formulation of the Child Labour act and its implementation in the Industry is another uncalled for interference by the government. . . . [The law is] totally impractical [in an industry] where artisans work at their own place and earn handsome wages irrespective of their being adults or children. (Carpet-e-World 1991)

In contrast, the industry now carefully argues against the prevalence of child labor and provides schools, health care facilities, and alternative labeling mechanisms. In a letter to the Chairman of the Human Rights Commission in New Delhi, AICMA (1998) asked that

children working for wages be identified, rehabilitated, given free education and a stipend to compensate for wages lost. The industry, through the Carpet Export Promotion Council (CEPC), alive to its social obligations, has already set up a corpus for this. It has opened several schools in this area and proposes to expand its welfare activities further.

AICMA (1999) also provides a list of social and educational activities—"a free in-house health clinic," "free mobile medical van-cum-ambulance," support of a "primary educational programme," assistance in the "reg-istration of looms," and an "awareness campaign"—carried out under its aegis. Further, other institutions, such as the Kaleen (carpet) label sponsored by CEPC, seek to provide an alternative labeling system to Rugmark.[21] Care and Fair, sponsored by other German importers, collects money from importers and uses it to create social welfare projects in India and Nepal.

Although the work of transnational movements against child labor led to change in the case of the carpet industry in India, it has also raised as many issues as it has addressed. The success of transnational movements in inducing behavioral change may be more appropriately described as interest driven rather than norm driven. Certainly, one factor influencing the carpet industry's reported change in child labor employment was the fear of losing material benefits. Further, it is important to remember that the flow of human rights norms related to children, in the Rugmark case, was not from the liberal states to India; rather, it was the effort of social activists from India that initially guided German responses to child labor in the carpet industry. As the movement unfolded, an Indian-German coalition, and later a more inclusive transnational coalition, evolved. This involvement cannot adequately be characterized as reminding "liberal states of their own identity as promoters of human rights" (Risse, Ropp, and Sikkink 1999). By implicating Western consumers, through the buying of carpets, in the exploitation of child labor, the movement seriously subverted the identity claims of Western citizens as the promoters of human rights. Reclaiming this liberal identity required international aid organizations and citizens concerned about human rights to become political and, in part, involved in the new business practices promoted by Rugmark.

Notes

1. Only Somalia has neither signed nor ratified the convention. Although the United States signed the convention in the United Nations, it has not ratified it. The Senate Foreign Relations Committee, chaired by the conservative gerontocrat Jesse Helms, has impeded ratification by stalling introduction of the convention.

2. Transnational social movements are communities of common-minded individuals "whose commonality depends less on coresidence in 'sovereign' territorial space and more on common worldviews, purposes, interests and praxis" (Rudolph and Piscatori 1997, 2).

3. Although interdependence and pluralist scholars have included nonstate actors in their study of international relations, including the analysis of transboundary capital and pollutant flows, the literature on transnational social movements has emerged recently.

4. The agenda of Greenpeace has often been described as progressive. However, Greenpeace has been critiqued for its policy stand on immigration to Western countries. Using environmental and resource overuse arguments, Greenpeace has argued for curbing immigration. Many have seen this stand of Greenpeace as Malthusian-induced displacement. Like Malthus, Greenpeace focuses on population growth as the root cause of resource overuse, while neglecting the consumption patterns of Western publics and global elites.

Some transnational religious movements, like the pan-Islamic (fundamentalist), pan-Christian, and pan-Hindu (Hindu right) movements, have been based on chauvinist understandings of Islam, Christianity, and Hinduism as well as on the denigration of nonbelievers.

5. Keck and Sikkink (1998) further clarify that epistemic communities or communities of science exclude activists. These communities include only those who share common beliefs in technical evidence and who address technical issues (n. 54).

6. Unlike Keck and Sikkink (1998), Rudolph (1997) does not distinguish between epistemic communities and transnational communities.

7. Risse, Ropp, and Sikkink (1999) have narrowly operationalized human rights violations as "extrajudicial execution and disappearance" and "freedom from torture and arbitrary arrest and detention." This limited operationalization of human rights may have influenced their decision to restrict their analysis to states as human rights violators.

8. Human rights legislation does not guarantee that a state will actively enforce human rights. This is true both for Western societies and non-Western societies.

9. This section draws heavily from Chowdhry forthcoming.

10. India Constitution, Article 24 ("No child below the age of fourteen years shall be employed to work in any factory or mine or engaged in any other hazardous employment").

11. Tucker (1997) lists the 25 industries in which child labor is prohibited as *beedi* making (an indigenous type of cigarette); carpet weaving; cement manufacture; cloth printing; dyeing and weaving; manufacture of matches, explosives, and fireworks; mica cutting and splitting; shellac manufacture; the building and construction industry; manufacture of slate pencils; manufacture of agate products; manufacturing processes using toxic metals and substances, hazardous processes as defined by section 87, and printing as defined by section 2(k)(iv) of the Factories Act of 1948; cashew and cashew nut processing; soldering processes in electronic industries; railway transportation; cinder picking, ash pit clearing, and building operations; vending operations in railway premises; work on ports; sale of fireworks; and work in slaughterhouses.

12. According to D. N. Saraf (1986), the Mughal empire was responsible for the start of an organized carpet industry in India. Even though "Sir George Birdwood in the Industrial Arts of India (1880) believed that carpet manufacturing existed here before the Moughals

there is hardly any evidence to show that it was an organized industry" (49).

13. There are at least two different accounts related to the arrival of the weavers in the villages of Madhosingh-Ghosia. According to one, the weavers were escaping the violence of the 1857 war of independence when they arrived at the villages of Madhosingh and Ghosia (Waziri 1986). Another account suggests that the artisans were soldiers traveling in a Mughal caravan that was waylaid along the Grand Trunk road. They then sought refuge in the villages of Madhosingh-Ghosia.

14. H. Tellary was created by Mr. A. Tellary, whose grandson Otto Tellary became the founding member and first president of the All India Carpet Manufacturer's Association. Obeetee was founded by Okay, Bowden, and Taylor. Interestingly, the name Obeetee stands for their initials.

15. According to Juyal (1993), many British traders were involved in the carpet trade, particularly because revenues from the indigo trade were not forthcoming. The success of Indian-made "oriental" carpets at the Great London Exhibition in 1851 cemented the involvement of British merchant traders in the carpet industry.

16. The modernization drive of the Shah of Iran, which banned child labor below the age of 18; the economic boom resulting from the export of oil; and the low wages paid to labor in the carpet industry led to a labor shortage in the carpet industry and a decline in carpet production in Iran. In addition, with the increase in domestic income, the domestic share of demand for carpets also increased, leading to a declining share of the world market. India captured the vacuum left by Iranian carpet manufacturing.

17. Other importers are Britain, Japan, Canada, Sweden, Italy, Australia, France, and Switzerland.

18. Preprocessing activities involve opening yarn to make balls (*kablis*) and sorting yarn (*berai*). Weaving involves sitting at the loom and knotting the carpets.

19. In an interview, Kailash Satyarthi recalled an incident after seven children had been returned to their parents by the BLLF. While waiting at the train station to take the train from Mirzapur to New Delhi, he noticed 40-50 children getting down from the train with two adult males. It was obvious to Satyarthi that these were bonded children being brought to work in the carpet industry, yet the men claimed that they were a group coming to attend a marriage in the area. It was obvious to Satyarthi that the police knew what was going on since they let the men go and arrested Satyarthi instead. Humiliated and despondent, Satyarthi started to think about a more broad solution to the child labor problem. Since the carpet industry was export dependent, a consumer campaign in Germany would be useful to pressure carpet manufacturers to not use child labor (Satyarthi 1999).

20. Chowdhry accompanied inspectors to several loom sites in the Mirzapur Badohi villages in June 2000. She also visited Balashraya, the rehabilitation center for children in Gopigunj.

21. Rugmark has raised concerns that Kaleen does not have a systematic inspection system.

References

All India Carpet Manufacturers Association. 1998. Letter to the National Human Rights Commission, New Delhi, India on Child Labour in the Carpet Industry. Badohi, India, 27 Jan.

———. 1999. Status of Indian Carpet Industry vis-a-vis the Problem of Child Labour and the Action Initiated by Trade and Govt. for Elimination of Child Labour and Their Welfare. Position paper, Badohi, India, 21 Nov.

Boulding, Elise. 1997. Foreword. In *Transnational Social Movements and Global Politics: Solidarity Beyond the State*, ed. J. Smith, C. Chatfield, and R. Pagnucco. Syracuse, NY: Syracuse University Press.

Brandstater, Johannes. 1991. Presentation at the Child Labour Seminar held in New Delhi, 15-16 February, 1991. In *Proceedings of the First National Workshop on Eradication of Child Labour*. New Delhi: National Labour Institute.

Brysk, Alison. 1993. From Above and Below: Social Movements, the International System, and Human Rights in

Argentina. *Comparative Political Studies* 26(3):259-85.

Byrne, Iain. 1998. *The Human Rights of Street and Working Children: A Practical Manual for Advocates*. London: Intermediate Technology.

Carpet-e-World. 1991. *International Annual Journal*. Varanasi, India: Varanasi University Press.

Chadha, T. S. 2000. Interview with Carpet Export Promotion Council Executive Director, June.

Chowdhry, Geeta. Forthcoming. Postcolonial Interrogations of Child Labor: Human Rights, Carpet Trade and Rugmark in India. In *Power in a Postcolonial World: Race, Gender and Class in International Relations*, ed. G. Chowdhry and S. Nair. New York: Routledge.

Cox, Katherine. 1999. The Inevitability of Nimble Fingers? Law, Development and Child Labor. *Vanderbilt Journal of International Law* 32(1):115-50.

Dutt, Ela. 1995. Rug Firms with No Child Labor Need Help. *India Abroad*, 3 Feb.

Haas, Peter. 1992. Introduction: Epistemic Communities and International Policy Coordination. *International Organization* 46:1-35.

Juyal, B. N. 1987. *Child Labour and Exploitation in the Carpet Industry: A Mirzapur-Bhadohi Case Study*. New Delhi: Indian Social Institute.

———. 1993. *Child Labour in the Carpet Industry in Mirzapur-Bhadohi*. New Delhi: International Labor Organization.

Keck, M. and K. Sikkink. 1998. *Activists Beyond Borders*. Ithaca, NY: Cornell University Press.

Kruijtbosch, Martine. 1995. *Rugmark*. New Delhi: South Asian Coalition on Child Servitude.

Kuppers, Barbara. 2000. A New Partnership for Children's Rights: Linking Business to Combat Child Labour. Workshop organized by Terre des Hommes et al., 29 June.

McDonald, Hamish. 1992. Boys of Bondage: Child Labour, Though Banned Is Rampant. *Far Eastern Economic Review*, 9 July.

Mehta, Pradeep S. 1994. Cashing in on Child Labor. *Multinational Monitor*, Apr.

Mishra, L. 2000. *Child Labour in India*. New Delhi: Oxford University Press.

Misra, S. D. 1999. Indian Carpet Industry vis-a-vis the Problem of Child Labour in India. Position paper, Carpet Export Promotion Council, 26 Dec.

Puetter, Benjamin. 2000. Interview by Geeta Chowdhry. Cologne, 5 July.

Risse, T., S. C. Ropp, and K. Sikkink. 1999. *The Power of Human Rights: International Norms and Domestic Change*. Cambridge: Cambridge University Press.

Rudolph, S. H. 1997. Introduction: Religion, States, and Transnational Civil Society. In *Transnational Religion: Fading States*, ed. S. H. Rudolph and J. Piscatori. Boulder, CO: Westview Press.

Rudolph, S. H. and J. Piscatori, eds. 1997. *Transnational Religion: Fading States*. Boulder, CO: Westview Press.

Rugmark. n.d. The Rugmark Initiative. New Delhi. Pamphlet.

———. 1999. Rugmark Germany Annual Report. Rugmark International, Cologne.

———. 2000a. Rugmark Facts and Figures. Rugmark International, Cologne.

———. 2000b. Rugmark at a Glance. Rugmark International, Cologne.

Rugmark-India. 1998-99. Progress Report. Rugmark International, Cologne.

Saraf, D. N. 1986. Indian Carpets. In *Silver Jubilee Special*. Badohi: All India Carpet Manufacturers Association.

Satyarthi, K. 1992. Welcome Address. South Asian Consultation on Child Labour in Carpet Industry, 11-13 July.

———. 1999. Interview by the Geeta Chowdhry. New Delhi, 23 June.

Sikkink, K. 1993. Human Rights, Principled Issue Networks, and Sovereignty in Latin America. *International Organization* 47:412-41.

Smith, J. 1997. Characteristics of the Modern Transnational Social Movement Sector. In *Transnational Social Movements and Global Politics: Solidarity Beyond the State*, ed. J. Smith, C. Chatfield, and R. Pagnucco. Syracuse, NY: Syracuse University Press.

Smith, J., C. Chatfield, and R. Pagnucco. 1997. *Transnational Social Movements and Global Politics: Solidarity Beyond the State*. Syracuse, NY: Syracuse University Press.

Smith, J., R. Pagnucco, and G. Lopez. 1998. Globalizing Human Rights: The Work of Transnational Human Rights NGOs in the 1990s. *Human Rights Quarterly* 20:379-412.

Tucker, Lee. 1997. Child Slaves in Modern India: The Bonded Labor Problem. *Human Rights Quarterly* 19:572-630.

United Nations. 1989. *United Nations Convention on the Rights of a Child*. UNGA Document A/RES/4425.

Walker, R.B.J. 1993. *Inside / Outside: International Relations as Political Theory*. Cambridge: Cambridge University Press.

Waziri, A. A. 1986. A Brief History of Carpet Weaving in Bhadohi-Mirzapur Belt. In *Silver Jubilee Special*. Badohi: All India Carpet Manufacturers Association.

Williamson, Hugh. 1995. Stamp of Approval. *Far Eastern Economic Review*, 2 Feb.

ANNALS, *AAPSS*, **575**, May 2001

Approaches to Children's Work and Rights in Nepal

By RACHEL BAKER and RACHEL HINTON

ABSTRACT: Current economic and political trends present particular challenges for countries dealing with the development of industry without the social infrastructure needed to uphold citizens' rights. As free trade demands competitiveness in global markets, so the demand for cheap labor rises. This has specific implications for children. This article argues that despite new legislation to fulfil the requirements of international mandates (such as the U.N. Convention on the Rights of the Child and International Labor Organization Convention 182 on the worst forms of child labor), rights-based programming does not sufficiently incorporate the perspectives of poor children and their family members. This article draws on recent ethnographic research that pioneered a collaborative model in which government, voluntary, private, and trade union organizations conducted research to compare the impact of current approaches to child labor on the livelihoods of working children. It shows that in failing to incorporate sociocultural understanding in program planning, services fail to maximize their potential in offering children opportunities to end the cycle of poverty.

Rachel Baker and Rachel Hinton are anthropologists currently teaching at the University of Edinburgh. Rachel Baker researches issues of migration and identity among Nepali children. Rachel Hinton's research investigates health systems among refugee children in Nepal.

NOTE: Funds for the present study were provided by the U.K. Department for International Development. The views and opinions expressed are those of the authors alone.

C HILDREN, and the rhetoric of children's rights, currently have a high profile in Nepal.[1] Due to the economic and political significance of international development in Nepal, the discourse that accompanies development interventions has had a significant influence on the way in which positive change is viewed by Nepali society. Important elements of this discourse are the internationally ratified human rights documents, including the U.N. Convention on the Rights of the Child. The active presence of child-focused organizations such as UNICEF and the Save the Children Fund has meant that Nepali adults and children have become part of strategies to improve the well-being of children. The question remains, however, as to how far these strategies correspond to the current aspirations of poor children as they move into adulthood and to the employment and educational opportunities open to them.

The aim of this article is to explore how specific Western interpretations of children's rights influence practice in Nepal. In particular, we will focus on the approaches taken by a six key stakeholders[2] to the problems associated with child labor. We will ask how policymakers understand the problem and hence define the route to a solution. Using recent research findings, we will draw upon the experiences of development practitioners implementing programs to tackle child labor as well as the views of working children and their families. This article poses the following question: To what degree does rights-based programming incorporate the perspectives of poor children and their family members? We suggest the need for new research frameworks in which children are considered with respect to their roles within the family, the peer group, and wider processes of social change in Nepal.

This article draws on two bodies of ethnographic research generated during a collaborative action research project in Nepal between March 1999 and May 2000. The ethnographic study of organizations engaged in policy and implementation relating to child work provides insight into the perspectives of these change agents on Nepali childhoods. The ethnographic study of children engaged in carpet production and their families offers their views, experiences, and aspirations. The research team explored these two areas simultaneously on the premise that the knowledge within organizations that is applied to programs to assist children will have a direct influence on the changes brought about in the lives of those children. Within the last decade, communication technology has enabled knowledge to be shared between countries and cultural environments at an unprecedented level. Key children's rights policies are generated by an international consortium of experts, yet it is widely recognized that local realities cannot be captured in universal legislation. This raises questions as to the source of knowledge used in programming and whether sufficient resources are invested in scrutinizing how best to apply international mandates. The challenge lies in importing the principles while ensuring that local knowledge is prioritized. The next section discusses globalization and the impact on children's livelihoods at a macro level.

IMPACT OF GLOBALIZATION ON CHILD LABOR

It has been argued that globalization is widening the income gap between the wealthy sectors and poor sectors of populations. A UNICEF document analyzing issues relating to child labor in South Asia argues that fiscal reforms have curtailed government spending in the public sector (Vidyasagar 2000). The author of this report states that "this is a direct result of efforts in reducing fiscal deficits and tax/excise concessions to private sectors, both national and foreign" (4). There are multiple implications of globalization processes for children who work. Children's livelihoods, like those of their parents, often depend on volatile employment markets that can produce hazardous and exploitative working conditions.

There is evidence from India, Nepal, and other countries within South Asia that increasing numbers of children migrate from their natal homes as opportunities for work expand in nearby towns or distant cities (Sharma, Shrestha, and Cross 2000). Improved communication and transportation have facilitated migration, which appears to produce both positive and negative outcomes for children. In most cases, migrant working children forego school, as urban jobs require a full-time commitment. A small proportion face extreme exploitation (for example,

trafficking in the sex trade), especially where they are outside networks of relatives or friends who can protect them (Acharya 1997). Few countries have established trade union movements that span all industries or work locations. Where trade unions do exist in the region, they are rarely able to protect the interests of informal-sector workers or children. Yet there is documentation to show the importance of the trade union movement in Europe in protecting children's interests (Morice 2000).

UNICEF estimates that some 600 million children live on less than a dollar a day. This represents 40 percent of all children in developing countries. Just over half (53 percent) of Nepal's population live below the poverty line (defined as living on less than a dollar a day), with women and children representing the majority of this group (Human Development Centre 1999). Donor organizations providing funds for development initiatives highlight the potential that globalization has to enhance the welfare of children. In recent years, there has been a noticeable shift in donor policy from direct service provision to enabling the processes needed for citizens to demand their rights (Department for International Development 1998). This policy change has meant that governments in developing countries now have even greater responsibilities to provide basic services. The World Bank's poverty reduction strategy process has the potential to incorporate the perspectives of the poor in reforms required to meet the international development target of halving the proportion of the world's population living in extreme poverty by 2015. However, there is no history of listening to the citizen's voice, and there are few mechanisms to hear children's views.

THE HISTORY OF CHILDREN'S RIGHTS IN NEPAL

The emergence of children's rights as a social issue in Nepal is closely tied to the political movement that led to the restoration of multiparty democracy in 1990. Early statements from the government and major donor agencies mentioned children as a special target group within the broader development aim to focus on the grass roots. In 1991, the U.N. Development Programme's statement of priorities for the new government began, "Programmes to alleviate poverty [are] to receive the highest priority. The requirements of women, children and economically and socially disadvantaged citizens will be paramount in determining the design of Nepal's development programmes" (Seddon 1993, 142).

Within the last decade, local and international nongovernmental organizations (NGOs), in coordination with the media, have played the greatest part in publicizing the notion of rights for working children. In 1990, tight state control over the media was replaced by a lively exchange of ideas about general social issues in Nepal, one of which is children's rights and the responsibilities of the government, voluntary sector, and general public in meeting children's needs. The loudest voice has often been that of local NGOs, whose number and power have dramatically increased over the past decade (Maskay 1998). The mushrooming of NGOs is attributed to the general desire for equality, freedom, and social justice that characterized the movement against the one-party system of government (Child Workers in Nepal 1995, 4); it is also the product of large sums of international aid channeled through the voluntary sector. In other words, the simultaneous impetus of national political change and international debate toward the U.N. Convention on the Rights of the Child has had a mutually reinforcing effect on the present policy environment. As we would expect, these agendas for change were set by adults concerned with setting right the power imbalances that have allowed the exploitation of children.

There is no evidence that consultation with children in Nepal was undertaken in the process of planning the practicalities of what should be done to assist children. In the last five years, there has been plentiful debate on the need for children's participation in programming, which has led to significant changes in practice. The reason we mention the absence of children's consultation is to add emphasis to growing concern that decisions about children's lives continue to be based on a set of norms surrounding children's competencies and vulnerabilities, without adequate questioning of the appropriateness of these norms to children's realities.

In the following sections, we will examine the particular actions taken to improve the lives of children working in Nepal's carpet industry. We focus on this work sector because the carpet industry, along with tourism, is a major source of foreign income (Centre for Policy Studies 1999). Thus the carpet industry's employment of children has received considerable attention from the media and development actors. Development organizations participating in the research are keen to learn how their interventions have affected children's lives and how best to tailor their provisions to achieve children's best interests. The high levels of trust and cooperation we gained with these organizations[3] through the collaborative research model meant that we were able to ask questions about the basic aims, premises, and effectiveness of each approach to deal with the problem of child labor. The interactive and collaborative research model enables employees of these organizations to conduct primary research with the children who are actual or potential participants in their programs. The objective of this model is to establish a dialogue about the relationship between theory and practice in achieving the rights of working children.

PROPOSED SOLUTIONS TO
THE PROBLEM OF CHILD LABOR

A range of approaches to address child labor have been supported by the Nepalese government and foreign donors (International Labor Organization [ILO] 1999). The rationale presented for each approach illustrates the differences in understandings of children's best interests between policy actors. Before consid-

ering the impact of each approach on children's lives, it is important to take stock of these trends in policy and practice. For the purposes of debate, the interventions to assist children in Nepal's carpet industry can be grouped into three approaches. As will become evident, the following approaches are in practice linked and mutually interactive:

1. the elimination of hazardous child labor through factory inspection and licensing schemes;
2. the rehabilitation of working children by removing them from the workplace and into temporary hostels, then placing them back with their families or in boarding school; and
3. the protection of working children through the provision of basic education and welfare facilities for children and families within the vicinity of work.

It is important to note that, as elsewhere, the backdrop to Nepal's trends in program approach has been the difference in two broad policies. The first is to eliminate child labor across the board, and the second to eliminate children's participation in hazardous employment. Proponents of the first policy argue that no form of work for children under the ILO's minimum age of work can be condoned, whereas advocates of the second policy argue that child work is diverse and that a general policy is inappropriate. As pointed out by Vidyasagar (2000), the debate between these two positions in the South Asian region has been unnecessarily polarized and reflects differences in rhetoric rather than in objectives and priorities for children. In the case of Nepal, discussion with key policy advisers indicates that there has been a shift in thinking within the past decade from eliminating child labor to appropriate actions to safeguard the well-being of working children in the short and long term.

Elimination of child labor

In 1993, the newly established Child Labour Unit in the Ministry of Labour began conducting factory inspections with the objective of fulfilling the concurrent policy of eliminating child labor. The Child Labour Unit's primary objective has been to enforce the law that dictates that no child under 14 years of age should work and that children between 14 and 16 years of age may work only under certain conditions relating to time, payment, and the work environment. This year, new legislation came into force in Nepal stating that children under the age of 16 are not allowed to work in certain occupations that are defined as hazardous, including the carpet industry. This change in national law is part of the Nepalese government's response to ILO Convention 182 to eliminate the worst forms of child labor. It was drawn up following a consultation process that involved international and local NGOs working with children as well as trade unions. The government, supported by the ILO, is now working to build structures for enforcement.

The enforcement of this law poses significant challenges to the state and the industries concerned. It is important to note that the extent to which laws are enforced is in part reflective of historical and cultural factors that define norms for children's lives. As Qvortrup (2000) points out, regulative influences on children have often grown out of norms and values. Research on attempts to globalize standards for children's lives is now exposing the fact that actions to improve children's quality of life are being taken within a patchwork of different cultural values and ideals associated with childhood (for example, Boyden, Ling, and Myers 1998; Burman 1996; Ennew 2000).

Due to the small size of the government's inspection team, a large proportion of Nepal's medium and small carpet industries have never been inspected, and employers remain ignorant of the law or able to avoid its enforcement.[4] There is evidence, however, that owners of large factories have ceased to recruit children following inspection work and international media coverage of exploitative child labor in Nepal's carpet industry during the early 1990s. It is hoped that this reflects a change of attitudes among employers toward childhood rather than purely the fear of being caught breaking the law. It is not known whether law enforcement has led to this broader shift in norms and values, due largely to the fact that employers are rarely consulted.

Turning now to children's experiences, it is worth noting that those who were expelled from factories directly encountered a set of regulations disallowing them to spend time generating an income. Although there was sufficient evidence from small-scale research that the physical environment posed serious health risks, little consideration was given to the relative risks of alternative livelihoods or to the potential benefits to children of a working role. It is interesting to note that a document produced by the Ministry of Labour in 1997 outlines the complexity of child labor and acknowledges the positive aspects of child work as part of a "gradual initiation into adult life" (Vaidya 1997, 20). The fact that the government responded first and foremost with a legislative approach indicates the power of media representations of the problem in countries that both buy Nepal's carpets and provide significant amounts of aid money.

During the mid-1990s, policy debate turned to the limitations of a purely legislative approach. First, it was felt that children expelled from factories were likely to move into hazardous jobs in the informal sector, where working conditions are much harder to regulate. Second, debate between exporters and U.N. policymakers revealed the need for a strategy that prioritized promotion of the carpet industry. The Nepal Rugmark Foundation (NRF) was established to enable factory owners to attach "child-labor-free" labels to their carpets if they sign an agreement with NRF. This agreement binds them to international employment standards and the payment of 0.25 percent of the export value of their carpets as a contribution to the running costs of the foundation. To regulate the use of the Rugmark label, NRF also operates an inspection team. When inspectors find children working illegally, they take them out of the factory and enroll them in a rehabilitation program.

*Rehabilitation of
  working children*

The rehabilitation approach is thus part of the policy to eliminate hazardous child labor. Children are provided a place in a residential hostel with health care, nonformal education, and counseling. Staff members investigate children's family circumstances and, when considered possible, take children home to their families, most of whom live in rural areas. Children without family members able to care for them are placed in boarding schools or vocational training institutions. On paper, this model of rehabilitation seemed to be an appropriate strategy to meet the needs of working children in the same way that many programs to reunite street children with their families seemed to make sense at the planning stage. Clearly, these programs are driven by norms relating to what children need for the best possible well-being both now and in the future. Questions are now being raised by staff as to the appropriateness of reversing the migration process for all children, particularly those who are over 12 years or who have missed large amounts of school. These point to the lack of attention to structural factors affecting poor children's lives, ranging from caste, ethnicity, and gender to access to quality education and employment opportunities in the rural environment.

Protecting working children

It is only recently that policymakers and donors have given serious consideration to initiatives designed to protect children and their families within the work environment (for example, Reddy 2000). In the past, this approach could not have been entertained, as it ran against policies to prevent children working, whatever the circumstances. Interestingly, in Nepal, the protective approach grew out of initiatives on sexual health awareness and literacy for women working in carpet factories. Staff members were aware that many children worked alongside their mothers, fathers, or older siblings. It was recognized that, for some children, the move to the urban environment is positive because it opens opportunities for informal apprenticeship and employment in sectors unavailable in rural areas (Boyden, Ling, and Myers 1998).

To ensure that the family unit remained intact, crèches and nonformal education and health facilities were provided within or near the factories. Employers were encouraged to be flexible with working hours so that children could be released to attend school for about two hours a day. Yet even now, no comprehensive strategy exists, and there is remarkably little debate among donors and implementers about the potentials of a protective approach, despite growing support for programs promoting children's right to work elsewhere in South Asia.

The current position of several major donors, including Deutsche Gessellschaft for Technische Zusammenarbeit (the German Development Organization) and UNICEF, is that programs to address problems in the workplace can never prevent children from working in exploitative environments (UNICEF 2000). Following research showing continuing high rates of child migration from villages to the city to find work (Centre for Policy Studies 1999), donors are increasingly supporting programs within villages that are designed to reduce the pressure on children to migrate for economic reasons and to warn them of the conditions they may face in city jobs. Components of these programs include income generation and literacy for adults, children's clubs, and resources to improve the quality of schooling. With the goal of reducing inequalities, these programs are designed to tackle some of the structural features of rural communities that discriminate against certain families and children on the basis of caste, ethnicity, gender, or family stature. While this year has seen the emergence of such programs aimed specifically at reducing child labor, similar community-based interventions have long been part of rural poverty reduction programs run by local NGOs and international organizations, including ActionAid and CARE. Research suggests that both poor children and children from comparatively wealthy families migrate for work (Baker, Panter-Brick, and Todd 1997). While both groups are at risk of exploitation in the workplace, children from higher-status, educated families are more likely to have the means to protect themselves, whereas poor children are unlikely to have such a protective net.

This brief overview of trends in policy direction on child work in Nepal reveals changes in attitudes toward childhood and what is considered good for children. The legislative and rehabilitative models are based on the premise that the work is harmful to children's physical, mental, and emotional health. Rehabilitation assumes that children will be better off in the safe and structured environment of a hostel and in their natal homes rather than in the work setting. The underlying rationale is that work in the carpet industry has predominately negative effects on children and that they are better off attending nonformal education programs or, preferably, formal school. Programs protecting children in the work setting acknowledge that children's work can be a crucial contribution to household income, but few go so far as to challenge the laws that prevent children younger than 14 from working. Rather, these programs aim to minimize the negative consequences of work in the carpet sector through broadly educational and health-based services for parents who work as well as for their children. Interestingly, working children, like working adults, are keen on taking educational opportunities that are compatible with their work schedules.

While sensitivities to the law have so far prevented initiatives that allow children younger than 14 to combine work and education, the value of this combination is borne out by the fact that some children and

minors (14-16 years) with full-time jobs in carpet factories have sought out nonformal education provided in the local community. Questions have been raised about the underlying assumption of the protective approach, namely, that parents do not know how to bring up their children in the city or how to protect themselves or their children from HIV/AIDS and other health hazards. Initiatives that aim to enable children to stay in their rural communities recognize that there are particular socioeconomic and cultural factors affecting poor families that have consequences for children. Implicit assumptions within this approach are that the family is the best environment for children and that the rural setting can provide learning and work opportunities for the future.

CHILDREN'S EXPERIENCES
OF LABOR PROGRAMMING

To understand how work, and the interventions to prevent work, impinge on children's lives, we selected some basic social and economic indicators that are meaningful to Nepali children and their families (see Table 1). The first of these is time, the second is income, and the third is access to education or learning opportunities for future livelihoods. The ethnographic data presented here comprise children's reflections on work as well as other features of their lives. Their words raise questions about children's participation in decision making in both institutional and family settings and

TABLE 1

THE EFFECT OF CHILD LABOR PROGRAMMING
ON THE LIVES OF WORKING CHILDREN IN NEPAL

	Legislation: Work in a City Job Following Expulsion from a Carpet Factory	Rehabilitation: Shelter in a Hostel and Provision of Nonformal Education and/or Schooling	Protection: Support in or Near the (usually urban) Workplace	Community-Based Intervention: General Community Development in Rural Hill Villages
Physical environment and safety	Health risks in carpet factories removed but nothing to prevent similar risks at child's next workplace	Removal of health risks posed by dust, long work hours, and poor diet; basic needs met in hostel	Setting minimum standards by raising awareness among parents and employers	Preventing child migration, assuming that the village environment is safe
Social environment	Children free to choose next social network	With peers but without family or community	Among family and community	With village community; includes many returnee migrants
Use of time	Over half spend more than 6 hours per day in productive work, but 70% have more than 3 hours of free time each day	Most children spend no time in productive work; due to nonformal education classes and cleaning duties, only half reported over 3 hours of free time per day	Over half spend more than 6 hours per day in productive work for their households; domestic duties and schooling meant that only 7% had over 3 hours free time per day	Only 20% spend more than 6 hours per day in productive work for their households; domestic duties and schooling meant that only 3% had over 3 hours free time per day
Income*	Average income exceeds the minimum wage by 408 rupees per week; large variation (150-1100 rupees) shows unpredictability of some urban jobs	As most children are not earning, the average income exceeds the minimum wage by only 25 rupees per week[†]	Average income exceeds the minimum wage by 114 rupees, with some degree of variation (−50-500 rupees)	Average income exceeds the minimum wage by 295 rupees, but large variation (−200-800 rupees)

*Nepal's national minimum wage for minors (age 14-16 years) is 1025 rupees per month (approximately 256 rupees per week).

[†]Evidence suggests that this loss of income affects both the household's ability to provide basic needs and the individual child's status within the family.

the comparative influence of two generations, namely, adults and the children's peer group.

Use of time

Of the research sample comprising 162 children and youths, all of those still working in the carpet industry spend more than six hours per day engaged in productive work (defined as work for an income in cash or kind). The same working hours were reported by just over half of children now working in other city jobs after having been expelled from the carpet industry and 60 percent of children who are protected in the work context through health and nonformal education programs. Only 20 percent of rural children reported working for over six hours per day, and only 8 percent of "rehabilitated" children worked for such long hours. At first glance, these figures suggest that children would prefer to be in the village or in the rehabilitation center where the workloads are significantly lighter. What they do not reveal is the high levels of household work done by children in rural homes, which many consider to be dull and unproductive in terms of future opportunities.

Jobs in the city, including shopkeeping, begging, and selling scrap to recycling yards, appear to enable children to have more free time than carpet weaving or agricultural work in the village. One former carpet weaver now working as a helper in a shop commented, "I now sleep for ten hours because I don't have to work at night."

In general, neither children nor adults placed significant emphasis on the proportion of the day spent working. While all children said that they liked to *"gumne janne"* (wander about and see things) in their spare time, especially in the city area, there was a wide range of responses regarding the extent to which work restricted their free time. Some children engaged in agricultural work with their families were disappointed when work demands prevented them from going to school. Youths still working in the carpet industry work very long hours, but their communal cooking arrangements and regular days off ensure that they have free time to watch television, shop for clothes at the bazaars, and watch movies. The piece-rate payment system of the carpet sector means that weavers can opt to increase their income by working longer hours or, after finishing one loom, take time off to visit relatives in rural areas during festivals. This system also allows some young women to attend a locally run nonformal education program.

Nevertheless, children reported that even by doing 16-hour work shifts, their pay was insufficient for anything more than basic needs. The sense of limitation and shame of being in a job that paid little for large amounts of time is illustrated in the following two quotations: "You cannot earn much from carpet weaving, as it does not give a good income. It is limited and I can't save, as I spend it all on my daily needs." "I don't like to narrate my past history because I used to work most of the time, but in return I earned very little."

Income

As shown previously, level of income is important to children in terms of their self-respect and for providing basic needs such as food and clothes. Findings suggest that young people who have remained in the carpet industry since middle childhood are now earning over the minimum wage for minors (14-16 year olds), whereas of those who left the carpet industry and took up other work in the city, a small proportion earn more than the carpet workers, but some earn much less than the minimum wage for minors. As would be expected, only a small proportion of children placed in hostels, schools, or with their family members were earning even minimal amounts. Their basic needs were largely filled by institutions; however, questions arise over the loss of control over income and expenditure experienced by these children. Only those children who had been rehabilitated and returned to their families made explicit reference to the loss of income. Given that children in the residential hostels have been provided with their daily needs and are surrounded by those who see this as an entirely positive experience, we can understand their reluctance to express any complaints. Yet boys in their mid-teens who wanted vocational training in order to leave street work were quick to point out that they were not prepared to live in a residential hostel that paid them a small sum of pocket money and

forbade them to leave the premises to earn more.

The research indicated that both adults and children are exploited by the employment system of the carpet industry. Employers hire contractors to secure the cheapest labor possible in order to keep production costs low. One child who was removed from a factory and placed in a hostel explained why he began weaving: "We did the work the contractor told us to. My mother used to say that if we didn't follow him, then she would not be able to feed me. That is why I started to work."

Rural immigrants to the city are often unaware of extra costs that are deducted from wages (for example, food and accommodation) or feel powerless to challenge their employers. In this respect, lack of city know-how and a sense of inferiority as a rural immigrant can expose adults to exploitation in the same way that the generational boundary causes children to be vulnerable. Here we see evidence that age or the notion of generational difference may not be the most powerful structural factor that prevents children from influencing decisions affecting their lives. Rather, their rural origins, caste, ethnicity, or gender may be more powerful determinants of how they are treated in the work context.

The reason most children begin working in the carpet sector is to provide a cash income for their families. At first, trusting the contractor's word that he will send their salaries back to their parents, children work for little or no personal income: "The contractor gave me 20 to 25 rupees (20-25 pence) once a week and he said he was sending 700 rupees to my family every month." Upon discovering that their salaries never reached home, some children left the carpet industry to find a job in which they would have control over their incomes.

It is clear that parents consider their children to be making vital contributions to the household economy, whether in terms of time or cash. A mother explained her young daughter's involvement in wool spinning as follows: "I have five daughters and three sons. This is my last daughter; if she does not work I will be dead. I have difficulties surviving so I need some work from my daughter."

Tensions can arise when children opt for work that allows them to immediately spend their incomes on food and entertainment. Children who left the carpet factory and began working on the streets reported being scolded by their parents for roaming about, but we do not know whether parents were more concerned about their children's safety or their early financial independence. Boys have a degree of freedom in terms of the location and nature of their work, so long as they maintain their filial obligations to provide for their parents in their old age. Parental ideals are that girls work at home or in closed environments where they can be supervised by relatives or trusted neighbors. Interestingly, older girls working in the carpet factory had considerably more spending power than their male peers, who were sending large proportions of their money home. Girls spend their extra cash on clothes, jewelry, makeup, and movies, all of which

portray an image of the middle-class urban resident that is vastly different from their siblings or friends who remain in hill villages.

Learning opportunities

Within the last decade, constructive policy debate on improving the lives of working children has been hindered by the existence of two separate debates on child labor and education (Fyfe 1999). Moreover, the debate on education has tended to focus on schooling and nonformal education rather than on the broader learning environment, which could include the workplace. A close look at Nepali children's comments about work and school shows a certain ambiguity about its value to them now and in the future. Working children who have never had the chance to attend school feel that they have missed out on an opportunity to gain basic literacy skills. However, children who have experienced school feel under pressure to perform well even when they have very little support. The sense of obligation to parents comes through in the following quotations from children who live and work in rural villages: "Studying is difficult. If I could not pass my parents will not send me to school." "No one stops me going to school, so I have to study to become a great person. Then in the future I will be able to care for my parents."

There is no doubt that the majority of rural and urban parents place a high value on formal education. Yet it is clear that there are other competing factors, such as marriage and work opportunities, that may mean that schooling has to be fitted around other commitments, as illustrated in the following comments of a father in his early forties:

My wife and mother died last year so I was left with the responsibility of two children. My 15-year-old son is soon getting married, but he will still be able to go to school. I am thinking of sending my 6-year-old daughter next session, and I will educate my children even if I am in debt. Even if my daughter has finished her education, I won't let her marry until she is 20, but if she elopes, I cannot do anything.

Many parents have a view of education that goes beyond schooling. The benefits of travel and experience are reflected in the following words of a father from the Tamang ethnic group of Nuwakot district: "A son has got to travel. By traveling a certain amount, we gain that much knowledge. It is not enough to learn from a book, so we must go to different places. There, the eyes can see and the hands can learn to do."

The ethnographic literature covering youth in Nepal points to the importance of access to social networks in the transition to adulthood (Sagant 1996). Similar observations have been made about access to career opportunities in the West. However, the extent to which one is connected in Nepal has greater significance in both gaining access to opportunities and securing a position, whether this is related to renting a flat, securing a job, or entering a school. Our research shows that access to social networks is particularly important for urban migrants who are looking to establish a career and an identity within a new

community. According to young adults who have been working in the carpet industry since they were children, it is difficult to find better work elsewhere because the skills are not transferable. However, children are very aware that building a good rapport with one's employer can lead to greater opportunities to move into better-paid and higher-status employment. One former carpet weaver observed, "Auto-mechanics garages are better places to work than carpet factories, and mechanic jobs are sometimes available because garage owners may also be carpet factory owners." The chance to link into social networks is an important reason why children consider work in the city preferable to agricultural work in rural areas.

CHILDHOOD OR TRANSITION TO ADULTHOOD?

In this final section, we raise questions about the extent to which development initiatives under the umbrella of children's rights have been able to incorporate the perspectives of children and their families. These are important questions because without such a process the everyday realities of children who have few alternatives are not prioritized in the programming arena.

It is clear from this article that generational factors are rarely considered in decisions concerning children's lives. The ethnographic data presented here indicate that policies to assist working children are based on assumptions of differences between generations. These norms say that children are not physically or psychologically mature enough to be involved in gainful work, to properly deal with money, or to have access to certain provisions procured through their own earnings. In Nepal, the capacity to work is not intrinsically linked to the move into the adult generation (as indicated by marriage and childbearing). Rather, it is part of the maturation process in which children participate with peers and older relatives. Observed trends toward models of practice that protect children at work show that practitioners are becoming increasingly aware that policy models do not accurately reflect children's competencies and the positive potential children see in a fulfilling working role.

These shortcomings of children's rights policy have been attributed to the dominance of the modern Western model of childhood within the global context (Burman 1996) and to the exclusion of children in the making of policy documents (Ennew 2000). Critical analysis of international conventions points out that the ideal childhood is one free of responsibilities, which would include work, and dominated by education and leisure within the family context. Ethnographers studying childhood in varying cultural contexts have exposed a very different set of ideals of childhood. Research in South Asia points out that children are considered members of the joint family and therefore have a set of associated obligations as they grow older (Baker 1998; Nieuwenhuys 1994). These roles influence decisions made by parents, other relatives, and children themselves regarding their education, residence, and contributions to the household economy. Childhood studies make a distinction between the traditional model of childhood, in which children perform a working role on family farms, and a modern childhood that tends to see children as requiring protection. These models have been further analyzed and developed in more recent years (James, Jenks, and Prout 1998). Within analyses of the traditional model of childhood (for example, Baker 1998; Hinton 2000), there is greater recognition of children's capacities to look after themselves, to care for siblings, and to perform a working role within the household.

Current research shows that the polarity that has developed between a traditional model and an imported modern model of childhood is not helpful. Broad social and economic changes, including the increasing availability of schooling and prevalence of migration, have blurred the distinction between these two models. Conversations with Nepali parents showed that they espouse elements of the modern childhood, for example, formal education, yet at the same time advocate the values and practices that are bound up in the childhood that they themselves experienced. With global developments in communication and media, children in Nepal are interacting with images from very different cultures. In this context, it can be argued that their material expectations differ from those of their parents. Currently, social status among young people is achieved by wearing clothing, body decoration, and jewelry akin to that of film stars from Bombay and Hollywood, in addition to other historically rooted forms and sources of status.

CONCLUSION

Reflecting on the current climate within the policy arena, we are struck by the prevalence of debate between development actors on the meaning of "child-centeredness" for everyday practice. The interesting question here is, Why do adults who understand the rationale then experience problems when converting it to practice? We suggest that the difficulties experienced by adults in crossing the generational divide are due to concepts of children as "other," the target group for their interventions as "the poor," as opposed to people with whom they share fundamental experiences, hopes, and fears. Program managers are often more concerned, or have more experience, with supporting work that follows standards laid out in the U.N. agreements than with exploring the fit between these standards and those of children and parents in the program area. In contrast, field-level staff members who interact with children and their families on a day-to-day basis are more in tune with their priorities and any conflicting objectives to those laid out in the U.N. Convention on the Rights of the Child. Yet structural factors, including caste and gender hierarchies, often prevent their knowledge from being shared with those who make decisions that will affect the lives of many children. The collaborative research process undertaken in Nepal has opened up some new channels of communication. Thus, in conclusion, we offer some ideas for furthering the rights of working children that have been generated during the research period.

In recognition that support to the national government is the only way to maintain national unity and cohesion in child labor policy, organizations participating in the study (among other key policy actors) aim to help enforce the new legislation on minimum ages for children working in hazardous industries. Their challenge is in devising a plan for enforcement that is feasible for all concerned parties. So far, carpet factory owners have shown little desire to engage in debate with the government over the changes in legislation for fear of raising any international publicity on child labor that could negatively affect the national economy. It is therefore vital that the relationships of trust and sharing between organizations in different sectors that were established in the collaborative research are strengthened by continued communication and action.

Some activists have emphasized that the cultural acceptance of child labor is the greatest hindrance to progress in children's rights. Reflecting on 10 years of campaigning for children's rights, Gauri Pradhan, head of one of the largest Nepali children's organizations, maintains that a fundamental shift in attitudes and behavior was needed before children's lives would improve (personal communication, 1999). But our research begs the question, Is it always the case that acceptance of child work equates with views of children as subordinate and exploitable?

Early anti–child labor campaigning focused on instances where industries were employing children for little or no wage and under deplorable conditions. Social activists have been slow to recognize the critical role of trade unions that could have great influence across many employment sectors around the country.

There is now scant evidence to suggest that employers do not merely see children as a cheap and malleable workforce but recognize the role that nonexploitative work can play in assuring the physical and psychological well-being of children. Examples include employers who support children through nonformal education classes run in large factories and financed by their owners. Research on child domestic servants shows that a small proportion of employers take steps to ensure that children working for them have access to education, good quality diet, and shelter, as well as time to play with their peers. Further work is needed to explore the extent to which employers are sensitive to their potential role in fulfilling children's rights.

This research has identified structural and cultural constraints within organizations to the systematic incorporation of local knowledge in children's rights programming. Where knowledge is being generated about children's roles in the family and community, mechanisms are needed to bring these to the decision makers. If the effectiveness of programs is to be improved, there needs to be a reappraisal of how local sociocultural concerns and priorities can be incorporated. There is clearly scope for greater collaboration and investment in working with the private sector in creating environments that can meet the best interests of children in a sustainable manner.

Notes

1. See, for example, Tuladhar 1997.

2. These six stakeholders are the Central Carpets Industrialists Association, the Child Development Society, the General Federation of Nepalese Trade Unions, the National Society for the Protection of Environment and Children, the Nepal Rugmark Foundation, and the Ministry of Labour of HMG-Nepal.

3. Participating organizations contributed resources and expertise toward the research.

4. Personal communication, Sakaya, Central Carpets Industrialists Association.

References

Acharya, U. D. 1997. *Country Report on Trafficking in Children and Their Exploitation in Prostitution and Other Intolerable Forms of Child Labour in Nepal.* Kathmandu: International Labor Organization.

Baker, Rachel. 1998. Runaway Street Children in Nepal: Social Competence Away from Home. In *Children and Social Competence: Arenas of Action*, ed. I. Hutchby and J. Moran-Ellis. London: Falmer Press.

Baker, Rachel, Catherine Panter-Brick, and Alison Todd. 1997. Homeless Street Boys in Nepal: Their Demography and Lifestyle. *Journal of Comparative Family Studies* 28(1):129-46.

Boyden, Jo, Birgitte Ling, and William Myers. 1998. *What Works for Working Children*. Smedjebacken: Save the Children Sweden.

Burman, Erica. 1996. Local, Global or Globalized? Child Development and International Child Rights Legislation. *Childhood* 3(1):45-66.

Centre for Policy Studies. 1999. Situation Analysis of Child Labour in the Carpet Industry of Nepal. Research report submitted to Nepal Rugmark Foundation and supported by UNICEF Nepal, Kathmandu.

Child Workers in Nepal. 1995. Background and Scenario of CWIN. *Voice of Child Workers*, Dec., 3-11.

Department for International Development. 1998. *Nepal, Country Strategy Paper*. London: DFID.

Ennew, Judith. 2000. The History of Child Rights. Whose Story? *Cultural Survival Quarterly* 24(2):44-48.

Fyfe, Alec. 1999. Child Labour and Education: Revisiting the Policy Debate. Paper presented at the IREWOC Workshop, 15-17 Nov., Amsterdam.

Hinton, Rachel. 2000. Seen but Not Heard: Refugee Children and Models of Intervention. In *Abandoned Children*, ed. C. Panter-Brick and M. Smith. Cambridge: Cambridge University Press.

Human Development Centre. 1999. *Human Development in South Asia 1999: The Crisis of Governance*. Karachi, Pakistan: Oxford University Press.

International Labor Organization. 1999. *IPEC-Nepal Implementation Report 1998-1999*. Kathmandu: ILO.

James, Alison, Chris Jenks, and Alan Prout. 1998. *Theorizing Childhood*. Cambridge: Polity Press.

Maskay, B. K. 1998. *Non-Governmental Organisations in Development: Search for a New Vision*. Kathmandu: Centre for Development and Governance.

Morice, Alain. 2000. Paternal Domination: The Typical Relationship Conditioning the Exploitation of Children. In *The Exploited Child*, ed. B. Schlemmer. London: Zed Books.

Nieuwenhuys, Olga. 1994. *Children's Lifeworlds: Gender, Welfare and Labour in the Developing World*. London: Routledge.

Qvortrup, Jens. 2000. Macroanalysis of Childhood. In *Research with Children: Perspectives and Practices*, ed. P. Christensen and A. James. London: Falmer Press.

Reddy, Nandana. 2000. The Right to Organize: The Working Children's Movement in India. *Cultural Survival Quarterly* 24(2):44-48.

Sagant, Philippe. 1996. *The Dozing Shaman: The Limbus of Eastern Nepal*. Delhi: Oxford University Press.

Seddon, David. 1993. Democracy and Development in Nepal. In *Nepal in the Nineties: Versions of the Past, Visions of the Future*, ed. M. Hutt. New Delhi: Paul's Press.

Sharma, Murari, Shraddha Shrestha, and Jamie Cross. 2000. Weaving Carpets, Weaving Lives: Childhood and Ethnicity in Downtown Kathmandu. Paper presented at the IAUES Inter-Congress on Metropolitan Ethnic Cultures, Maintenance and Interaction, 14-28 July, Beijing.

Tuladhar, J. 1997. *Situation Analysis of Child Labour in Nepal*. Report submitted to the National Planning Commission Secretariat. Kathmandu: Centre for Women/Children and Community Development.

UNICEF. 2000. Towards a Strategic Framework for UNICEF Contribution to the Elimination of Child Labour in South Asia. Draft, UNICEF Regional Office of South Asia, Kathmandu.

Vaidya, S. N. 1997. *Child Labour: Protection and Promotion of Their Rights in Nepal*. Kathmandu: HMG-Nepal Ministry of Labour/ILO-IPEC.

Vidyasagar, R. 2000. Issues Relating to Children and Work in South Asia. Working paper. Kathmandu: UNICEF-ROSA.

ANNALS, *AAPSS*, **575**, May 2001

Child Labor in Pakistan:
Coming of Age in the New World Order

By SAADIA TOOR

ABSTRACT: The issue of child labor in Pakistan's export industries has become the topic of much controversy and in some ways has triggered the debate over trade and labor standards. Consumer protests and boycotts in the North have led to initiatives being taken by various national and international organizations. However, this article takes issue with the current projection of child labor as a function of children's poverty and lack of education and families' lack of awareness. The author argues that it is impossible to understand and even address the child labor problem without placing it against the backdrop of the dynamics of the current neoliberal international political economic system. She concludes by arguing that the only way in which the issue of social and labor rights can be once more given precedence in an increasingly socially disembedded world economy is through political engagement with the forces of globalization: the World Bank, the International Monetary Fund, and the World Trade Organization.

Saadia Toor is a doctoral candidate in the Department of Rural Sociology at Cornell University. Her dissertation research is on the political economy of national culture in Pakistan between 1958 and 1975. Her other research interests include feminist theory, international political economy, and development theory.

WHEN I began this article, my reference points for a critique of globalization were the riots in Seattle and the World Bank's newest World Development Report on Poverty. Since then, the world has witnessed yet another clash between the forces of labor and those of capital. I refer to the recent meeting of the International Monetary Fund (IMF) and the World Bank in Prague and the brutal crushing of protest, ironically (or perhaps poetically), by the government of Vaclav Havel, sometime dissident and leader of the "democratic" movement against the old Communist regime in the former Czechoslovakia. The manner in which the activists—gathered from across the world—were treated by the Czech Republic outdid even the manner in which the Seattle police crushed its local protests. In the process, these two events have done much to expose the iron hand within the velvet glove of globalization, as represented by the current triumvirate of the IMF, the World Bank, and the World Trade Organization (WTO).

This article deals with the issue of child labor, particularly the case of Pakistan, but within the framework of a new world order defined by the politics of the WTO. It argues that the way the debate over child labor has progressed, and the agents or actors involved in it, has presented a distorted picture of the real issues at stake: the fact that the rights of labor (or social rights more generally) matter little (if at all) in a world where the rules of the game are increasingly being defined by multinational capital. The debate over child labor

at the international level has thus been highly revealing in a number of ways. For instance, it has shown how consumer power (through boycotts and the like) can be channeled to pressure multinational corporations to show some corporate responsibility in this age of fly-by-night capital. However, ultimately, this article argues that demanding social rights—especially labor rights of any sort—in the current international political economic scenario increasingly dominated and defined by the WTO and its constituency is a losing battle and that even if these rights were granted in some limited fashion (for instance, by ensuring that children's rights are implemented vis-à-vis labor, by making industries child-free) it accomplishes no more than papering the cracks being produced by a system premised on the existence and perpetuation of inequalities—an intensified and increasingly global capitalism.

This article is thus less about the specifics of child labor in Pakistan and even less about the state of child labor in any one industry in Pakistan, which would amount to an important, but ultimately misplaced ethnographic exercise. Of necessity, we need to place the issue of child labor in Pakistan against the global context within which it exists. By not addressing the structures and interests that produce, support, or encourage the practice of child labor, we run the risk of engaging in superficial analyses and reaching irresponsible conclusions. Instead, I aim to address the connections between child labor and globalization by highlighting and examining the contributions of various institutions to this debate as well as the interests and structures that are at work. This article therefore pertains specifically to the analysis of child labor in export industries but can be applied to—indeed, must be applied to—other sectors and industries because the effects of the same forces suffuse society at large.

LINKING POVERTY, GLOBALIZATION, AND DEVELOPMENT

The World Bank's 1997 World Development Report sustains the myth of globalization as the new development strategy—the path to economic well-being. The most recent World Development Report, on the other hand, is forced to deal with the issue of increasing and intensifying poverty across the world. However, in their infinite wisdom, World Bank economists insist that the answer to this is more, not less, globalization or, at the very least, "globalisation with a human face."

In the late 1950s, John Kenneth Galbraith noted that "the transition of the very poor from a majority to a comparative minority position", through the spread of general affluence in society, had caused "a profoundly interesting although little recognized change in what may be termed the political economy of poverty." This change amounted to the poor ceasing "to be automatically an object of interest to the politician" because to speak for the poor was to speak "for a small and also inarticulate minority." The "poverty-stricken," he went on, were "further

forgotten because it is assumed that with increasing output poverty must disappear" (Galbraith 1958, 254). Even at that time, at the height of the Keynsian-Fordist state, Galbraith noted that "this is not be expected or, in any case, it will be an infinitely time-consuming and unreliable remedy" (255).

Again, contrary to the popular wisdom of neoclassical development economics institutionalized in the World Bank, which proposes an initial inverse relationship between economic growth and equality in a developing society (extrapolated from the experience of industrialized countries and presented as a universal model by followers of the Nobel Laureat Simon Kuznets), Gunnar Myrdal (1970) proposed altogether different relationships between economic growth and equality when he said that "greater equality is a precondition for lifting a society out of poverty" where "economic and social inequality may itself be not only a cause of the prevailing poverty, but also, at the same time, its consequence" (57).

Although even the World Bank has been forced to acknowledge that economic growth does not, by itself, bring automatic prosperity for all people of the world (see the most recent World Development Report), it continues to insist that it is at least a necessary condition. Putting the matter this way obscures the fact that both the question of what kind and form of economic growth—absolute versus relative, for one—is desirable as well as the ways in which it should be pursued remain open. Although economic policies and theories of the past have been severely criticized for their role in exacerbating inequalities within and across nations, and for increasing both relative and absolute poverty, the present neoliberal regime continues to tout them as the only way out of the poverty trap, despite the fact that the IMF recently admitted that "in the recent decades, nearly one-fifth of the world population have regressed"—arguably "one of the greatest economic failures of the twentieth century" (quoted in Palast 2000). A secret internal IMF document on Ecuador reveals that "by 1 November this year . . . [Ecuador's] government is ordered to raise the price of cooking gas by 80 per cent. It must eliminate 26,000 jobs and halve real wages for the remaining workers by 50 per cent in four steps in months specified by the IMF." Palast (2000) notes that the IMF and World Bank

have effectively controlled Tanzania's economy since 1985. . . . Their experts wasted no time in cutting trade barriers, limiting government subsidies and selling off state industries. This worked wonders. According to bank-watcher Nancy Alexander of the Washington-based Globalisation Challenge Initiative, in just 15 years Tanzania's GDP has dropped from $309 to $210 per capita, the literacy rate is falling and the rate of abject poverty has jumped to 51 per cent of the population.

Need we still wonder, then, where poverty comes from in this present historical conjuncture? Palast (2000) remarks sardonically that "in all, the IMF's 167 loan conditions look less like an assistance plan and more like a blueprint for a financial coup d'etat." However, in what amounts to bizarre logic lifted from *Through the Looking Glass*, neoclassical economists continue to insist that what is needed is actually more of the same medicine. The problem with neoliberalism, it appears, is that there just has not been enough of it.

Another example of fantastic logic—or willful distortion, depending on one's politics and ethics—comes from the hallowed halls of U.S. business. Tom Niles, of the U.S. Council for International Business, recently cited a UNICEF study that concluded that only 5 percent of the children in developing countries were engaged in export-led industries. No doubt, in his view, this constituted proof positive that globalization—and the international trade regime—was not responsible for the child labor phenomenon. "He inferred," we are told, "that the rest of the child workforce was employed elsewhere," which seemed sufficient basis on which to conclude that "it was poverty and nothing but poverty that forced parents to make their children do demeaning, dangerous and unpaid jobs" (Pakistan's Anti-Child Labour Project 2000). On that much we can all agree, but why so mum over the reasons behind such an overwhelming increase in poverty worldwide?

CHILD LABOR, POVERTY, AND FREE TRADE

Poverty, not trade, is the main cause of unacceptable working conditions and environmental degradation. And the answer to poverty is more trade and business, not less.

—Mike Moore, addressing a
conference organized
by trade unions on
globalization and
workers' rights
(WTO 1999)

If the free traders cannot understand how one nation can grow at the expense of another, we need not wonder, since these same gentlemen also refuse to understand how in the same country one class can enrich itself at the expense of another.

—Karl Marx ([1848] 1969, 223)

In the "regime of truth"[1] (Foucault 1980), which legitimizes the neoliberal project, development and globalization are understood as synonymous; the latter is only the latest stage of the former. In actual fact, of course, globalization is the latest stage in a process of backlash against the Keynsian-Fordist project that began with the structural adjustment program initiated by the IMF and the World Bank in the wake of the oil crisis of the late 1970s. The mainstream development project had been largely articulated within the economic framework provided by the Keynsian-Fordist model and the international context characterized by the Cold War. The resurgence of neoliberalism (embodied in the Thatcher-Reagan regimes), beginning around the late 1970s, and the end of the Cold War, with the breakup of the Soviet Union, were fundamental to the rising hegemony of the neoliberal project. Just as structural adjustment—although presented as a part of the development process and crucial as a correcting mechanism for the ills of the welfare state— actually undermined the gains of the latter and increased poverty and insecurity wherever it was implemented (Bello 2000a, 2000b), the current neoliberal project of globalization is not a newer and better stage of developmentalism but has brought the development project into severe crisis both at the level of academic work on the subject and on development practice itself.

Of all the aspects of the neoliberal globalization process, free trade is the one being most directly linked with development and prosperity for all. It thus becomes important to deconstruct the arguments being given in favor of free trade and analyze the WTO—the institutional apparatus behind it—as well as understand the larger project of neoliberalism within which these discourses and practices are being shaped.

The issue of labor rights has become highly contentious. Neoliberal globalization's regime of truth is hard at work to characterize all efforts at enforcing labor rights— and social rights in general—as part of a conspiracy against the poor. The issues of child labor and labor in developing countries are being recast in the dominant framework in terms of either social dumping,[2] protectionism, or comparative advantage, obscuring the fact that the battle is not between North and South but between the interests of capital and those human beings who, in a capitalist system, can only be conceptualized as labor.

Under the present regime, those who argue that globalization and the free-trade regime is detrimental to human, child, and labor rights are represented as naïve, elite activists who are unknowingly doing more harm than good by insisting—in Seattle, Prague, and elsewhere—that multinational corporations and their platform, the WTO, be held accountable for their actions (see An Unjustified Sense of Victory 1999).

Mike Moore, director general of the WTO, said as much in a much earlier address: "There are those who would like to put the clock back, to wish away the mutual dependence of nations [achieved through trade]. But no-one can stop the course of history" (WTO 1995).

Luckily, we are simultaneously reassured that the mutual dependence of nations (achieved through trade) is the best possible solution for all the world's ills—from conflict to poverty. If that sounds like so much déjà vu, it should: these were precisely the arguments presented by free traders in the time of Marx.

In the same speech, Moore stated that the participation of the developing countries in the world trading system was tantamount to a "geopolitical revolution" because of how it has "chipped away the old North-South divide." In what precise way, we are not told. The coercive terms and conditions under which this has occurred are completely obscured: "Over the last decade or so, dozens of developing countries have shifted towards liberal trade policies and greater reliance on international competition to generate money and growth" (WTO 1995).

Moreover, we are assured, globalization is about the free market, which is on its way to becoming a level playing field. Unfortunately, some countries still obstinately refuse to share in the increased prosperity promised by globalization. But luckily, we know how to "provide the conditions for such countries to get themselves off the floor. . . . we must do our utmost to see that [they] are able to diversify their export production and expand their export markets on a competitive basis" (WTO 1995).

In this scheme of things, all those who refuse to play by the rules of the game are either just very bad losers or subversive terrorists bent on sabotaging the true agenda of globalization: prosperity and peace. In a conference on globalization and workers' rights, Moore told unions that "there are dangers to this backlash against globalization which we ignore at our peril" because, although it was "true that the benefits of the global economy are not evenly shared," the vulnerable "are not helped by blocking trade, restricting investment, and making economies poorer" (WTO 1999). And for those tougher nuts to crack in the audience, Moore has another card up his sleeve:

There is also a darker side to the backlash against globalization. For some, the attacks on economic openness are part of a broader assault on internationalism—on foreigners, immigration, a more pluralistic and integrated world. Anti-globalization becomes the latest chapter in the age-old call to separatism, tribalism and racism. (WTO 1999)

Once upon a time, when Moore was a young man, "the word internationalism was a noble word . . . but now the idea of internationalism has become something to be feared or attacked" (WTO 1999). Well, Mr. Moore, we can easily explain that: in your youth, "internationalism" was a word that connoted the solidarity of working people across the world, whereas what we are now faced with is the internationalization of capital.

In a press release issued by the International Union of Food, Agricultural, Hotel, Restaurant, Tobacco and Allied Workers' Association (2000), much of the detritus that has collected around the issue of the WTO, labor rights, and developing countries was cleared away. This statement reiterated that the main conflict—the principal contradiction, in Mao's terms—in this conjuncture (and, indeed, throughout the history of capitalism) was between capital and labor, and not—à la dependency theorists of yore—between rich countries and poor countries. The latter conflict was there, but it was an effect of the former:

While we respect the call by developing nations for an end to exclusion and for equal rights at the negotiating table, we must continue to expose and refute the position of governments whose opposition to a social clause conceals a "comparative advantage" based on repression, bonded and child labour. . . . The issue is not, as some governments and NGOs would have [us] believe, conflict between "North" and "South." It is how to defend the democratic and trade union rights of workers on both sides of the development divide from a globalization process which is undermining these rights while ravaging living and working conditions, public services, and the environment around the world.

The statement shows that protests against globalization—and their suppression—are not limited to the North: it exposes the "oppressive reality behind [developing countries'] ideological posture" with regard to excluding labor rights from the WTO's agenda through the example of the government of India's use of the armed forces to break strikes by workers seeking a moratorium on privatization (International Union of Food, Agricultural, Hotel, Restaurant, Tobacco and Allied Workers' Association 2000). The same forces are at work in Pakistan.

Of course, the intensification and internationalization of the free-market system has not happened seamlessly. There have been severe reactions by an increasingly aware— if only selectively so—consumer public in the North against multinational corporations' poor record vis-à-vis labor (for example, the GAP issue) and the environment (for example, the demand for turtle-safe shrimp nets). The campaign against child labor has been part of this larger demand for social responsibility and transparency from multinational corporations. Of course, when multinational corporations do respond, it is only to counter the bad publicity through better public relations, hence the phenomenon of "greenwashing." Often this does not go beyond launching a new ad campaign that projects the multinational corporation in a better, more responsible, and altogether benevolent light. Sometimes this involves actually doing something, because the international media attention is so severe or because the corporation has no choice in the matter. This is what happened in the case of the soccer ball controversy in Pakistan. First, media attention was unprecedented: the 1998 soccer World Cup was due to take place when the exposé regarding child labor in the soccer ball industry in Pakistan hit international headlines. The fact that the controversy involved children was instrumental in building the campaign, which spread across schools in the United States.

In this age of fly-by-night capital, it is usually easier for multinational corporations to pack up and leave undesirable areas for greener pastures. However, Pakistan has somewhat of a monopoly on the production and export of soccer balls. Thus sports industry giants such as Nike and Adidas, among others, were forced to address the issue or at least be perceived as doing so. Enter various certifying agencies with labels testifying to a product's child-labor-free status.

However, we need to keep in mind that even behind this show of corporate responsibility exist the primary interests of capital. When the latter are threatened through bad press and consumer boycotts, it makes good economic sense to invest in better publicity campaigns. As Jean Baudrillard warns us,

in this "capitalist" society, capital can never actually be grasped in its present reality. It is not that our Marxist critics have not run after it, but it always stays a

length ahead of them. By the time one phase has been unmasked, capital has already passed on to another. . . . Capital cheats. It doesn't play by the rules of critique. . . . By reinventing capital in each successive phase on the basis of the primacy of political economy, [these theorists] simply confirm the absolute initiative capital enjoys as a historical event. (quoted in Kincaid and Portes 1994, 1)

The standoffs and organized boycotts and protests, whether in Prague or Seattle or in the form of strikes against liberalization and privatization across the world, and their aftermath expose globalization's reality not as ultimately empowering—or at the least benign—but as a consciously institutionalized political project backed by the military and police forces of the advanced industrialized North/West. As a political project, then, it can only be countered through political engagement and direct political action and not, as has been proposed, through the addition of social clauses within the WTO's mandate itself. This is a contradiction in terms because of what the WTO is and the interests it is there to protect and promote.

The protests in Seattle and Prague have historical significance because they rent asunder the elaborate veil of illusion so elaborately constructed by the propagandists of free trade and globalization. But these hard-working people are not to be outwitted—the process of damage control begins immediately after a crisis, despite the fact that even the most promising public relations exercises manage to backfire: the much-publicized recent e-discussion on the World Bank's Report on

Poverty organized and moderated by the Bretton Woods Institute is a case in point.[3] Although supporters of the international market system (often actual World Bank employees) often resorted to airing shrill defenses of the World Bank and globalization, they were overwhelmingly drowned out by a passionate, well-informed group of detractors ranging from academics, nongovernmental organization (NGO) workers, activists, and concerned individuals from the North and South who could, and did, present empirical evidence against the World Bank's claims to have increased economic growth and prosperity and against its current poverty alleviation agenda and its development policies historically. Thus there is good reason why the unholy trinity's supporters cannot actually afford to give space to "democratic" critique emanating from "civil society," no matter how much they may sell these concepts to the South. The kind and amount of human and social wreckage that the globalization project leaves in its wake is beyond even that captured by the imagery of Walter Benjamin's "Angel of Progress" (1969) and is getting harder and harder to sweep under the carpet.

What has emerged systematically from such contemporary and previous critiques of the mainstream development project represented by the World Bank, and the crisis in development inaugurated by the structural adjustment policies of the IMF and World Bank in the late 1970s, is the stark reality that both absolute and relative poverty as well as inequality—whether between states or within them—have dramatically and tragically increased, not decreased. There are a number of studies that directly connect this rise in the impoverishment of the world's masses with the policies of these multilateral institutions that now include the WTO. The World Bank itself is forced to acknowledge the increase in poverty, and the latest World Development Report admits that the one-point agenda of economic growth has not resulted in increased prosperity for most people. However, the report ends by prescribing more of the same medicine by arguing that the problem has been not too much but not enough globalization. What these organizations do not tell us is that the fact that trade is outstripping production across the world is not a cause for celebration—it reflects the closure of hundreds of factories and speaks of mass unemployment created through the liberalization process. It speaks of the decline of productive investment, of the relative importance of productive capital versus finance capital, and of the increasing disembeddedness of the global economy. Moreover, although there is much talk of whether economic growth through the World Bank's policy prescriptions has trickled down to the majority of the people, there is little focus on the fact that economic growth itself has declined, largely as a result of the debt trap (see Kincaid and Portes 1994, 8).

The WTO is the culmination—the crowning achievement—of a newly consolidated global market. Prior to the Uruguay Round, the General Agreement on Tariffs and Trade

(GATT) was a minority club that had no power to enforce its recommendations. Alan Freeman (1998) writes that, in the WTO, "the GATT has been transformed from an effectual chamber of commerce into a powerful device for restructuring the world market in the commercial and financial interests of the leading powers" (81). GATT also "marked two decisive changes. Firstly it moved from 'result-orientation' to 'rule-orientation'. . . . This extends to legal trade regulations which the WTO obliges member countries to write into their own laws. Most significantly, these rules are now policed" (83).

Following the breakup of the Soviet Union and the consequent end of the Cold War, the advantages of a bipolar world came to an abrupt end. No longer was there an alternative economic system or trading bloc for developing countries: there was, instead, a new world order. During the neoliberal counterrevolution, there is a switch from negotiation to aggressive, threat-based U.S. policies; debt crisis; and the draconian intervention of the IMF with its structural adjustment, export-oriented programs. The counterrevolution process went so far as to replace "Keynesians . . . on the leading world financial institutions, and wave after wave of neo-liberal advisers and political regimes came to the fore in development economics and in the Third World countries themselves" (Freeman 1998, 85). This is hardly surprising if looked at within the framework of a Gramscian analysis. Every attempt at hegemony by a historic bloc requires a fight at the ideological level. Scientists, academics, and other intellectuals are the main actors who set the terms of this "war of maneuver." Thus the new world order did not just happen as a result of the arrival of the "end of History"—it was consciously and forcefully put in place. Since hegemony in the Gramscian sense is always already an unstable state (see Gramsci 1971)—that is, it needs to continuously and constantly be won anew—we have the numerous media blitzes, academic conferences, and special reports supporting the neoliberal project and its specific components, often in the face of all evidence to the contrary.

Freeman (1998) is correct to some extent when he argues that producing consent through ideological manipulation is no longer necessary because "it no longer matters whether the hapless victims [of the multilateral agencies' erroneous policies] believe them or not" and because the WTO can enforce them "by threats and blackmail" (85). However, the ideological manipulation is not meant for them—it is meant for all the workers and well-meaning citizens of the North who, at least for now, could rock the boat by pressuring their own governments. The propaganda in the North is directed, as we saw, not against the South or southern activists (who disappear from view) but against misguided activists and NGOs in the North.

The fact is that the WTO's policies are creating conditions for the accentuation of poverty and the decline in the condition of workers everywhere. Child labor is one manifestation or effect of the demands being placed on the majority of the world's population under a neoliberal economic regime. In fact, just as the feminization of the labor force across the world went hand in hand with the end of the family wage, the use of child labor works to depress wages across the board. In an exposé of the child labor industry in Pakistan, Jonathan Silvers (1996) argues that "as long as children are put to work, poverty will spread and standards of living will fall." He points out that "in many regions the surplus of cheap child labour has depressed the already inadequate adult wage to the point where a parent and child together now earn less than the parent alone earned a year ago."

Children workers are also preferred by employers—Third World firms and multinational corporations—for many of the same reasons that women workers are: they are nonunionized, pliant, and have "nimble fingers" (a major consideration in both the carpet and soccer ball industries in Pakistan) (see Silvers 1996). Moreover, in Pakistan, children workers are usually beholden to their employers, who have more often than not "leased" them from their parents. They are, effectively, bonded labor. In Pakistan, NGO efforts recently brought about legislation outlawing the *pagri*, or advance, given by the potential employer to the family of the young worker. This advance was supposed to be adjusted against the child's wages, but the fact that all the expenses that the employer incurs vis-à-vis the child, including any losses due to his or her work, functions to keep the child forever in debt to the employer. Despite the outlawing of this practice, there is not sufficient awareness about the law's passage, and even if there is, increasing poverty and the lack of alternatives force people into the same cycle.

The WTO in fact is only drawing on the work already done by the World Bank and IMF's structural adjustment policies and the development project itself in terms of drawing the majority of the world's population directly into a market system characterized by the Thatcherite and Reaganite ideological revolutions. The dependencies created and now actively perpetuated by the neoliberal project in the name of internationalism and solidarity[4] have made it impossible for people or governments to even imagine, for example, the kind of alternative once proposed by Samir Amin (1990): delinking. If anything, the system itself spits out those areas and regions that it considers worthless for its purposes; sub-Saharan Africa is one example. The areas are then casually designated as being beyond development, which is not surprising in an age when development and globalization are considered synonymous. Any area that is useless in terms of the global market and multinational corporations is thus by definition beyond development. The fact is that we are now in a stage of indifferent imperialism, where the world powers need only exploit some of the world, not all of it.

As Walden Bello (1991) argues,

The crisis of the developing countries of the South is not simply one of exposure to unregulated financial flows—a problem that can easily be fixed with controls on speculative capital at the global and international level. The financial deregulation of these economies that has proven so devastating is simply the latest phase of a development model that they have internalized over the last two decades under the aegis of the IMF and World Bank structural adjustment programs—one in which foreign markets and foreign capital serve as the twin engines of development.

Because the issue of child labor took American public opinion by storm in the mid-1990s, the federal government was forced to take a stand on it. And through pressure judiciously applied, other key people (and people in key institutions) have also found themselves cornered in a way that made the issue of turtle-free shrimp fishing nets fade into the background. Nothing makes the American public's heart melt like the idea that there are children in this world for whom—shock! horror! surprise!—labor is a fact of life and education a luxury. Nobody questions why these children are forced to grow up before their time, because that would involve questioning the systemic and structural issues that force them into the labor market. Most of the attention focuses on social values and the awareness level of families and communities, as if child labor was a function of ignorance and not of political economic systems such as feudalism and capitalism (or, as in Pakistan, an articulation of the two). In no time, the word had spread far and wide, and schoolchildren were organizing protests and boycotts against big names like Nike and Adidas and demanding an end to child labor.

THE RETURN OF NEWSPEAK

There is a tendency for all knowledge, like all ignorance, to deviate from truth in an opportunistic direction.

—Gunnar Myrdal (1970, 3)

Ultimately, neoliberalism is more than just an ideological assault. It is a regime in which the ideological doublespeak is backed, as in all systems of power, by an apparatus of repressive force. The agents of this repressive apparatus are the WTO, the World Bank, and the IMF, with the firepower of advanced capitalist countries like the United States never far behind (see Bello 2000b). The fate of Iraq under economic sanctions serves as a gruesome cautionary tale for all those countries that entertain ideas of disregarding the dictates of these forces of global capitalism. The WTO has been given the legal right to impose sanctions on any country that refuses to ratify—and, more crucially, implement—its conventions, hence the regular reviews of countries. Keeping in mind this thinly veiled threat of force, it is nevertheless important to examine and deconstruct the ideological strategies of this regime.

But what do these people actually have to say about the issue of child labor, or labor rights, in general? There are a few interesting themes. One, of course, is the ubiquitous use of the statement that poverty is the root of the problem. The other is that globalization—and especially free trade—is actually going to solve problems such as poverty, unemployment, and child labor. Another is the attempt to cast globalization in a positive light by co-opting the rhetoric of the Left—of social justice and international solidarity.

Mike Moore of the WTO did his bit for damage control in the wake of the Seattle protests by telling trade union workers that as far as he was concerned there simply was not any contradiction between trade and labor (WTO 1999). "Open economies, imperfect as they are have delivered more jobs, opportunities and security to more people than alternatives." Here the veiled reference is clearly to the centrally planned economies because we are immediately informed that countries that have "embraced openness and freedom have increased the real incomes of their workers, which in turn has raised labour standards and reduced poverty. Countries that remain closed, remain poorer, underdeveloped, cut off from the world of rights and freedoms." This is, of course, patently false. The greatest tragedy of the 1990s has been the massive decline of welfare in the countries of Eastern Europe and Central Asia, many of which have experienced increases in mortality, illiteracy, crime, malnutrition, and gender inequality (see, for example, Palast 2000). As an internal secret IMF report reveals, and as I have tried to show here, the exact opposite of what Moore claims has been happening across the world. Unemployment is on the rise everywhere, except perhaps for information technology workers, who constitute a very small percentage of the world labor force. Real incomes have declined as poverty has risen exponentially. That Moore can still manage to face trade unions and lie brazenly in the face of contradictory evidence speaks volumes for the relations of power embodied in the new world order.

One major problem at the international level is that national governments continue to be seen as representing their people—a fact that may or may not be true of formally democratic governments but is simply not the case in Pakistan, which vacillates between civil and military bureaucratic authoritarianism. Thus if the official representative of Pakistan declares that free trade is good, it supposedly follows that Pakistani public opinion is behind this decision. Conflating the vast majority of the world's people with their respective governments or their states is a convenient discursive move that, by affirming nationalism and nationalist ideology, obscures the divisions and contradictions that do matter: those between the exploited and the exploiters and between labor and capital. In fact, Myrdal (1970) correctly points out that

the goal of the developed countries and, in particular, the United States has not been that the masses should be awakened in order to make possible genuine democracy and the radical reforms needed [for development]. All their sympathies have been with the privileged classes in the underdeveloped countries and not with the impoverished masses. They were readily prepared to condone the absence of reforms, preferring stability. (435-36)

When developing countries—or rather, the comprador bourgeoisie—argue that the noise against child labor and the accusations of social dumping by advanced industrialized countries amount to little more than protectionist measures, they are technically correct. In fact, it is on the issue of social dumping and social clauses in general that the real powers at work behind the WTO reveal themselves. Because, in true Chinese-box style, the WTO is not just an agency that protects the interests of capital at large regardless of their national origin. The WTO is an agency that has been set up to protect the interests of particular capitals. No prizes for guessing which (see Freeman 1998; McMichael 2000).

The fact is, of course, that free trade is only one aspect of the neoliberal package of the free market. In a market economy, the only important freedoms are the freedom of the capitalist to exploit workers and the freedom of workers to let their labor be exploited. As has amply been pointed out by scholars such as Polanyi, the entire package of rights and freedoms in liberal political philosophy were to the advantage of the industrial capitalist system: the freedom (and right) to own private property, the freedom to trade one's labor for wages, and the right of the capitalist to increase his profit margin by the extraction of increasing amounts of surplus labor. Marx ([1848] 1969), in a speech to the Democratic Association of Brussels, had this to say on the subject of free trade after the repeal of the corn laws in England:

To sum up, what is free trade, what is free trade under the present condition of society? It is freedom of capital. When you have overthrown the few national barriers which still restrict the progress of capital, you will merely have given it complete freedom of action. So long as you let the relation of wage labor to capital exist, it does not matter how favorable the conditions under which the exchange of commodities takes place, there will always be a class which will exploit and a class which will be exploited.

What has changed from those early days is that, as far as the capitalists are concerned, the world is their oyster. Samir Amin (1997) has pointed out that one of the major effects of the globalization of the world economy has been to extend the reserve army of unemployed persons across the world. And just as the reserve army of the unemployed within a national economy gave the capitalist the leverage he needed, vis-à-vis labor, to depress wages, so is the case today for multinational firms in an increasingly globalized world economy. Chossudovsky (1997) has called this the globalization of poverty, arguing that the

IMF structural adjustment programs . . . have generated a global cheap-labour economy through the decomposition of the national economy of indebted states. . . . The WTO, in turn, uses a vehicle for generalising the "free trade zone" to the entire country. . . . material production takes place off-shore in a Third World cheap-labour economy, yet the largest increases in GDP are recorded in the importing country . . . [where] cheap-labour imports (in primary commodities and manufacturing) generate a corresponding increase in income in the services economy of the rich countries. (86)

If any doubt remains as to the relationship between free trade and poverty, we can always turn to Myrdal, speaking in 1970: international trade theory, he states, was biased from its inception within the ideological predilections of classical liberalism, which assumes that "there are certain elements of social reality which can be characterized as 'economic factors,' and that it is defensible to analyze international trade while abstracting it from all other factors." "Biased in this way," he continues, "international trade theory developed the thought that trade worked for the equalization of factor prices and incomes [yes, but in which direction?], in the first instance wages of labor" (277). In fact, what we observe "is indeed a very strange thing. International inequalities of income have been increasing for a long time and are still increasing" (278). In effect, "contrary to the theory, *international trade—and capital movements—will generally tend to breed inequality, and will do so the more strongly when substantial inequalities are already established*" (279). Thus, even if we absolve the IMF and the World Bank of the responsibility of creating and/or intensifying such inequalities across the world through their structural adjustment policies, we cannot forgive the WTO for establishing a system of world trade that assumes a level playing field (interestingly, the WTO policies are being called "structural adjustment for the North").

But again, as Marx ([1848] 1969) warned, free trade has never been and never will be about any such thing:

The whole line of argument [of the free traders] amounts to this: Free trade increases productive forces. If industry keeps growing, if wealth, if the productive power, if, in a word, productive capital increases, the demand for labor, the price of labor, and consequently the rate of wages, rise also. The most favorable condition for the worker is the growth of capital. This must be admitted.

But what happens when capital grows? Marx continues,

Competition among the workers grows in a far greater proportion. The reward of labor diminishes for all, and the burden of labor increases for some. . . . This law of commodity labor, of the minimum of wages, will be confirmed in proportion as the supposition of the economists, free-trade, becomes an actual fact. Thus, of two things one: either we must reject all political economy based on the assumption of free trade, or we must admit that under this free trade the whole severity of the economic laws will fall upon the workers.

Hence the need for more and better marketing of the free-trade system highlighting its multiple benefits for society at large and for workers in particular. This is, after all, what is called a hard sell.

DREAMS OF FORDISM PAST

This is why we cannot expect any respite from within the system: the brief period of relative prosperity and mass consumption made us forget the iron law of wages articulated by Ricardo and then taken up by Marx. The worker under the capitalist system will be

kept on the margin of destitution . . . because of his utter weakness in dealing with the capitalist employer and because the system won't work if he is well paid. On occasion he may get more than the bare minimum, but is for the same reason that the dairyman feeds his cows more than the maintenance ration—they give him more milk. (Galbraith 1958, 60)

Or, these days, because if the animal rights activists discovered the subsistence condition in which he kept the cows, the dairyman's milk would be boycotted. Crucially, though, it must be remembered that "the bargaining position of the worker vis-à-vis the employer is the same as that of the cows vis-à-vis the dairyman" (60).

Thus, for all its obsession with lofty ideals such as equality, freedom, and rights, the liberal creed (and even less so the neoliberal creed) cannot be trusted to ensure workers' rights. Galbraith (1958) points out that "the formal liberal attitude towards inequality has changed little over the years. The liberal has partly accepted the view of the well-to-do that it is a trifle uncouth to encourage a policy of soaking the rich" (72). The difference between the liberal and the neoliberal is that the former will wring his hands in despair over the gap between the rich and the poor without really having the guts or motivation to engage in anything

more than palliative measures; the neoliberal is wont to shrug his shoulders expressively and tell you that this is simply the natural order of things. What we are witnessing in the present period of neoliberal hegemony is a return of the good old-fashioned differentiation between the deserving and the undeserving poor; expressed within a resurgent social Darwinism, the gap between the rich and the poor within and across nation-states becomes nothing more and nothing less than the result of natural selection, à la Herbert Spencer.

In trying to prove that the trade-versus-labor issue was a false one, Moore pointed to the fact that most of the 135 members of the WTO are also members of the ILO. In true (neo)liberal fashion, he neglected to mention the absence of a level playing field between these same 135 countries as well as the fact that most of them are trying to play by rules that they had no part in drafting, rules made for living in a world order that was put in place without their input and sometimes despite their active resistance. The notion of the end of history has done incalculable harm in discrediting any and all alternatives to capitalism—the resurgence of neoliberalism with the intensification of globalization was not a coincidence. Neoclassical economists and other neoliberal ideologues fully exploited the window of opportunity provided by the breakup of the Soviet Union in the form of a renewed ideological assault on Fordism-Keynsianism. The result, as we know, was the new world order and the WTO. Just as the Keynsian-Fordist welfare state was never more than a historic compromise between labor and capital that left the issue of a capitalist economic system untouched, any dreams of a new Keynsianism on a global level must come to terms with Dani Rodrik's (1998) definition of global Keynsianism as "a regime of peaceful coexistence among national capitalisms." Those who realize that the logic of capital is what, first and foremost, drives capitalism would not have been surprised by the breakdown of the Keynsian compromise once the age of affluence was over. They will also realize that given capitalism's crisis-prone nature, there will always be a danger of any compromise reached between labor and capital to be subject to retrenchment.

Moore says much the same. He frames the issue in terms of that basic and ubiquitous tenet of the liberal creed: freedom. We are told that "there is a profound connection between economic, political, social and industrial freedom and economic development. Indeed, there is an argument that freedom is a pre-requisite for economic success" (WTO 1999). Note that there is no indication that these different freedoms may come in conflict with one another. "Freedom," in the neoliberal, as in the liberal, creed is in fact a highly selective category and one that rightfully only makes sense from the perspective of the capitalist: it means freedom for workers to sell their labor ("free" labor), the freedom to own property, and so forth. And

lest we forget, it means the free market.

And how does this paean to globalization gel with Moore's admission— almost immediately afterward— that "productivity is being decoupled from employment—growth from redistribution. Both within and across nations the gap is growing." Moore is obviously a consummate politician. Since he is addressing trade unions, he has to admit that all is not well—but he does so in such a way that actually undermines this admission. "Not all our critics are wrong," he says. "We live in a time when we have never had so much but we've never felt so insecure" (WTO 1999). One may well question if the "we" in the first and second part of this statement are the same—in fact, they are not. The people who are feeling insecure are not the ones who have never had it this good—certainly not those workers who have seen an effective decline in their real wages, that is, if they're lucky enough to have jobs.

Moore then appeals to those socialist concepts that are sure to resonate with his audience of trade union members:

All of these governments [in the WTO] are signatories to the United Nation's Universal Declaration of Human Rights. These rights are not the property of one organization, one culture, or one country, but of all people. . . . *It was trade unionists who stood as internationalists in solidarity for freedom everywhere.* Why? Because there were universal values at stake in all these places. Now we should we shrug off their needs for markets and jobs? (WTO 1999; emphasis added)

The internationalism and solidarity that trade unionists have stood for is suddenly presented as having been in the service of nothing but universal freedom, an essentially liberal creed! What Moore is doing, and not coincidentally, is nothing short of conflating internationalism with globalization. The sleight of hand is so seamless, it leaves one breathless.

Moore would have us believe that he joined the WTO because he "saw the WTO as a way of lifting living standards for working people everywhere" and that he believed the multilateral trading system was "fundamentally about international solidarity, interdependence, breaking down barriers between people as well as economies. Prosperity and peace" (WTO 1999). Hence those who argue against the WTO and all it stands for are fundamentally aligning themselves against prosperity and peace. But we have all heard this one before—free trade has been aligned with peace ever since the nineteenth century. History speaks for itself. The connection between free trade and prosperity is a more complicated one because, of course, free trade and neoliberalism in general do bring about prosperity. The question, of course, is prosperity for whom? And at what and whose cost?

In one of his many caustic remarks directed at the free traders of his time, following the repeal of the corn laws in England, Marx ([1848] 1969) said, "Cheap food, high wages, this is the sole aim for which English free-traders have spent millions, and their enthusiasm has already spread to their brethren on the Continent. Generally speaking, those who wish for free trade desire it in order to alleviate the condition of the working class." But,

strange to say, the people for whom cheap food is to be procured at all costs are very ungrateful. Cheap food is as ill-esteemed in England as cheap government is in France. The people see in these self-sacrificing gentlemen, in Bowring, Bright and Co., their worst enemies and the most shameless hypocrites.

Compare this to Moore's statement to unions that "trade is the ally of working people, not their enemy" (WTO 1999).

The fact is that a disembedded world economy cannot be expected to address the needs of people. Only a socially embedded economic system can do that. The self-regulating market always was and will continue to be a convenient myth—a will-o'-the-wisp that people have been persuaded, in the tried and tested style of Goebbels,[5] to believe in. In any case, "market rule rests on institutionalised coercion in a world of unequal states" (McMichael 2000, 8).

THE VIEW FROM PAKISTAN

Time now to shift gears and link this macro critique of neoliberal globalization and its free-trade regime to the particular situation of Pakistan. In 1996, Pakistan was one of the first countries to be reviewed by the WTO (1995). As with all other reviews, the WTO highlighted a long list of protectionist measures that it considered potentially in violation of its rules under the trade-related investment measures clause. Pakistan is also a country with one of the worst child labor problems—both in terms of quantity and quality—in the world.

It is against this that statements and policies issued by the Ministry of Finance should be read. For instance, in the beginning of the millennium year, the ministry issued a statement that announced that

Pakistan's economy is facing multidimensional challenges which include restoring investor's confidence, reinvigorating investor's confidence, reinvigorating growth, restoring macroeconomic stability, reducing poverty, improving social indicators, and improving governance. . . . A concerted and sustained effort is required to steer the economy towards growth and stability.[6]

Next, consider the presentation of the trade policy for the year 2000 by the finance minister of Pakistan, in which he declaims,

I [present this policy] at a time when the global trade environment poses challenges that are matched only by the opportunities that it offers. On the one hand it induces a vigorous competition for our Industry, on the other it promises a greater market access than ever before. There is a huge market out there. It is entirely up to us to remain at less than a quarter of one percent—0.16% to be precise—of world exports, or to make our presence felt; to stagnate at the 8 billion dollar mark, or to achieve a quantum leap; to restrict 60% of our exports to Textiles alone and just eight markets, or to diversify; to live with prices that are amongst the lowest in the world, or *to prove to the world, and to ourselves, that the Pakistani nation thrives upon competition*; and that it loves to convert every challenge into an opportunity.[7]

The minister declared that he was confident that the Pakistani nation could rise to the occasion, but note under what conditions he considers this possible: "We can do it if every Pakistani—the worker, the farmer, the producer, the exporter, the civil servant, the house wife—everyone—is committed to the cause of exports," but "we can not hope to make a break through in exports unless we make our agriculture an industry more efficient; more competitive." A commitment to exports becomes the sine qua non of the national interest, and all class and gender distinctions are flattened in its face.

A recent advertisement placed in national dailies by the Export Processing Zones (EPZ) Authority of the Ministry of Industries and Production, Government of Pakistan, declares Pakistan a haven for foreign investors (of course) and urges a "closer look at EPZ—now more investor-friendly and one of the freest in the world." Moreover, it announces that Pakistan's EPZ is the place where foreign investors "have all the rights and no duties," since nuisances such as import duties and sales tax (even on utility bills) have been abolished and "one Window operation for all your infrastructure needs, including gas, telephone, electricity, etc" is just one of the "many, many more incentives and facilities" that include "production-oriented labour laws" and "exemption from foreign exchange control." The oft-quoted idea that neoliberalism amounts to welfare and subsidies for multinational capital at the expense of labor rights finds empirical justification here.

In such an atmosphere, where economic growth (and often survival) in an increasingly competitive world market is presented as being synonymous with the national interest, it follows that any move that threatens the competitiveness of industry or agriculture will be brutally suppressed. (This resonates with the way in which the butchering of mining communities in England in the early part of this century was seen in the context of "mere economic necessity" and "their defence as something akin to treason" [Corrigan and Sayer 1985, 1]). Under such discursive and political economic regimes, labor rights are the first set of social rights and civic freedoms to be compromised, all in the name of a greater organizing national myth, a myth that is a cover for a very old class struggle. Indeed, the government of Pakistan has made strikes illegal and has termed them and go-slows terrorist acts. Strikes have been brutally broken up, protesting women are dragged off by the hair, and protestors are hauled in before antiterrorist courts. The rate of suicide and public self-immolation citing economic reasons skyrocketed last year, eliciting editorials and op-ed pieces in major dailies across Pakistan (Human Rights Commission of Pakistan 2000).

If we needed more proof of this race to the bottom, we can review the most recent report on the state of human rights in Pakistan:

Worsening of both the economic situation and labor practices contributed to the declining fortune of labor during 1999. Virtual suspension of investments, further contraction of industrial activity, and decline in the agricultural sector brought the gross domestic product growth rate to as low as 1.3 percent, down from an average in recent years of between 5 percent and 6 percent. In the industrial units, cost cutting led to a further shift of activity from the shop floor to small shops and the informal sector and to the contracting and subcontracting of various segments in the production process. (Human Rights Commission of Pakistan 2000, 204)

It should be noted that this informalization of labor makes unionizing impossible under Pakistan's labor laws. The report also cites 4000 industrial mills as being sick, of which 152 were in the textile sector—one of Pakistan's export-oriented sectors. Out of a total of 442 spinning units with over 1 million spindles, 90 were shut down. And that all occurred in one year alone (Human Rights Commission of Pakistan 2000, 206). Meanwhile, the labor force is growing at the rate of over 3 percent—about 1.25 million new entrants to the labor force every year. Meanwhile, unemployment and underemployment are at about 28-30 percent, mostly due to the shrinking economic base and "privatisation of public sector, premature retirements, retrenchment and golden handshakes" (Ali n.d.).

What effect does this have on workers? "Recession, new surcharge on utilities and revision of such prices of petroleum products caused a notable decline in real wages" and the ratio between the richest 10 percent and the poorest 10 percent of the population was calculated by the World Bank to be 7.4 to 1 in the 1990-1996 period (Human Rights

Commission of Pakistan 2000, 207). Ali also points out that child labor has increased in proportion to declining family income, although in a tragic twist, the low wages of children and women serve only to depress the average wage rate further.

The issue of child labor and the efficacy of ILO conventions must be seen in this context. Recently, the ILO passed its Convention on the Worst Forms of Child Labour, Convention No. 182. Pakistan has yet to ratify it, although nongovernmental children's rights organizations and movements against bonded labor have been exerting pressure on the government for years. Pakistan's minister for manpower (and, significantly, industries, among other portfolios), Umar Asgher Khan, disclosed early in the year that Pakistan was seriously considering its ratification (Pakistan to Ratify 2000).

The minister's understanding was that "the main causes of poverty in Pakistan were abject poverty, illiteracy, social attitudes and ignorance about the rights of children" (Pakistan to Ratify 2000), a view shared by most individuals and organizations working in the field of children's rights in Pakistan. For example, the annual report of the Insan Foundation (2000), one of the more high-profile NGOs, claims to want to break the myths about the relationship between child labor and poverty:

The State as a Strategy [sic] and general public as clichés, pronounce poverty as the reason for poverty. Insan Foundation-Pakistan, however, sees the problem with a different angle. If . . . we believe that poverty is the reason [for] child labor, we cannot ignore the other side of the picture that Child labor perpetuate[s] poverty. Both poverty and child labor promote literacy and ignorance that is again reason for child labor perpetuates poverty.

The report continues with a diagrammed representation of this cycle between child labor, poverty, illiteracy, and ignorance. The accompanying text explains that "the poor families socially are less inclined towards education and do not hesitate in sending their children to labor" and that " 'ignorant people' are unaware of economic opportunities" and the "real benefits of education" and so send their children to work. This is a fairly typical example of the way the relationship between child labor and poverty is understood, as is the proposed solution: education (whether it is education of families, of communities, or of children). Nowhere do we see any connection to the structural adjustment policies of the World Bank and IMF, which have severely reduced employment opportunities, or the link between poverty and globalization through the internationalization of the division of labor.

Of course, no one can deny the importance of education and literacy and their connection with social development, especially in a country like Pakistan where "the rate of enrollment at the primary level actually declined over the past ten years— by as much as 3%" and where the ratio of illiterate 15-year-olds was 86 percent for girls and 59 percent for boys (Human Rights Commission of Pakistan 1998, 253). But to argue that education alone is responsible for the existence and perpetuation of child labor is a form of alienation in the classic Marxist sense. The fact is that it is impossible—and irresponsible—to try to understand child labor in Pakistan outside the context of a globalized world economy and its articulation through certain class interests in Pakistan. Silvers (1996) writes that "few countries have done less to abolish or contain the practice than Pakistan. And fewer still have a ruling class that opposes workplace reform and human-rights initiatives as vigorously."

As Silvers (1996) points out, the unpleasant truth is that

despite its modern views on warfare and industrialization, Pakistan remains a feudal society, committed to maintaining traditions that over the centuries have served its upper castes well. The lords—factory owners, exporters, financiers—reflexively oppose any reforms that might weaken their authority, lower their profit margins, or enfranchise the workers.

Silvers (1996) quotes an industrialist as saying that

there is room for improvement in any society. . . . But we feel that the present situation is acceptable the way it is. The National Assembly must not rush through reforms without first evaluating their impact on productivity and sales. Our position is that the government must avoid so-called humanitarian measures that harm our comparative advantage.

How can we expect the use of child labor to be effectively curbed when there remains "little doubt that inexpensive child labour has fueled Paki-stan's economic growth [such as it is]" and the government remains committed to the cause of exports?

Article 11(3) of the Constitution of Pakistan declares that no child below the age of 14 years shall be engaged in any factory or mine or any other hazardous employment. Article 35 states that "the state shall protect . . . the family, the mother and the child," while Article 37(e) declares that "the state shall make provisions for . . . ensuring that children . . . are not employed in vocations unsuited to their age." Yet Pakistan's child labor force is estimated at around 30 million in the 5-18 age group or 20 million in the 5-15 age group (Human Rights Commission of Pakistan 1998, 226), most of it in the urban informal and agricultural sectors, so these children are not covered by Article 11(3). However, even those forms of child labor that are covered by these constitutional provisions are not curbed, due to the lack of political will on the part of state elites.

When the use of child labor in Pakistan's soccer ball and carpet industries hit the headlines in the industrialized North in 1996-97, the public's reaction was very strong. The international exposure given to Iqbal Masih—a child laborer freed by the Bonded Labour Liberation Front (BLLF) from bondage and subsequently killed by person or persons unknown—through the BLLF platform helped to highlight the problem of child labor across the world in general but particularly in Pakistan. The extent of public reaction to this issue can be gauged by the fact that school-children across the United States started campaigns against the use of child labor in the soccer ball industry. As a result, carpet exports fell precipitously, and the soccer ball industry appeared to be in trouble as well.

With the annual retail market in soccer balls standing at $1 billion (Pakistan accounted for 55-75 percent of the world's export) and with the football World Cup approaching in June 1998, the unthinkable happened (Human Rights Commission of Pakistan 1998, 202). The large multinational sports franchises with factories in Pakistan, like Nike, Reebok, and Adidas, took it upon themselves to institute greater checks—with the help of independent investigators—against child labor in the soccer ball industry in Pakistan. The result has been a process whereby soccer balls produced without child labor are certified as child-labor-free. Not surprisingly, this certification has become an added value in marketing terms, much as the label "no animal testing" is for cosmetics. In the carpet manufacturing sector, this has resulted in the launch of four international monitoring and certification organizations: Rugmark, Care and Fair, Qualite France, and STEP. The result has been one of the most successful attempts at greenwashing ever instituted by multinational corporations. Obviously, the reason for this is not altruism or the sudden realization of corporate responsibility but the imperative of saving the brand name—and the industry—from bad publicity.

Since Pakistan was also in the unusual position of having a large majority of the world's export market in soccer balls—which require very skilled work—the multinational corporations concerned could not engage in the kind of fly-by-night tactics that they otherwise engage in. It was no doubt easier on the pocket, and good for business besides, vis-à-vis the good publicity, to invest a little in Pakistan itself in the way of certification and education. Cynicism aside, this case shows how much public opinion in the North can make a difference in terms of holding multinationals accountable. This is of course only possible because countries in the North happen to be representative democracies in which public opinion carries political weight, and this is precisely why the U.S. State Department also got involved in the issue of child labor in Pakistan's export industries, particularly those of direct relevance to the United States, such as soccer balls. Under pressure from the State Department and the ILO, the government of Pakistan has set up schools of its own in partnership with UNICEF and NGOs.

These, then, were the reasons behind the sudden flurry of interest in Pakistan's child labor problem and the sudden influx of both financial and technical aid from sources as diverse as the ILO, the U.S. State Department, and the concerned multinational corporations. I present this not as a fairy-tale ending but in order to add a dose of much-needed cynicism to some very highly publicized initiatives. First, these initiatives remain concentrated only on export industries. As the Human Rights Commission of Pakistan's (1998) report for 1997 points out, "little or nothing has been done to begin to alleviate conditions in the 2,000 brick kiln factories or in the agricultural sector where child labour was endemic, and where child bondage in one form or another remained widespread" (203). When we talk about globalization creating the conditions (through the disembeddedness of the economic from the social) for the increasing exploitation of child labor in countries of the South, it does not mean only in the export sector, although the export sector is perhaps the most direct link. What I have attempted to show in this article is the link between increasing poverty and the intensification and spread of neoliberalism as doctrine and project. Thus all forms and means and sites of the exploitation of vulnerable sections of the labor force (which is pretty much all of the labor force) are connected to the global economic order through the state class and its allies. Establishing schools, no matter how noble an initiative, does little more than paper over the cracks being made and being widened under the neoliberal world regime.

It is of course always possible that international bodies like the ILO will keep a check on such schools and put pressure on the government of the day, but the fact is that the ILO in the present global economic scenario is an organization increasingly without any teeth, whereas the forces of globalization, such as the WTO, are growing increasingly new ones. ILO regulations on child labor go far back in ILO history, and they have been recently updated to address the current international child labor

situation. Pakistan was a signatory to the original ILO regulations, although it has not yet ratified the new convention. But the ILO has been powerless against the resurgent forces of neoliberalism and its powerful ideology of the free market. Internationally, labor rights have suffered massive blows as countries scramble to offer the best terms to multinational capital. And in such a scenario, most developing countries (especially those that have not invested in social sectors, such as education, in the past) have found that their only comparative advantage lies in cheap (trouble-free, or as the EPZ advertisement puts it, "production-oriented") labor.

Neoliberalism has exposed the seams within the historic compromise between capital and labor, and with it the ideological and political basis of the ILO. The contradictions inherent in trying to accommodate the needs and rights of workers and the poor in a socioeconomic system based on the accumulation and realization of profit and surplus value have now become painfully exposed. The irony of the matter is that the only institution capable of and likely to exert the right kind of pressure is the WTO—if allegations of social dumping by developing countries and their cry of protectionism begin to be taken seriously. Because the WTO does not even really operate by its own rhetoric of free trade, it is, as many of its detractors, from activists to academics to southern country representatives, have pointed out, a platform to serve the interests of multinational capital based in the North. This is more than adequately testified to by the terms of the now-defunct Multinational Agreement on Investment (MAI)—the notorious MAI that was exposed by activists in the United States and now widely accepted as the blueprint for the evolution of the WTO in the coming years.

Lest we stand accused of falling into the *dependencia* trap of looking only at external pressures, we need to understand the structural and historical reasons for the high incidence of child labor in Pakistan. (South Asia in general and Pakistan in particular hold the doubtful distinction of having the highest incidence of child labor per capita in its worst forms.) The sad fact is that despite critiques of the dependency school for taking the category of nation-state for granted as a monolithic structure without internal class antagonisms and pressures, this fallacy continues to define discussions of international political economy. It is of course mostly conveniently—and most problematically—invoked by Third World state elites and is particularly problematic when used by nonrepresentative governments and their officials, which has invariably been the case in Pakistan. Policies enacted in the name of the people have invariably been anti-people and anti-poor and have historically had the approval—and often the impetus or expertise—of the United States (see Myrdal 1970, 435-36).

The short history of Pakistan must be looked at as the resultant of complex domestic and international conditions. The containment politics of the Cold War meant the artificial

(because unpopular and unrepresentative) installment and support of right-wing, authoritarian—whether civilian or military—governments and their anti-people policies all over the world. This was particularly true of Pakistan. The civil-military bureaucracy and the landed elites have benefited under every regime in Pakistani history, with a few shifts in the balance of power between them but no serious threat to their overall status. This has resulted, among other things, in the continuation and intensification of existing feudal structures; there have never been more than cosmetic land reforms under any regime, ensuring that the feudal power structure remains undisturbed. This has severe implications for the incidence and forms of child labor and labor practices in general. Moreover, labor laws have been draconian, even under the populist "socialist" government of Zulfiqar Ali Bhutto. It is only recently that NGOs and movements such as the BLLF and the Bhatta Mazdoor Mahaz have been able to pressure the government to pass a law such as the Bonded Labor (Abolition) Act. Although we cannot look upon this as an absolute victory—laws are, after all, only as good as their implementers, and the implementers are still feudal/tribal elites—this act has enabled thousands of bonded laborers to be freed by lawyers working with the BLLF.

Moreover, the national bourgeoisie in Pakistan has been historically weak, especially as compared to the comprador class. There has thus never been any real initiative or motivation, private or public, to develop the domestic/national market and local industry and to encourage the latter to produce for the former. The focus in Pakistan from the very first has been export-promoting industrialization as opposed to the import substitution industrialization (ISI) policies followed by most developing countries in the 1950s and 1960s. (This occasions the repetition of another oft-quoted factotum: that South Korea used Pakistan's first five-year plan as a model.) However, there has never been any serious attempt to diversify Pakistan's exports or, indeed, to impose any effective quality control on them. The end result has been that Pakistan has a very narrow export base composed of textiles, carpets, surgical instruments, and soccer balls. The profit margin in these industries has been ensured overwhelmingly by low wage rates. Thus it is no accident that all these industries employ disproportionately large numbers of women (in textiles) and children, the two categories of labor with the lowest wage rates.

STATE AND CLASS
IN THE PERIPHERY

The classic analyses of state and class under conditions of peripheral capitalism hold particular resonance for a study of Pakistan. Here, "even more than in the First World, the state . . . denotes a category of class power, namely the structural power of an (external and internal) capitalist class standing in fundamentally antagonistic relationship to labour"

and "class power . . . still stands in roughly isomorphic correspondence with state power" (Graf 1995, 153) such that we can talk, justifiably, of a state class. This class is one "whose linkages and dependencies extend outward (in the form of economic and political dependence) and who therefore operate 'their' state at the sub- and supra-national levels" (153). And this remains true despite globalization's claims to be strengthening the industrial and commercial bourgeoisie at the expense of regressive state classes. Here, capitalist classes have also "lack[ed] the socio-economic 'base' to sustain and develop an autochthonous capitalism and so [have relied] mainly on political means, in collaboration with external class allies, to create the preconditions for, and to promote, private accumulation" (154). This state class, according to Petras, is best conceived of as "a precarious coalition of 'collaborator classes' whose function is to 'organize the state and economy in accordance with core definitions of the international division of labour.' It assumes a double role—exploitation within the society and exchange outside the society" (as quoted in Graf 1995). This state class "cannot ally itself, either totally or a combination of segments, with the popular classes since any strategy promoting mass economic well-being or development [or better working conditions and better wages] would, ipso facto, undermine the basis and rationale of the peripheral state" (Graf 1995, 155). Thus it has "a vested interest in suppressing basic human needs and in perpetuating the existing international division of labour"; this basic conflict of interest between the state class and state comprador elites and the majority of the population, and the increasingly obvious and brutal exploitation in this society, makes legitimation more and more impossible, hence the central role played by coercion (156). It should not be surprising, then, if under the extreme polarization of societies affected by globalization, we should find the elites becoming "more parasitical, more repressive and less 'attached' to societies under their control" (158).

Capitalism operates by creating and working through differences and inequalities—be they based on class, gender, race, or whatever—and in articulation with existing systems of power and exploitation, even as it occasionally comes in conflict with them. In Pakistan, this has meant the marriage between international capitalism and a political economy characterized by severe polarizations of power, particularly an extremely brutal feudal system of which bonded labor is a part. However, these elites "do not accumulate within the confines of the borders of the state. Peripheral (state) capital stands in a subordinate relationship to the capital at the centre, and reproduction processes at the periphery, mediated by the world market, are overwhelmingly determined by valorization processes emanating from the centre" (Graf 1995, 154).

This is why schools suddenly sprang up for ex–child laborers in certain export industries only after pressure from consumers in the center. For instance, the Child Care Foundation, a much-touted initiative (as an NGO!) by the Export Promotion Bureau in 1996 was launched with the "cooperation of the private sector at a time when *propaganda against Pakistan on the child labour issue was at its peak* . . . and Pakistan was made a target of international media campaign" (Child Care Foundation 2000; emphasis added). The advantages of such an initiative are obvious: the *Business Recorder* reported that Pakistan's carpet exports rose to $194.5 million during the first 10 months of the current fiscal year, from $148.2 million during the same period last year. Addressing a meeting of the Pakistan Carpet Manufacturers and Exporters Association (PCMEA), its vice chairman said "that the positive work done to address the child labour issue in the carpet industry had . . . had a salutary effect on carpet exports. . . . [as did] the CCF activities and the ILO-PCMEA project for the rehabilitation of child labour in the international market" (Carpet Export Earnings 2000).

Although there is of course some truth to the knee-jerk apologia stand of representatives of these Southern states who claim that childhood did not exist as a separate and special category even in Europe until sometime in the early twentieth century and so it cannot be applied as a universal category, this does not explain why the practice of child labor has been increasing over the past few years. In any case, it is highly problematic to use the cultural relativism made fashionable of late (and which is gaining currency) by certain kinds of postmodernism to justify exploitative practices in any society; the danger of doing that has been amply demonstrated over the past several decades vis-à-vis women's rights, with everything from the banning of abortion to female genital mutilation being turned into sacred cows once they are labeled cultural (or traditional) practices. This is not to say that there is not a "political economy of human rights"—to borrow a phrase from Noam Chomsky and Edward Herman's book of the same name (1979)—in which "human rights" is used selectively by developed countries (particularly the United States) as a stick with which to beat those states that it needs to bring (back) into line. This has been amply documented elsewhere and need not be addressed here (see, for instance, Chomsky 1978, among others).

It is undisputably true that child labor is not an aberration due to lack of awareness of the sanctity of childhood or the importance of education. On the contrary, studies have shown that poor, rural people have a conscious critique of the kind of education imparted by government and private schools alike, which neither prepares children for the future nor corresponds with their reality and is hardly ever a means of social mobility. Lubna Chaudhry (2000), in her exploratory study of formal education in the Punjab, writes that "in the villages, education was not perceived as an antidote to poverty. Even those who professed a belief in the enlightenment aspects of education were not very convinced of its practical use in their lives" (10).

All these explanations for the existence of child labor have important implications because they form the basis of particular policies designed to address this issue. Thus if child labor is caused by poverty, then we must have poverty alleviation programs and development (once again understood as economic growth). If child labor is part of a vicious cycle that is caused by lack of education or primary schooling, then we must ensure that children go to school. And there are several initiatives, both local/domestic and international (and usually a combination of the two), specifically geared to address this lack.

The real issue is, of course, that child labor is a function of poverty but that poverty is not just an unfortunate feature of life in Pakistan. Poverty is structurally created, maintained, and now under the process of intensifying. The structural reasons are both domestic and international and, under the current international political regime, are unlikely to be reversed without political intervention.

It follows then that institutions such as the WTO, which are the handmaidens of this new economic order, cannot be expected to address the issues of labor—be it workers in the Third World, women, or children, be it through social clauses or other means. If the overarching structural framework of the institution remains the same, social clauses will always be nothing more than a bargaining chip between warring national capitals. What is needed are external pressure and institutions that can provide an effective counterbalance to these forces of neoliberalism—institutions with more than just their heart in the right place—institutions with teeth. The ILO is an existing institution with a history of work on behalf of labor, but activists, intellectuals, and critical development experts need to think seriously about either turning it into a more powerful organization or designing and establishing a new institution that can work as a watchdog on behalf the world's exploited workers. Bloody protests against authoritarian and absolutist regimes may be rousing in a general sense, and the ones in Prague and Seattle have served their purpose of exposing the brutal nature of this current international regime. But now what is needed is an organized effort to provide alternatives.

In the words of the Prague Declaration,

A revolution in economics is called for, one that returns control of economies to the people who live in them. The time has come to put economics at the service of the people, rather than entire societies at the service of economic models that have failed for over 20 years.[8]

Notes

1. The term is Foucault's. In "Truth and Power" (1980), he states, "Each society has its regime of truth, its 'general politics' of truth: that is, the types of discourse which it accepts and makes function as true; the mechanisms and instances which enable one to distinguish true and false statements, the means by which each is sanctioned; the techniques and procedures accorded value in the acquisition of truth; the status of those who are charged with saying what counts as true. In societies like ours, the 'political economy' of truth is charac-

terised by five important traits. 'Truth' is centered on the form of scientific discourse and the institutions which produce it; it is subject to constant economic and political incitement. . . . it is the object, under diverse forms, of immense diffusion and consumption (circulating through apparatuses of education and information whose extent is relatively broad in the social body, notwithstanding certain strict limitations); it is produced and transmitted under the control, dominant if not exclusive, of a few great political and economic apparatuses. . . . lastly, it is the issue of a whole political debate and social confrontation."

2. "Social dumping" is the term applied by developed countries to the export of competitively priced products by developing countries to the global market. The argument is that developing countries are able to do so only because of low social and environmental standards applicable domestically. The debate is between whether this constitutes developing countries' comparative advantage or whether it qualifies as an unlawful practice under WTO rules and regulations.

3. See http://brettonwoodsinstitute.org.

4. The efficacy of the ideological assault of the neoliberal project must also not be underestimated. Even in politically correct academic circles, one finds the tendency to understand globalization in terms of the information or communication revolution—a highly questionable and naïve liberal idea that is also intellectually irresponsible when it fails to frame this against the imperatives of the international political economic order. It is interesting to find even such a renowned left theorist as Anthony Giddens talking about globalization in these terms (see Palast 2000).

5. Joseph Goebbels, Hitler's right-hand public relations man, is famous for his theory of propaganda: that a lie repeated often enough eventually attains the status of truth.

6. At http://www.finance.gov.pk.

7. At http://www.epb.gov.pk/tpl.htm; emphasis added.

8. At http://www.globalexchange.org/wbimf/prague092800.html, 28 Sept. 2000.

References

Ali, Mir Zulfiqar. n.d. *Asian Economic Crisis and Its Social Impact on Child*

Labour: Roles and Responses—The case of Pakistan. Available at http://www.cwa.tnet.co.th/booklet/pakistan.htm.

Amin, Samir. 1990. *Delinking: Towards a Polycentric World.* Trans. Micheal Wolfers. London: Zed Books.

———. 1997. *Capitalism in the Age of Globalization: The Management of Contemporary Society.* London: Zed Books.

An Unjustified Sense of Victory: Pressure Groups in Rich Countries Have Succeeded Only in Mobilizing Poor Nations Against a WTO Hijack. 1999. *Financial Times* 21 Dec.

Bello, Walden. 1991. Strategies and Alliances for Effective Action. Paper presented at Economic Sovereignty in a Globalising World: Creating a People-Centered Economics for the 21st Century, 23-26 Mar., Chulalongkorn University, Bangkok.

———. 2000a. From Melbourne to Prague: The Struggle for a Deglobalized World. Speech delivered at a series of engagements on the occasion of demonstrations against the World Economic Forum (Davos), 6-10 Sept., Melbourne, Australia. Available at http://focusweb.org and http://www.50years.org.

———. 2000b. The Prague Castle Debate: A Few Questions for Mr. Wolfensohn and Mr. Kohler. Available at http://www.50years.org.

Benjamin, Walter. 1969. *Illuminations.* Trans. Harry Zohn, ed. Hannah Arendt. New York: Schocken.

Carpet Export Earnings up at $194.5 Million. 2000. *Business Recorder,* 20 May. Available at www.brecorder.com.

Chaudhry, Lubna Nazir. 2000. On the Verge of the "New Age." *Resistance* 1(1):10.

Child Care Foundation to Set Up More Schools for Carpet Weaving Children. 2000. *Business Recorder,* 23 May. Available at www.brecorder.com.

Chomsky, Noam. 1978. *"Human rights" and American Foreign Policy.* Nottingham: Spokesman Books.

Chomsky, Noam and Edward S. Herman. 1979. *The Political Economy of Human Rights.* Boston: South End Press.

Chossudovsky, Michel. 1997. *The Globalisation of Poverty: Impacts of IMF and World Bank Reforms.* Penang: Third World Network.

Corrigan, Philip and Derek Sayer. 1985. *The Great Arch: English State Formation as Cultural Revolution.* Oxford: Basil Blackwell.

Foucault, Michel. 1980. Truth and Power. In *Power/Knowledge: Selected Interviews and Other Writings, 1972-1977,* ed. Colin Gordon. New York: Pantheon Books.

Freeman, Alan. 1998. Fixing Up the World? GATT and the World Trade Organisation. *Links,* Mar.-July.

Galbraith, John Kenneth. 1958. *The Affluent Society.* New York: Mentor Books.

Graf, William. 1995. The State in the Third World. In *Why Not Capitalism,* ed. Leo Panitch. London: Merlin Press.

Gramsci, Antonio. 1971. *Selections from the Prison Notebooks of Antonio Gramsci,* ed. and trans. Quintin Hoare and Geoffrey Nowell Smith. New York: International Publishers.

Human Rights Commission of Pakistan. 1998. *State of Human Rights in 1997.* Lahore: HRCP.

———. 2000. *State of Human Rights in 1999.* Lahore: HRCP.

Insan Foundation. 2000. *Breaking the Poverty Myths in Education: Report on the Child Rights Education and Literacy Project, 1997-1999.* Lahore: Insan Foundation.

International Union of Food, Agricultural, Hotel, Restaurant, Tobacco and Allied Workers' Association. 2000. Seattle and After. *IUF Bulletin,* 11 Feb.

Kincaid, Douglas A. and Alejandro Portes. 1994. Sociology and Development in the 1990s: Critical Challenges and Empirical Trends. *Comparative National Development: Society and Economics in the New Global Order*, ed. D. A. Kincaid and A. Portes. Chapel Hill: University of North Carolina Press.

Marx, Karl. [1848] 1969. On the Question of Free Trade. In *The Poverty of Philosophy*. New York: International Publishers.

McMichael, Philip. 2000. Globalisation: Trend or Project? In *Global Political Economy: Contemporary Theories*, ed. Ronen Palan. London: Routledge.

Myrdal, Gunnar. 1970. *The Challenge of World Poverty: A World Anti-Poverty Program in Outline*. New York: Vintage Books.

Pakistan to Ratify ILO Convention on Child Labour. 2000. *Business Recorder*, 24 June. Available at www.brecorder.com.

Pakistan's Anti-Child Labour Project Spotlighted at a World Conference. 2000. *Business Recorder*, 20 May. Available at www.brecorder.com.

Palast, Greg. 2000. Inside Corporate America. *Observer*. 8 Oct. Available at http://www.guardianunlimited.co.uk/Archive/Article/0,4273,4075049,00.html.

Rodrik, Dani. 1998. The Global Fix. *New Republic*, 2 Nov.

Silvers, Jonathan. 1996. Child Labour in Pakistan. *Atlantic Monthly*, Feb. Available at http://www.theatlantic.com/issues/96feb/pakistan/pakistan.htm.

World Trade Organization. 1995. Growing Complexity in International Economic Relations Demands Broadening and Deepening of Multilateral Trading System—WTO Director. Press Release 25, 16 Oct.

———. 1999. Labour Issue Is "False Debate," Obscures Underlying Consensus, WTO Chief Mike Moore Tells Unions. Press Release 152, 28 Nov.

Book Department

INTERNATIONAL RELATIONS AND POLITICS

CAMPBELL, JAMES E. 2000. *The American Campaign: U.S. Presidential Campaigns and the National Vote*. Pp. xxii, 314. College Station: Texas A&M University Press. $34.95. Paperbound, $18.95.

Like many scholars, political scientists often find things to be more complicated than they seem at first. Take political campaigns. With over $200 million having been raised just to secure the party nominations for the 2000 election, campaigns must surely be important. But not to some political scientists. To hear them tell it, because so many factors are already built into the political system—things like partisan ties, economic class, as well as racial, regional, and gender peculiarities—campaigns alone cannot possibly dislodge such long-standing influences.

James Campbell understands these arguments and reprises them in *The American Campaign*. He also surveys the opposing view: that campaigns are determinative. Journalists, says Campbell, see campaigns as spectacles pitting powerful forces against one another in a drama punctuated by sudden, unexpected events. Campbell rejects both the feckless and all-powerful models of campaigns, insisting that "the effects of presidential campaigns are smaller and much more systematic than the journalistic view would have it, yet larger than supposed by the conventional wisdom of political science." Campbell's "theory of the predictable campaign" is a compromise model.

The American Campaign provides an exhaustive reanalysis of existing polling data. Among Campbell's findings are these: (1) two-thirds of all Americans know whom they will vote for before the first campaign cantata is sung; (2) after Labor Day, campaigns affect the outcome by about 4 percent, which is sometimes enough to change things dramatically; and (3) the gap between presidential candidates inevitably narrows as they approach election day because of three factors: the economy, incumbency advantages, and the two-sidedness of U.S. campaigns. Campbell also notes that late-deciding voters are especially affected by the strength of the economy, that party conventions almost always produce a "bump" in the polls (usually about 7 percent), that Labor Day front-runners almost never lose the presidential race, and that most of the 12 nonincumbent elections between 1968 and 1996 resulted in either a dead heat or a very close race.

The American Campaign is not meant for the casual reader. Its tables and charts are often daunting, and its prose, intimidatingly technical. Yet it is also an honest book that rewards the assiduous student of campaigns with well-reasoned findings. But some of Campbell's best insights are offered only in passing. He notes, for example, that campaign messages that could make a difference are almost never uttered, largely because candidates are so threatened by the mathematics of the modern, poll-driven campaign. He also notes that each campaign is part of a continuing battle for control of government and that these serial reassertions of partisanship are what give the American polity its dynamism.

For most political scientists, campaign effects are equated with survey data. James Campbell follows in that tradition. But a different measurement tool might produce a less cramped view of campaigns. What if one asked, for example, how campaigns affect the philosophical worldview of a nation or its very model of leadership? What new latent political assumptions do campaigns engender, what habits of lay discourse do they inspire? What sudden fears are generated in campaigns? What sudden hopes? Do campaigns produce new ideas, new methods of problem solving, new items for future discussion? Do campaigns make better the angels of our nature? Do they soothe the savage beast?

Admittedly, campaign effects like these are hard to measure, but that is not to say they are unimportant. All too often, scholars study that which can be studied rather than that which should be studied. It is time to go beyond opinion polls, to find new and richer ways of judging politics. *The American Campaign* is an important study, but it is not the only sort of work that must be done.

RODERICK P. HART

University of Texas
Texas

COHEN, SHARI J. 1999. *Politics Without a Past: The Absence of History in Postcommunist Nationalism.* Pp. xiii, 281. Durham, NC: Duke University Press. $54.95. Paperbound, $18.95.

The post-Communist world has been widely interpreted as an instance of either radical reversion or progressive evolution. Some observers saw a "rebirth of history," in which ancient enmities and pre-Communist politics would reemerge. Others expected that East European political systems would develop in roughly the same way as earlier transitions to democracy in southern Europe and Latin America. In this stimulating work of political sociology, Shari J. Cohen takes issue with both views. She argues that the post-Communist landscape is one in which the absence of "historical consciousness," a void created by Leninist systems themselves, allowed a particular brand of politician to come to the fore: a member of an opportunist "mass-elite" with few ideological convictions, no link to the traditions and history of the country he represents, and no clear vision or program for the future. Cohen places her work within a growing body of sophisticated, historical-institutionalist research that focuses on the experience of communism and the ways in which the institutions, identities, and incentives forged by that system continue to shape politics today.

The object of Cohen's research is Slovakia. The Slovak case is a wonderful instance from which to build a theory about the interplay of history and post-Communism; it is, in fact, probably a far better one than its overstudied Central European neighbors, since most post-Communist states are, like Slovakia, undergoing processes of both state- and nation-building. Vladimir Meciar, until recently Slovakia's prime minister, was the quintessential product of a Leninist system, a figure with few ideological attachments but able to wield nationalist discourse to silence potential opponents. And the problems the country still faces—democratization, economic reform, minority-majority relations—are the same as those across most of the post-Communist world.

Cohen's argument in large part depends on how well she is able to conceptualize the idea of historical consciousness, which she holds is especially weak in the Slovak case, both among average Slovaks and among the mass-elite who ruled them for much of the 1990s. It is a slippery notion to be sure; it is not completely clear how one would know consciousness if one saw it. Indeed, one of the mass-elite's key traits is its ability to offer a simulacrum of historicity devoid of real content. Still, Cohen's book raises a host of essential questions about the nature of politics after communism and, more broadly, about the ability of political scientists to model behavior in contexts in which preferences, incentives, and outcomes are all fluid. Now, more than a decade after communism's end, the most important question raised by this book is why some countries have been able to move out of the post-Communist malaise and others remain mired in a "politics without a past."

The author and publisher have stretched the book's central argument nearly to the breaking point by giving an overly broad and provocative title to what is really a deep but comparatively minded case study. Still, Cohen's work has resonance far beyond Slovakia. Moreover, in a political science field increasingly dominated by a mania for comparison at the price of really understanding individual cases, Cohen's book represents the best of what Central and East European studies can be: a nuanced investigation based on serious engagement with primary sources, foreign-language skills, historical sensitivity, and an almost anthropological commitment to explaining politics from the perspective of those who engaged in it.

CHARLES KING

Georgetown University
Washington, D.C.

KENDALL, KATHLEEN E. 2000. *Communication in the Presidential Primaries: Candidates and the Media, 1912-2000.* Pp. xiv, 257. Westport, CT: Praeger. $69.50. Paperbound, $24.95.

Kendall's is the first book to systematically analyze U.S. presidential primary contests via an examination of public communication media. She selects primary contests at 20-year intervals—1912, 1932, 1952, 1972, and 1992—to provide a longitudinal overview of speeches, print and electronic advertising, and newspaper, radio, and television coverage of campaigns. Those studies are framed by two introductory chapters treating the presidential primary as rhetorical situation and reviewing the evolution of primary rules and by a concluding chapter reporting what she has learned about the game.

The book does not deal with primary-period caucuses, which are dismissed as too controllable by party officials and more productive of lower voter turnout than primaries proper. Nonetheless, the book delivers a fascinating story about the rise, development, and regular repair of the presidential primary system.

The first presidential primary law was Florida's in 1901, and by 1912 at least 13 primaries—perhaps as many as 21, depending upon one's definition—were in place. By 1992, 37 Republican and 38 Democratic primaries in the states, as well as two more in the District of Columbia and Puerto Rico, faced candidates. Chapters 1 and 2 review the background for battles in the selected years and the rule changes—especially those for 1972 and later primaries—that regularly remade the contests. Kendall sees those changes as encouraging more candidates, wresting power from national party committees, and rebalancing state party organizations in favor of popular constituencies. More emphasis on the accompanying campaign refinancing reform would have been helpful, but generally those chapters are informative.

Chapter 3 is a gold mine for students of political speech, especially its background on campaign rhetoric before the television era. The research base of Chapter 4 creaks with its emphasis on 1980s research, but the narratives on advertising through the five presidential contests complements Kathleen Hall Jamieson's *Packaging the Presidency* (1984) thanks to Kendall's sorting of ads. One wishes only that Kendall had better information on actual play schedules in sample markets for individual ads. Most valuable are the two chapters on newspaper, radio, and television coverage and polling, covering the periods 1912-52 and 1972-92. While Kendall might have done more on newsreels (see candidate biographies and Raymond Fielding's *American Newsreel*) and on campaign film (see Joanne Morreale's books), she makes a valiant effort to review major newspaper stories, radio reporting and commentary, and especially the remanufacture of campaigns in the television era. She is especially convincing with respect to the media's construction of expectations-for-candidate-performance in the winnowing process. More attention to the financial framework governing candidates' capabilities for sustaining their campaigns would have rationalized some findings, but Kendall has judiciously outlined the rise and fall of major-party candidates across the century.

Kendall too easily dismisses the impact of computerized media on campaigning by working primarily from early-1992 projections of computer access to campaign materials. Campaign 2000 demonstrated the range and potency of computer technologies in assembling constituencies, constructing electronic chat groups, providing opportunities for near-instant responses, and organizing far-flung voters and financial supporters. Otherwise, her conclusions—that primaries were important politically long before 1972, that horse race coverage has been with us throughout the century, and that candidate- and media-controlled messages vied with each other from the start—are convincing, and her proposals for candidate debates throughout the primary period are both thoughtful and helpful.

Overall, Kendall's archival and secondary-source research provides long-needed historical grounding, multiperspective reconstructions of campaign communication processes, and balanced, sensible generalizations about why American presidential primaries are unique, frustrating, and yet finally determinative of electoral outcomes. Students of both communication and electoral politics need this work on their bookshelves.

BRUCE E. GRONBECK

University of Iowa
Iowa City

LIBBY, RONALD T. 1998. *Eco-Wars: Political Campaigns and Social Movements*. Pp. xiv, 256. New York: Columbia University Press. $45.00. Paperbound, $21.50.

In *Politics and Markets* (1977), Charles Lindblom argued that business enjoys a "privileged position" in American politics. His assertion—one more subtle than critics portray—added fuel to the debate about the relative power of business in American democracy.

Ronald Libby contributes to this debate in *Eco-Wars*, an odd title insofar as the book's focus is more on the impacts of social movements in American politics. Libby examines Lindblom's assertion by looking at five campaigns that ran contrary to the priorities of the business community: the effort to ban BST in milk; an animal rights initiative in Massachusetts; environmental and antismoking initiatives in California; and, from a different angle, the conservative attack on the Endangered Species Act. Libby seeks to understand why the campaigns succeeded or failed, concluding that they succeeded when social movement activists were able to control the definition of the issue, set the agenda for debate, and paint opponents into untenable political positions. In sum, he argues, business does not always win.

It is hard to disagree with this assessment. Indeed, compared to 40 or 50 years ago, business interests do have to work harder to maintain their advantages. And Libby is correct in asserting that noneconomic interests have reshaped the political landscape. However, the reader is left with some questions.

First, is Libby correct in concluding that expressive groups provide an effective counterweight to economic interests? It is hard to say. For one thing, Libby sets up simplistic renditions of the interest group literature in order to knock them down. Too often he asserts some "conventional wisdom" about interest groups that few group scholars see as such. For example, he says that group scholars agree that noneconomic groups lack the resources to hire public relations firms or employ media campaigns (11). That he finds this "consensus" to be wrong is hardly a revelation to anyone who has spent any time on the topic. Nor does it advance our collective understanding.

Second, while Libby correctly focuses on the interplay between interest groups,

social movement activists, elected and appointed political leaders, and other allies, too often the "causal story" is not well told. In part, this is due to space limitations, but Libby also may have used too many cases. There is always a trade-off between having enough cases and being thorough, but in this instance the trade-off was too great. Fewer but lengthier case studies may have been better.

These are not simply stylistic grousings. They are methodological issues of some weight, since the overarching requirement when relying on case studies is to tell the story in such a way that any reader could come to the same conclusion. Lacking statistical proof, case studies are supposed to offer plausible causal stories. However, too often Libby offers pieces that are not knit together into a compelling whole, leaving the reader to wonder exactly what led to what.

Libby's case selection also leads to more analytical muddiness. It is easy to portray one side as bad in one example (tobacco), but in the four others, the issues are fuzzier and the balance between good and evil is less well fixed. That's fine, since we want to go beyond simplistic depictions. However, the only instance in which the "anti-business" side "won" was the tobacco case. In all the others, at least by my assessment of the outcomes, the campaigns essentially failed.

If this was so, what are we to make of Libby's main argument? Business may have to fight harder to maintain its privileged position, but this is hardly the same as asserting that expressive groups now neutralize business power. Business still has the edge in terms of mass public and elite support for business definitions of free markets and minimal government, or simply in terms of resources. The Sierra Club is big and well financed, but it or any other expressive group cannot match business dollar for dollar. Maybe

Lindblom's general argument still stands. Having privilege is no deterministic guarantee of success, but it sure beats the alternative.

These reservations aside, Libby's book is a good place to start for anyone who wants to understand the role of social movements in contemporary American politics. It is most useful for undergraduate courses on American politics or on interest groups and social movements more narrowly.

CHRISTOPHER J. BOSSO

Northeastern University
Boston
Massachusetts

MUELLER, JOHN. 1999. *Capitalism, Democracy, and Ralph's Pretty Good Grocery*. Pp. xi, 352. Princeton, NJ: Princeton University Press. $29.95.

John Mueller has written a fine book, destined to be a classic in the economics and democracy literature. He performs a great service by raising capitalism from the depths of popular contempt and lowering the heights of effusive praise for democracy. As at Ralph's Pretty Good Grocery in Garrison Keillor's fictional town of Lake Wobegon, capitalism and democracy give its customers—citizens in nation-states—what they need: economic and political freedom. What both systems lack, perfect equality, citizens can get along without. Mueller skillfully synthesizes these twin constructs and thus explains their growing global popularity. General readers and specialists alike will gain much from reading the book.

Mueller begins by stating two simple truisms: capitalism ultimately rewards honest business behavior, and democracy-in-action appears to be unproductive. The bulk of the book is then divided into two sections expanding on these truisms,

with a concluding synthetic chapter and an "inventory of propositions."

According to Mueller, capitalism has been given an unjustly bad reputation. It is not compelling enough to portray everyday business life in either good literature or other mass media. Michael Milkin's business behavior sells newspapers, and Michael Douglas won an Academy Award for portraying Gordon Gekko in *Wall Street*, whereas routine, ethical business ventures are simply routine and go unrhapsodized.

But it is those ethical businesses that earn the money in the long run, according to Mueller. The best business advertising winds up being word-of-mouth, whereas scam artists are shunned. Openness of communication in a capitalist system leads to widespread knowledge about business practices. Ethical businesses that treat customers humanely triumph. Further noting that advanced industrial economies set prices with no real haggling at the point of sale (with the major exception of the stock and commodities exchanges), Mueller finds that basic capitalist practice creates transaction efficiencies that encourage economic growth. Being nice pays.

Democracy, on the other hand, while much loved in the abstract, is in reality frustrating, messy, slow, and given to deciding political winners on the basis of petitioning by organized interests and not elections. Here Mueller departs from the democratic orthodoxy of the necessity of free and fair elections. While elections are useful for review and deciding questions of succession, they are hardly essential. Instead, what is necessary for democracy is that "the government be routinely and necessarily responsive." Contrary to popular belief about the necessity of an informed citizenry, Mueller radically posits that democracy works precisely because it does not place excessive demands on the public. The necessity of being responsive makes democracy cautious with respect to public opinion. Bad, unwanted, radical public policy thus becomes less likely.

Mueller further comments on what brings about democracy. While socioeconomic correlates are an important independent variable, ultimately it is elite behavior that decides whether a country becomes democratic or not.

Mueller on occasion seems too glossy in his discussion of democracy. He does not explain why countries retreat from democracy other than to say that "thugs with guns" overthrow democracy. At the same time, Mueller gives slightly less credit to the connection of democracy and capitalism than is warranted. Democracy seems at present to be more than fashionable in that it creates a better information climate for capitalism. (To be fair, Mueller acknowledges, though does not highlight, this in his concluding synthetic chapter.) Finally, Mueller neglects to fit capitalism and democracy into a burgeoning globalization.

Yet these small critiques detract little from the immense contribution of this witty, inviting book to both scholarly thinking about the economics-democracy relationship and to helping the general public to understand what these essentially appealing concepts mean for global society.

ROSS E. BURKHART

Boise State University
Idaho

SHATTUCK, GARDINER H. 2000. *Episcopalians and Race: Civil War to Civil Rights*. Pp. xiii, 298. Lexington: University of Kentucky Press. $32.50.

A product of admirably detailed research, and obviously a labor of love by a trained historian and Episcopalian minister, *Episcopialians and Race* explores a century of racial attitudes, policies, and conflicts among white Episcopalians with respect to their black brethren. Shattuck's introduction makes clear this is primarily the story about how white Episcopalians have responded to black Americans; it is not the story of black Episcopalians themselves (though they do make their presence felt in the narrative at various points), nor is it the story of Episcopalians and race from the broader multicultural perspective (hence Shattuck makes no attempt to cover Native Americans or others not white or black). Most of the story, save for the last chapter, centers on the South, from the response of white Episcopalians to the end of the Civil War and Reconstruction and through the dramatic events of the civil rights movement, when a number of Episcopalian clergymen and laymen, including such luminaries as Judge J. Waties Waring of South Carolina, Thurgood Marshall of the NAACP legal defense team, Ralph McGill of the Atlanta *Constitution*, and Pauli Murray (a black woman later ordained as the first female cleric in the church) were major players in the most important social movement in twentieth-century American history. Perhaps the work's most significant contribution is to provide the first scholarly history of the Episcopal Society for Cultural and Racial Unity (ESCRU), an informal fellowship formed by Episcopalian liberals (mostly white) in 1959 to advance the cause of racial integration in the South.

Throughout the work, Shattuck emphasizes how white paternalism—sometimes benevolent, sometimes antagonistic—treated African Americans as objects rather than as political actors in their own right. The traditional Episcopalian emphasis on the unity of the body of Christ made it difficult for churchmen and -women to comprehend fully the diverse needs of that body. Shattuck traces how overtones of racial paternalism affected the policies of church liberals in the civil rights years, making it difficult to see how calls for unity in the body of Christ could be seen by many blacks as the suppression of black cultural institutions, and how in the eyes of African American churchmen, "whites ... had always called the shots and simply expected blacks to follow their lead, even in matters that affected blacks more than whites."

Poignantly, white liberal churchmen and -women who followed their conscience in support of racial unity found themselves by the late 1960s the object of distrust by both white conservatives and black activists. At the end of that tumultuous decade, the House of Bishops chose conservative Mississippian John Allin to succeed a relatively more activist head of the church. Although resisted by the white liberal wing of the church, Allin correctly diagnosed that the church's view of itself as leading Christian activists "prepared for Zion's war" was chimerical, for Episcopalians as a whole were made up of men and women from the "silent majority," who "lacked the spiritual and theological discipline necessary to involve themselves in a radical process of institutional transformation." Allin's response to calls for unity was to recognize the diversity of the membership of the church, making this conservative far more accepting than his liberal forebears of separate black institutions within the church.

Shattuck's work is a major piece of scholarly research, which may overwhelm the general reader but will be essential reading for scholars in the field of religion and civil rights. Shattuck's personal sympathies are clear, but they never get in the way of his penetrating analysis of the good intentions, very real achievements, and yet ambiguous legacy of the believers who fought under the banner of unity.

PAUL HARVEY

University of Colorado
Colorado Springs

ZAKARIA, FAREED. 1999. *From Wealth to Power: The Unusual Origins of America's World Role.* Pp. x, 199. Princeton, NJ: Princeton University Press. No price.

Diplomatic historians and international relations specialists often express a wish to garner insights from each other. Few succeed in doing so. Historians start from archival findings and build inductively toward middle-level generalizations applicable to a specific time and place. Political scientists start with theory and sift the evidence for support. Even when they address similar subject matter, the two disciplines reflect conflicting methodologies. Fareed Zakaria has had superb training in both history and social science theory, and he offers an elegant contribution to what he deems a "necessary joint enterprise." This volume serves as an exemplar of the efforts that Zakaria and his fellow editors of the Princeton Series in International History and Politics are making to knit the respective fields together.

Zakaria examines American foreign policy from 1865 to 1908 and seeks to explain why the United States failed until the late nineteenth century to exercise its proportionate weight on the world stage. Classic realism, identified with Hans Morgenthau, posits a model in which material resources and military power shape the definition of the national interest. Although preferences differ, capabilities largely determine intentions. Ideology and the culture of the decision makers rate as secondary phenomena. Nearly all economically rising powers, Zakaria contends, expand territorially or in other forms of influence. Yet the United States after the Civil War seems to constitute an anomaly. Both distinguished publicists like Walter Lippmann and George Kennan and theorists like Stephen Walt and Steven Van Evera have drawn on American experience to develop an alternative theory, denominated defensive realism. According to that model, states should expand to defend their economic or security interests only when threatened. If nations irrationally exaggerate threats, pathologies of domestic political structure are usually to blame.

Zakaria is too good a historian to claim that one model fits all cases. He observes that definitions of national interests or threats are slippery and infinitely malleable. He concludes that a third theory, which he calls state-centered realism, resolves most of the apparent contradictions. Applying the analysis of Max Weber, he emphasizes that state structure limits the application of national power. The United States had a strong economy but a notoriously weak presidency and a small federal bureaucracy from 1865 to 1896. What Woodrow Wilson called "Congressional government" motivated the American understretch. Zakaria does not deny the fortunate geographical position of the United States before the development of steam navies, nor does he neglect domestic opportunities before the closing of the frontier in 1890. Nevertheless, in at least 15 out of the 22 cases in which the United States passed up a chance for aggrandizement after 1865, a weak executive provides the primary explanation.

Zakaria has read deeply in the literature of the period, and he almost always makes an intriguing argument. Many analysts assert that transnational institutions and the efflorescence of a global economy are currently eroding the boundaries of the traditional nation-state. Can we therefore expect a return, as the author suggests, of the "Tudor polity of the medieval world," with weakened capacity for interstate conflict? The evidence does not allow clear predictions. Zakaria concedes that McKinley appreciably strengthened the presidency. Still, he and his business allies could not withstand the emotional pressure of public opinion for war with Spain in 1898. Naval

threats from European powers best explain the "defensive" application of American force in the Caribbean under Theodore Roosevelt. No one model fully accounts for history's surprises. Zakaria shows admirable flexibility as a theorist by allowing himself to think outside the box.

STEPHEN A. SCHUKER

University of Virginia
Charlottesville

*AFRICA, ASIA, AND
LATIN AMERICA*

WIRTSCHAFTER, ELISE KIMERLING. 1997. *Social Identity in Imperial Russia*. Pp. xi, 260. DeKalb: Northern Illinois University Press. No price.

The subject of this book is elusive, and that is in a way the author's main point: both the state's official categories—the *soslovie*, or estate, system based on differential obligations to the state (service, taxes, military draft, and so forth)—and the informal social groupings on which they were superimposed were moving targets, constantly being redefined or evolving under the pressure of administrative and economic development over the course of the last 200 years of the Russian old regime's existence. The result, much helped along by the regime's political inflexibility—its persistent unwillingness to share governance with *Obshchestvo*, the mobilized elements of society, and its equally persistent disinclination to allow the formation of public organizations, from voluntary relief organizations to trade unions, for fear that they would lead to an expanded *Obshchestvo*—was a persistently fragmented society. This situation on the one hand allowed the old regime to survive a long time without serious challenges to its monopoly on power; on the other hand, when the political and economic orders unraveled in the course of World War I, society had little to fall back on and the consequence was anarchy. Such, at any rate, is my understanding of Wirtschafter's main conclusion.

Of course, this is not the discovery of America (as the Russians like to say) regarding the nature of the Russian revolution and the relationship between society and politics that lay behind it. The value of the book, in any case, does not hinge on the originality of its conclusions. In the author's own words, this is "an extended essay [that] explores the relationships between state building, large-scale social structures, and everyday life." Elsewhere she describes "the central subject of the book" as "the meeting of the social and administrative regimes." It seems to me that it could be even more accurately described as an extended review and evaluation of the scholarly literature that in various ways has endeavored to get at the elusive social and social-psychological *realia* behind the state's administrative and legal categories. Because of the aforementioned persistent state of flux and the fact that the bulk of the Russian population over most of the history of the old regime was illiterate, among other things, the debates and unresolved issues are many, to put it mildly. Wirtschafter wends her way through a vast literature with considerable skill and erudition, in four chapters devoted, respectively, to "The Institutional Setting," " 'Ruling' Classes and Service Elites," "Middle Groups," and "Laboring People," plus a general conclusion. The bibliography at the end of the book is a nearly exhaustive list of modern work on Russian social history.

For a work that operates, generally, at a fairly far remove from event history (*l'histoire événementielle*), this book is noticeably short on methodological preamble (less than one page). Perhaps this is as it should be. Any rigid method-

ological structure would have precluded the kind of sensitive, historiographically centered synthesis we have here.

TERENCE EMMONS

Stanford University
California

EUROPE

GIENOW-HECHT, JESSICA C. E. 1999. *Transmission Impossible: American Journalism as Cultural Diplomacy in Postwar Germany, 1945-1955.* Pp. xx, 230. Baton Rouge: Louisiana State University Press. $47.50. Paperbound, $22.50.

Having defeated the Third Reich, the Allies who occupied Germany in 1945 vowed not to permit any repetition of the aggressive nationalism and militarism that had instigated two world wars. In the American sector to which Jessica C. E. Gienow-Hecht's monograph pays special attention, the policy of denazification included the encouragement of democratic values through the example of an autonomous press. But that model newspaper, the *Neue Zeitung*, was also an instrument of the U.S. Army. Its key editors were GIs, whose job was to implement the foreign policy objectives of a conquering nation. Such journalists certainly wanted to exemplify the fair and free dissemination of news, in accordance with the elusive ideal of objectivity. But the government that they served also wanted them to wage psychological warfare, to propagandize overtly against the totalitarian practices that Germans had so directly experienced and perpetrated.

The direction of this newspaper, which was published in three cities (Munich, Frankfurt, and West Berlin), was therefore confused. Its editors wanted to show their readership what an independent organ might look like. But their superiors wanted an ideological case to be advanced on behalf of the American way of life and, beginning in 1947, against the Communist system that the Soviets had installed in the eastern zone of Germany. These journalistic aims simply could not be reconciled. But the struggle to split the difference makes for a fascinating case history of miscommunication, of muffled purposes and miscues, even as the *Neue Zeitung* especially distinguished itself for its cultural reportage. With crisp assurance and exceptionally thorough research, Gienow-Hecht illumines the brief but gallant history of the newspaper and suggests that so novel an experiment in a binational medium was destined to fail.

The advantage that it enjoyed was the familiarity of its key personnel with the populace that *Neue Zeitung* hoped to reach. Its dominant personalities were European born and German speaking and mostly Jews; the editor of the cultural section, Erich Kästner, had been a celebrated novelist during the Weimar Republic. Even those whom Nazi racial policy had evicted harbored considerable sympathies for the German citizenry, and these returnees not only repudiated the early prohibition against fraternization but also admired the *Kultur* that the Third Reich did so much to extirpate. Some of the staffers were socialists. They were at least ambivalent about the market economics that the Department of State increasingly wished to promote and also about the popular culture that seemed so tawdry and superficial in the shadow of Goethe and Kant.

From the very beginning, the operations of this newspaper were marked by friction between the editors, who claimed to know their audience, and General Lucius D. Clay and his staffers, who sometimes did not even speak German. When the Cold War exposed the cross-purposes that divided the Americans from the Soviets, readers of the *Neue*

Zeitung not only became a defeated people who had to be taught democratic values but were supposed to be mobilized as anti-Communists as well. That transformed the newspaper into a forum for propaganda—which meant that the most talented reporters and editors quit, were reassigned, or were fired. One of their successors had been an aide to Joseph Goebbels.

Though publication ceased in 1955, the newspaper had an impact—however, one impossible to measure with any precision. Political reeducation had been achieved, and the self-respect of a *Kulturvolk* was enhanced. In the decade covered in *Transmission Impossible*, West Germany hardly became "Americanized." But "the émigrés proved to be uniquely equipped to convey American values to a German audience," Gienow-Hecht concludes, and the *Neue Zeitung* thus contributed to the reintegration of the Federal Republic into the West.

STEPHEN J. WHITFIELD

Brandeis University
Waltham
Massachusetts

UNITED STATES

MICHEL, SONYA. 1999. *Children's Interests / Mothers' Rights: The Shaping of America's Child Care Policy.* Pp. xi, 410. New Haven, CT: Yale University Press. $35.00.

The title of Sonya Michel's powerfully written book reveals much about many historiographical, ideological, and programmatic divides and about Michel's own policy perspective. Children have interests; mothers have rights. I am not sure if the postmodern solidus is meant to be more or less than an "and," but it aptly conveys the tensions and ambiguities of issues concerning mothers and children. Michel analyzes other disjunctures as well: between women's public and private lives, between education and child care, and between the history of social welfare programs and the welfare state. Her main purpose is to explain why, unlike most other developed, democratic market societies, the United States does not have a system of publicly supported universal child care. The absence of such a system, according to Michel, deprives mothers of their rights to full social citizenship, by making it difficult for them to work outside of the home.

Whether or not one believes that the state should be responsible for making it easier for all citizens to work, Michel argues very persuasively that the lack of public child care did not happen accidentally. It might have been otherwise. There were choice points when other roads were not taken.

Michel emphasizes women's agency, both that of maternalist social reformers who opposed child care and that of poor mothers who exercised "maternal invention" to find care for their children. The elite mothers who led the day nursery movement, such as Josephine Jewell Dodge, who founded the National Federation of Day Nurseries in 1898, thought poor mothers should work only if necessary in times of emergency. Unmarried female progressive reformers such as Julia Lathrop, director of the Federal Children's Bureau, and Jane Addams criticized day nurseries as unhealthful environments for children and unfeasible arrangements for impoverished working mothers, whose low wages made supporting a family difficult. African American women, both society women and poor mothers, did support day nurseries, however, because they knew that most African American mothers had to work. Lathrop and Addams promoted mothers' pensions, which remained the dominant

public policy until the welfare reform act of 1996.

Although the number of day nurseries continued to grow after the enactment of mothers' pensions in many states in the 1910s and 1920s, the day nursery movement eventually declined. Michel describes other programs that might have evolved into child care, but she stresses that the federal government supported emergency nursery schools and children's centers during the depression and World War II only as stopgap measures, not permanent initiatives. When publicly funded child care was finally established in 1962 as an amendment to the Social Security Act, it was targeted at poor children as an antipoverty program.

One of the most fascinating parts of this impressive book is the concluding section, comparing child care systems in Sweden, France, Japan, Canada, and the United States. Interestingly, France, "one of the preeminent conservative-corporatist regimes," sponsors one of the most generous, comprehensive public child care systems, in part because of pro-natalism and the efforts of French feminists and socialists. This suggests that, as our birthrates decline, there may be more support for public child care, rather than less.

Could it really have been otherwise in the United States? The history of the public kindergarten movement shows that it was possible to garner public support for preschool education for 5-year-olds. Whether child care, which is viewed primarily as a service for working women, not their children, could have achieved universalization had reformers not chosen the strategy of mothers' pensions seems unlikely. It took the National Kindergarten Association more than half a century of state-by-state, town-to-town political lobbying, in coalition with other groups, to establish universal kindergartens, and cost was always the sticking point. As shown by *The Silent Crisis in U.S. Child Care*, the May 1999 issue of *The Annals* of the American Academy of Political and Social Science, edited by Suzanne Heburn, public child care would have been even more expensive.

I wish Michel had said more about local day nursery associations, some of which, as Elizabeth Rose documents in her 1999 book, *A Mother's Job: The History of Day Care*, were more successful than others in maintaining support. The current movement to universalize preschool education for 3- and 4-year-olds is growing through translocal initiatives and regional clusters of state-sponsored programs. With the recent turn against mothers' pensions, we may have a chance to replay history. Sonya Michel's timely book should be read by anyone concerned about the outcome of this next phase of welfare policy debate and about the interests of American mothers and children.

BARBARA BEATTY

Wellesley College
Massachusetts

O'BRIEN, GAIL WILLIAMS. 1999. *The Color of the Law: Race, Violence, and Justice in the Post–World War II South*. Pp. xiii, 334. Chapel Hill: University of North Carolina Press. $45.00. Paperbound, $19.95.

In this important and valuable book, Gail Williams O'Brien examines the racial violence that broke out in Columbia, Tennessee, in February 1946, along with the legal proceedings that followed. Trouble began with a fight in a store between James Stephenson, a black World War II veteran, and a white store employee. Stephenson was arrested, but a white mob began to form. Fearing a lynching, the sheriff released Stephenson to a group of black leaders who managed to spirit him out of town. Nonetheless, the white mob remained, and local blacks armed themselves in self-defense. When members of Columbia's all-white police force entered the town's black business district, gunfire broke out, leaving four officers wounded. The Tennessee State Guard and Tennessee Highway Patrol then intervened, and the next morning, members of the latter raided Columbia's black section, beating suspects and vandalizing homes and businesses. By the time it was over, more than 100 local blacks had been arrested, 2 of whom were later shot and killed while in custody. Once the violence ended, the U.S. Justice Department sought to obtain grand jury indictments against the state law officers for violating the civil rights of Columbia's black citizens, while the state of Tennessee sought to convict several black community leaders for inciting a riot. Both prosecutions failed.

In analyzing these events, O'Brien has selected a pivotal moment in American race relations. Although some aspects of the Columbia incidents are part of the familiar Jim Crow pattern of white violence and legal repression, the importance of the story rests in how this case deviates from so many that preceded it. O'Brien makes clear that the ideological, economic, and political changes wrought by World War II had made the Jim Crow system increasingly untenable. First, the war had elevated the consciousness, capacities, and expectations of Columbia's blacks. Indeed, the argument that set off the violence began when Stephenson, a Navy radio operator during the war, protested that his mother had been overcharged for what he knew to be minor repairs to her radio. Moreover, many of the blacks who armed themselves to defend their community were also veterans of the war. In general, blacks in Columbia and elsewhere were beginning to demand for themselves the same freedoms for which many had fought abroad.

The war also had a powerful impact on whites. For example, although the effort failed, the Justice Department's prosecution stands in contrast to that department's overwhelming indifference to civil rights violations before World War II and, as such, represents the beginning of a continuing (and ultimately more successful) effort at enforcing civil rights laws. Even ordinary whites seem to have been influenced by the war. O'Brien points out that the increased levels of social mobility created by the war made whites less willing to engage in racial violence. The war also seems to have helped alter white racial attitudes. According to O'Brien, in a closing statement, one of the lawyers defending the black leaders charged with incitement appealed to the all-white jury by comparing the state's prosecution to Nazi atrocities and by citing the service and sacrifices of black soldiers. In O'Brien's assessment, such appeals contributed to the jury's decision to acquit.

Drawing on a rich array of oral histories and written accounts, O'Brien not only provides a thorough description of the Columbia riots and their aftermath but also offers a rich and revealing analysis of the factors influencing these events and their participants. In doing so, she has made an important contribution to our understanding of this important moment in the history of American race relations.

PHILIP A. KLINKNER

Hamilton College
Clinton
New York

SOCIOLOGY

BERKOVITCH, NITZA. 1999. *From Motherhood to Citizenship: Women's Rights and International Organizations*. Pp. xii, 207. Baltimore, MD: Johns Hopkins University Press. $34.95.

Despite a rather conventional title, this book turns out to be an original and theoretically exciting treatment of the international women's movement between 1850 and 1990. Nitza Berkovitch, though still a new scholar, pursues a daring hypothesis in her book based on her 1994 dissertation at Stanford. She investigates the connection between the evolution of international women's organizations and the emergence of a global society in which both advanced and developing nations pursue the ideals of women's rights and human rights. Berkovitch contends that globalization and the international movement for women's equality pushed each other forward. Beginning in the nineteenth century with suffrage and peace organizations, and continued between the two world wars by international labor groups, this broad movement finally flowered in the 1980s with the United Nations Decade for Women.

Although Berkovitch does not cite the classic sociological theories of Durkheim and Parsons, her stunning synthesis bears out some of their central ideas. Durkheim, in the *Division of Labor in Society* (1893), argued that increasing societal complexity brings about both greater interdependence and greater individualism. As individual members of a society become more specialized, they also became more dependent on each other to supply their needs. In a similar vein, Berkovitch's book demonstrates that growing worldwide concern for women's equality, even in the most backward countries, is part of growing global interdependence. The economies of highly developed and less developed nations are ever more intertwined, and this fact makes them look beyond their borders to women's, children's, workers', and human rights elsewhere. The poorer countries try to achieve some of the same rights as enjoyed by women in the modern nations, while the advanced countries try to lift women's status in the developing world.

This story is well supported by the documentation about the growth of international women's organizations. However, Berkovitch makes more of a case for global influence on individual nations than the other way around. She shows how the rights of women as individuals and citizens were increasingly articulated and promoted by global actors so that equal employment policy, protective legislation, and expanded maternity provisions became an integral part of the labor code in most countries. But about her statistical analyses showing that "the process is not internally generated but is, rather, externally driven" (17), I am skeptical. Progressive and modernizing reforms are always the result of both tighter integration of a society at higher levels and of increased specialization of individuals and institutions that make up the whole. In *Societies: Evolutionary and Comparative Perspectives* (1966), Talcott Parsons described reform movements as efforts for "adaptive upgrading" that strive for full citizenship of formerly excluded persons or groups. The costs of exclusion become ever clearer as specialization and mutual dependence increase.

My skepticism about giving greater weight to global than country-level dynamics for gains in women's rights is also based on my knowledge of women's movements and women's changing lives in the United States and abroad. Leaders emerge, ideologies are formed, adherents are won, and legislation is passed because of powerful changes in the lives of the women who find a discrepancy between their rights and their responsibilities. They document and protest the injustice they encounter and in turn convince their brothers, husbands, fathers, and sons that women should have rights, too. The models and measures developed by Berkovitch therefore need to be closely inspected to account for what seems to be an overemphasis on a top-down dynamic of change, compared to the revolutionary potential of social protest from below. Nevertheless, *From Motherhood to Citizenship* remains a very impressive first book whose author will likely produce more such original and thought-provoking work in the future.

JANET ZOLLINGER GIELE

Brandeis University
Waltham
Massachusetts

HAGAN, JOHN and BILL McCARTHY. 1997. *Mean Streets: Youth Crime and Homelessness.* Pp. xv, 299. New York: Cambridge University Press. No price.

This book is an outstanding field study of adolescents who have left home and school for a potentially dangerous street lifestyle. Identifying the risk factors that forced youths in Toronto and Vancouver to abandon the safety and security of home for the mean streets of urban centers is the book's central focus. Hagan and McCarthy gathered data via street-based interviews and surveys of youths in Toronto schools and then use a qualitative and a quantitative analytic model to provide intensely interesting perspectives on the ecology of youth homelessness. Four key ideas are fundamental in this study: (1) that parental neglect and abuse effect dysfunctional psychological and emotional states in children; (2) that street life is a rational, viable alternative to parental abuse and neglect; (3) that street life leads to community marginalization; and (4) that such marginalization is worsened by harsh criminal sanctions. The strength of this book's analysis is its usefulness to researchers interested in the effect of multiple risk factors for delinquency and to practitioners in urban and suburban settings who struggle to support homeless youths. These research findings shed light on why youth homelessness is such a difficult challenge for those who wish to intervene and how a suppression-oriented approach, used to the exclusion of prevention and intervention, amplifies crime problems linked to homeless youths.

Hagan and McCarthy's integrated theoretical (social control, strain, differential association) approach sheds light on the complexities of youth homelessness, but the authors also expose street life to a social network perspective. Homeless youths are low on human capital, have been marginalized from mainstream institutions such as school, and have families that offer them little socioeconomic and emotional support. So here they are, standing on street corners, sleeping on sidewalks and in parks, panhandling for change, the community's teenaged school dropouts with emotional scars, struggling to stay alive on the street. The authors suggest, and I fully agree with them, that the street survival of these youths is predicated on criminal capital, that is, the knowledge and technical skills of street-based crime as well as the beliefs supporting such behavior. A cultural anthropologist like me would refer to criminal capital as street culture, and, as we discover, it takes time to assimilate street culture's rules and learn its behaviors. Street culture is not a default lifestyle, but rather it has social, economic, and ideological integrity, and trying to extract homeless youths from it can be difficult.

Gang researchers like me know that many of the multiple risk factors leading children to gang affiliation are shared by homeless youths: parental neglect and abuse, inadequate support mechanisms in schools, too little proactive involvement of community agencies with troubled children, and too much law enforcement suppression for the sake of punishment and teaching a lesson. This book is the single best road map to understanding the social services necessary to support homeless youths. If you are interested in the lives of children, read this book, give it to your students, send it to your elected officials, and then talk to community leaders and policymakers about rational, therapeutic, nonpunitive approaches to helping adolescents. A proactive strategic approach to nurturing our youths begins with *Mean Streets*.

MARK S. FLEISHER

Illinois State University
Normal

KENNEDY, LESLIE W. and DAVID R. FORDE. 1999. *When Push Comes to Shove: A Routine Conflict Approach to Violence*. Pp. xi, 199. Albany: State University of New York Press. Paperbound, $19.95.

When Push Comes to Shove breaks new ground in the arena of the rational choice theory of violence and the sociology of deviance with a well-written presentation of distinct and cogent social constructionist hypotheses of the origin of violent behavior. Breaking new ground, Leslie Kennedy and David Forde's study of two Canadian provinces is methodologically sophisticated and rich in thick description of the pervasiveness of interpersonal conflict in everyday life and how potentially violent behavior is conditioned by an individual's repertoire for reacting to conflict that is routinized across situational context. Their insightful and convincing argument that violence is a natural product of social interaction is buttressed by a sound contribution by Stephon Baron, of the

University of Windsor, on violence committed by street youths.

Kennedy and Forde begin by presenting a summary of the major assumptions of the social control, social learning, and criminal event theory of violence and aggression. They contend that these theories are limited, deterministic, and too specific. Moreover, they argue that, by examining specific crime types and offenders, too much emphasis is placed on generating explanations for senseless violence, and not enough attention is given to studying the victims of violence and the violence originating from low-intensity situations. In short, they conclude that violence is a dynamic and natural part of social interaction. Thus, to understand violence, researchers must examine the origins of everyday violent behavior. Toward that end, Kennedy and Forde present a routine conflict theory of violence, borrowing useful concepts from the social construction of violence, criminal event, and social coercion theoretical perspectives. This book continues the previous work of Forde and Kennedy with a renewed commitment to grand rational choice theories of violence. Although the grand theory approach is useful, it is often complex, ahistorical, and less likely to explain violent trends. However, the routine conflict theory does make important contributions to the field of violence research through its reasoned hypotheses of the role of choice in how violence evolves and changes.

When Push Comes to Shove presents research on a representative sample of Canadians. The authors employ survey methods, including the sophisticated factorial survey design, to test the routine conflict model. The core research is presented in chapters 4-6, which highlight evidence that conflict is common in a community sample; furthermore, the authors found a high acceptability of violence in society, violence that varies by social situations and the presence of third parties. A similarity between people's responses to hypothetical situational descriptions and their self-reported experiences of conflict and violence provides moderate evidence for the routine conflict model. More important, the study demonstrated that violence originates from a process of naming, claiming, and aggression. Evidence is presented that explains how individual's coercive intentions might increase or decrease the likelihood of violence. In chapter 7, Baron's work highlights important similarities and differences regarding how violence is sanctioned, experienced, and routinized by a subsample of male street youths compared to the general population of males. He found that the tolerance for the use of violence is more pervasive among male street youths for selective events compared to males in the general population, that many street youths experience conflict, and that their responses to conflict are routinized and more frequently result in aggression. Overall, this work is theoretically strong and presents evidence that people considered many situational factors when confronted with conflict.

The conclusion of When Push Comes to Shove is that not all violence begins with lethal intentions or is simply a behaviorist response to stimuli; rather, violence often begins as low-level conflict and emerges as a consequence of daily routines scripted by the previous actions of individuals involved in these behaviors. The study highlights the importance of understanding the complexity of violence as a product of choices made in the process of determining and responding to conflict, which is also conditioned by the circumstances of the event. It provides greater evidence on conflict and Canadians' attitudes toward the use of violence, including those of male street youths, than a rigorous proof of the thesis of the book. However, the research does further the knowledge about crime victimization, with a new analysis of the process involved in the development of conflict and violence, and of how the social interaction context conditions violent responses to social conflict. Suggestions for the prevention of violent acts include addressing the characterization of violence in the media and improving an individual's ability to manage conflict.

SEAN JOE

University of Pennsylvania
Philadelphia

LEISERING, LUTZ and STEPHAN LEIBFRIED. 1999. *Time and Poverty in Western Welfare States: United Germany in Perspective.* Pp. v, 379. New York: Cambridge University Press. $74.95.

The ongoing analyses of several large U.S. longitudinal data sets has led to a volume of research findings in the past two decades regarding the dynamics of poverty and welfare use. This work has primarily focused on the length and frequency of poverty spells and welfare use across fairly short intervals of time (for example, 5-10 years). Surprisingly, few researchers have taken full advantage of these data sets by placing the event of poverty within the context of the entire adult life course—in other words, to examine, as Ralf Dahrendorf writes in his foreword, "the place of such moments in people's life histories."

It is precisely such a life course perspective that provides the framework behind *Time and Poverty in Western Welfare States* by Lutz Leisering and Stephan Leibfried, which is an updated translation of their 1995 book published in Germany. The book is divided into four major sections. The authors begin by laying out the theoretical foundations of a life course perspective as it relates to poverty. In addition, they discuss social policy within the context of life course policy. That is, social programs dealing with education, employment insurance, or old-age pensions are intended to provide varying degrees of protection against the economic risks that occur across the life cycle.

The second section of the book provides a quantitative and qualitative analysis of welfare recipients in the Bremen Longitudinal Study of Social Assistance. This analysis looks at individuals who began receiving Social Assistance in 1989 in the north German city of Bremen and were followed through 1994. The authors argue that the "results of the analyses can be taken to be indicative of the structure of Social Assistance and poverty throughout Germany." They focus on the length of time individuals use welfare, their perceptions of welfare use, their life course patterns of welfare receipt (based upon current and retrospective data), and whether welfare utilization creates dependency.

The third section of the book reviews the German historical and societal context of poverty. Leisering and Leibfried discuss the ways in which poverty had been perceived and studied in post–World War II Germany, noting various shifts across the decades. They also consider how the unification of Germany has affected life course patterns and the risk of poverty, particularly for former citizens of the German Democratic Republic.

The final section of *Time and Poverty in Western Welfare States* develops some of the implications of using a life course perspective in order to study impoverishment. These include rethinking social policy approaches to poverty, new ways of conceptualizing social stratification and economic inequality, and laying out several challenges with regard to the future of Western welfare states.

Perhaps the most important contribution of this book is to illustrate the value of using a life course perspective to the study of poverty. In employing this perspective, a number of new insights are gained. For example, within the long-term context of the life course, poverty is an event that can touch the mainstream population. As the authors write,

Poverty is no longer (if ever it was) a fixed condition or a personal or group characteristic, but rather it is an experience or stage in the life course. It is not necessarily associated with a marginal position in society but reaches well into the middle class. Poverty is specifically located in time and individual biographies, and, by implication, has come to transcend traditional social boundaries of class. (239)

Indeed, recent life table analyses of my own have revealed that two-thirds of Americans will at some point during their adult life course experience at least one year below the poverty line.

This book is of clear interest to scholars and researchers studying poverty and welfare dynamics. In addition, those concerned with cross-cultural patterns of poverty and the welfare state will find this book invaluable. It would also prove to be a useful addition in graduate classes dealing with social stratification, poverty, and the welfare state.

MARK R. RANK

Washington University
St. Louis
Missouri

PORTZ, JOHN, LANA STEIN, and ROBIN R. JONES. 1999. *City Schools and City Politics: Institutions and Leadership in Pittsburgh, Boston, and St. Louis.* Pp. viii, 199. Lawrence: University of Kansas. $35.00. Paperbound, $16.95.

This book examines the fate of school reform in Pittsburgh, Boston, and St. Louis in order to understand why some cities have experienced more success than others in mobilizing support for public education. It starts by looking at the economic and demographic changes that have transformed these cities since World War II and by describing the effects of these changes on the condition of their public schools. Then it ranks each of the cities according to three indicators of local effort on behalf of public education: financial support, programmatic innovation, and interviewees' perceptions of effort. Based on these criteria, the authors conclude that Pittsburgh has made the most significant effort to support public education, followed by Boston, while St. Louis has lagged consistently behind. Finally, to account for these differences, the book contains three case studies that trace the political history of educational reform in each city over the last three decades.

The main theme of the book is the role of cross-sector alliances between business, government, and education (what the authors and others call civic capacity) in addressing urban problems and the importance of institutions and leadership in building, or failing to build, those alliances. For example, the authors argue that Pittsburgh outstripped the other two cities in its support for reform because it benefited from a long-standing alliance between business and city government that, together with strong leadership from the school superintendent's office, worked to activate public support for education. By contrast, they argue, reform has made little headway in St. Louis because city government there is fragmented and the local business community has shown little interest in educational issues. Lukewarm support from local business also stalled reform in Boston, as did a long-standing governance battle between the mayor's office and the school system. But the authors say that Boston has recently moved ahead of St. Louis because the election of a mayor committed to school reform coupled with a change in the structure of school governance has made it possible to break this stalemate and build an alliance of civic leaders in support of educational improvement.

As an analysis of the various ways in which cities have mobilized, or failed to mobilize, civic support on behalf of public education, there is much of value in all of this. But the application of this model of development to school reform is troubling to me. Not only does it privilege the interests of elites at the expense of other, less powerful groups, but because it assumes that civic elites have no vested interests of their own but speak for the public good, it valorizes them as well. Consequently, it tends to imply that elite involvement will necessarily lead to better schools, though there is little evidence that their agenda for school improvement has any place for reforms that address the sources of the problems currently plaguing urban education (such as the disparities in curriculum, teacher expectations, disciplinary practices in re-segregated city schools, and the financial inequities between cities and suburbs), since these reforms might also conflict with their goals of productivity, accountability, and change through privatization and increased competition.

This is not to deny that educational improvement in American cities today requires the support of civic leaders. The evidence the authors have gathered from Pittsburgh, Boston, and St. Louis makes clear that reform cannot proceed without them. But I can see no good reason to assume that building civic capacity by fostering elite support for public education will automatically make urban schools better or more equal. More likely, it will simply make them more efficient.

HARVEY KANTOR

University of Utah
Salt Lake City

OTHER BOOKS

ABERBACH, JOEL D. and BERT A. ROCKMAN. 2000. *In the Web of Politics: Three Decades of the United States Federal Executive.* Pp. x, 230. Washington, DC: Brookings Institution Press. $42.95. Paperbound, $17.95.

BAECK, LOUIS. 2000. *Text and Context in the Thematisation on Postwar Development.* Pp. 150. Leuven, Belgium: Leuven University Press. Paperbound, no price.

BECK, ROGER B. 2000. *The History of South Africa.* Pp. xxx, 248. Westport, CT: Greenwood Press. $35.00.

CARPENTER, WILLIAM M. and DAVID G. WIENCEK, eds. 2000. *Asian Security Handbook 2000.* Pp. xiv, 349. Armonk, NY: M. E. Sharpe. $89.95.

DALTON, RUSSELL J., PAULA GARB, NICHOLAS P. LOVRICH, JOHN C. PIERCE, and JOHN M. WHITELEY. 1999. *Critical Masses: Citizens, Nuclear Weapons Production, and Environmental Destruction in the United States and Russia.* Pp. xvi, 457. Cambridge: MIT Press. Paperbound, $27.50.

EKSTEROWICZ, ANTHONY J. and ROBERT N. ROBERTS, eds. 2000. *Public Journalism and Political Knowledge.* Pp. xvii, 198. Lanham, MD: Rowman & Littlefield. $65.00. Paperbound, $22.95.

FERNANDEZ, DAMIAN J. and MADELINE CAMARA BETANCOURT, eds. 2000. *Cuba, the Elusive Nation: Interpretations of National Identity.* Pp. 317. Gaines-ville: University Press of Florida. $55.00.

GLASSMAN, RONALD M. 2000. *Caring Capitalism: A New Middle-Class Base for the Welfare State.* Pp. vi, 266. New York: Palgrave. $69.95.

GVOSDEV, NIKOLAS K. 2000. *Emperors and Elections: Reconciling the Ortho-dox Tradition with Modern Politics.* Pp. 156. Huntington, NY: Troitsa. No price.

HARRIS, PAUL G., ed. 2000. *Climate Change and American Foreign Policy.* Pp. viii, 296. New York: St. Martin's Press. $49.95.

HOWELL, KERRY E. 2000. *Discovering the Limits of European Integration: Applying Grounded Theory.* Pp. xx, 216. Huntington, NY: Nova Science. No price.

JOHNSTON, VAN R., ed. 2000. *Entrepreneurial Management and Public Policy.* Pp. xvi, 281. Huntington, NY: Nova Science. No price.

KROES, ROB. 2000. *Them and Us: Questions of Citizenship in a Globalizing World.* Pp. xv, 221. Champaign: University of Illinois Press. $44.95. Paperbound, $18.95.

LASKY, MELVIN J. 2000. *The Language of Journalism: Newspaper Culture.* Vol. 1. Pp. xx, 478. New Brunswick, NJ: Transaction. $39.95.

MADDEN, FREDERICK, ed. 2000. *The End of Empire.* Pp. xxxv, 555. Westport, CT: Greenwood Press. $99.50.

OZIEBLO, BARBARA. 2000. *Susan Glaspell: A Critical Biography.* Pp. xiii, 345. Chapel Hill: University of North Carolina Press. $55.00. Paperbound, $22.50.

PERI, YORAM, ed. 2000. *The Assassination of Yitzhak Rabin.* Pp. viii, 386. Stanford, CA: Stanford University Press. $55.00. Paperbound, $19.95.

SOLOMON, PETER H., JR. and TODD S. FOGLESONG. 2000. *Courts and Transition in Russia: The Challenge of Judicial Reform.* Pp. xii, 222. Boulder, CO: Westview Press. Paperbound, $25.00.

WILSON, ANDREW. 2000. *The Ukrainian: Unexpected Nation.* Pp. xiv, 356.

New Haven, CT: Yale University Press. $29.95.

ZHAO, SUISHENG, ed. 1999. *Across the Taiwan Strait: Mainland China, Taiwan, and the 1995-1996 Crisis.* Pp. x, 306. New York: Routledge. $80.00. Paperbound, $24.99.

INDEX